My Rhonda

E-mails from the Hospital

Seven Years through the Valley of
Cancer by the Grace of Our Lord

SCOTT SMITH

ISBN 978-1-64003-306-1 (Paperback)
ISBN 978-1-64003-305-4 (Digital)

Covenant Books, Inc.
11661 Hwy 707
Murrells Inlet, SC 29576
www.covenantbooks.com

We want to dedicate this book of our story to the memory of our beloved surgeon, Dr. Joseph Kuhn, a man who was gifted in his skill, a nationally recognized leader in his field, and taken from us much too soon. He was also a man who understood his place as a "technician" while the healing of his patients was ultimately the work of the Great Physician, our Lord and Savior, Jesus Christ. We look forward to seeing you again one day, Doc, on the other side of this life of pain and suffering even as we are still basking in the Joy that we have in Him, and of being touched by His Saints such as you.

...about you both
...re healing. Our God is a

...or a good report. You both are such inspira-
...rly

Contents

The Reason for This Book

It was in December of 2016 when we saw the beginnings of our Lord's work in His way of engineering events and circumstances and pulling on our hearts and ultimately bringing all these together into what has become this book, this journal, this collection of e-mails and thoughts, which were born out of some of the most difficult and trying times of our lives.

Our first hint of what was to come was when I was tapped on the shoulder from the pew behind us after a morning worship service at our church. A man who I did not recognize told me, "We've been watching you and your wife for awhile. My wife has just been diagnosed with cancer. How do you do this?" My emotions nearly got the better of me as I attempted to share words that would somehow give this man an answer that would help to carry him and his wife and family through a time that we knew would be life-changing, possibly even to the point of death. Those who have heard their doctor say, "It is cancer," know what a devastating moment that is. It will ruthlessly take over your life, dictating your time and your finances, and it, along with the sometimes brutal treatments, will demand more strength from you than you ever thought you could muster. Our journey and experiences through these multiple diagnoses that our Lord had carried us through were now being redirected by Him, in His Grace, to share with others and to somehow be used by Him to encourage the hearts of others for the battle that lay ahead in their own lives.

Then there was what I can only say what I felt to be the Lord's leading. It started with an early-morning "impression" that I needed to begin compiling the multitude of e-mails that were sent out and received back from our wonderful support group of friends and family during the course of my Rhonda's illness. This "impression" was followed by comments of affirmation made by others during the course of normal conversation in the weeks following, especially as I shared about the tap on the shoulder I had received.

And so, still not knowing where this would lead me, I began the work of pulling all of these e-mails together. My first response to this task of reading through all of this history was intense grief and mourning and many tears. To relive these times and events was almost more than I could handle. The emotions of each circumstance, both good and bad, came flooding back, at times, in such an overwhelming way that I could only stop, put my face in my hands and sob. These years were so exhausting to us that many times my only memories are from these written notes. My conscious brain was too weary to register anything else or too traumatized to want to remember anything else. My Rhonda has very little memory from much of this time, which we see as mostly a good thing, a blessing from God. As we look back, it is mostly a blur of suffering and seemingly unending complications and setbacks. But now we are on the other side of it, and we can see more clearly how our Lord used us many times to reach out to others to share and show how His Love (and our love and caring for each other) served to carry us through these days and how He has greatly blessed and gifted us by bringing us through it all.

Which finally brings me to that underlying reason for this compilation of writings; the fact that our Lord did bring us through it all and that He stands ready to help and carry us all through such difficult and trying times. To Him, we freely give all Thanks and Glory and Praise. We share our story to glorify our Lord and Savior, Jesus, the Great Physician, our Healer, and our Only Hope. By His Grace, He carried us through this time of suffering and darkness and then finally back into the wonderful warmth of His Light. So we offer this as our testimony hoping that our Lord can somehow use our story to be an encouragement to those who are facing similar trials and difficulties in their lives. Jesus is there for all of us.

Yes, this was a sometimes overwhelming test of our faith, but our Lord gave us the Grace to stubbornly cling to Him during these times. This decision to hold onto His promises had to be made by choice for each day, each moment. During the course of these doctor visits, tests, surgeries and procedures, and hospital stays of weeks at a time, there were many times where I didn't feel like God was with us. It is not an easy thing to see your spouse suffer so much, and I was even angry and hurt at times. "Why must she suffer so?" But true faith is not a feeling, and we had both made that choice back when we first trusted Him for our salvation that we would trust Him through all and in all, and He always made a way and carried us through each day, each hour of this darkness. And our precious support team gave hands and feet and words of love and peace to beautifully reflect our Savior's care and loving kindness over us. Some may feel that it is difficult to admit to health or other difficult circumstances in their lives and share these with others, but those who choose to walk through such times alone are handcuffing our Lord's love and the help and support that He longs to give you because it is through the Love of His church, His wonderful body of true believers, that we feel His Love and compassion most strongly. It is as we freely confess our struggles to caring souls that He will Love us back through them. And if you don't feel that you have a support group, pray to our Father in Heaven, and He will bring them to you. We were blessed to experience that too—His Love and words of encouragement coming to us from "random strangers" that our Lord graciously sent to us when we needed it most.

You are never alone in your suffering if you will but have Faith in the One who cared deeply enough to also suffer and die for all of humankind… for you. His Love for us is an amazing gift that I am still unable to wrap my head around, but it is a wonderful and humbling feeling to be rescued by that Love many times over many years as it was poured out to us by His Holy Saints, our friends and family. Words cannot express our thankfulness for their gifts of His Love to us, but I know that their reward in heaven is great.

My Rhonda

I first met my Rhonda in September of 2004 through an Internet dating site. My first wife had succumbed to breast cancer in 2001. I remember watching the horrors of 9/11 unfold on the TV in her hospital room after her final surgery where the surgeon had told me that they "couldn't get it all." She passed away three weeks later. My father, who had been fighting lymphoma 800 miles away in New Mexico, passed away three days after that, the day before her funeral. I was left with my two teenage sons, David and Jordan.

Rhonda was a single mom of three (Stefanie, Julie, and Charlie) who had basically been abandoned in her marriage, only divorcing after years of being alone with the kids to make the separation finally legal so she could move on with their lives. After time to adjust, she had frugally used her accounting skills and school teacher income to build a new home and life for her family and signed up on the dating site in a quest for true companionship.

When we met, Rhonda had been on the dating site for around nine months. She had signed up for a year, knowing that it would be a process that would take time to find the soul mate she had been praying for all of her life. Our Lord knows that I was more impulsive and had a ways to go in learning the grace of patience. I had signed up for a month, and Rhonda was one of the first matches that came across when I'd only been on the site for a couple of days.

We had both been frustrated in our search for the right one. When my first wife became ill, our marriage was not in great shape. Years of financial distress had built a wall between us with cycles of conflict that we couldn't overcome. We had tried counseling, but it had gotten to the point where my soul had just given up. I wasn't angry; I was numb and indifferent. We actually got along better after that point because I had lost the will to fight anymore, but our hearts were no longer one. After she passed away, I was overcome with the guilt that she not only suffered from the cancer that ended her life, but she also suffered from a husband who was unable to give her the love and support she deserved and needed during her illness. I also felt guilt from not being able to be there for my mom with my dad's illness and death. I couldn't be in two places at once, and I thought it was a cruel way of losing two of the most important people in my life. After a couple of years, I dated some and pursued a relationship or two but never found a good match for the person I was wanting to be.

So God had his work cut out to get me through this mess and to a place where I would be ready for another relationship, and by the time I signed up on the dating site, I was a different guy. Through loving friends and coworkers, a men's Sunday school class, a cloistered Christian weekend, playing guitar in the church praise band, and even being a volunteer counselor at Billy Graham's last Dallas crusade, God had taught me much about loving Him and loving people.

Rhonda had compiled her list for her perfect match and had been praying patiently, even setting out two fleeces (as Gideon had done in Judges), and God had been working on me for three years to fulfill her list and prayers. I guess I was a slow learner.

After I initiated contact (which fulfilled Rhonda's first "fleece"), we felt each other out through the website e-mail. It didn't take us long to figure out that we were both looking for the same thing. When reading through the extensive profiles that we both had to fill out to be on the website, the responses were almost identical. We couldn't tell whose we were reading. They were that close. Soon we shared our personal e-mail addresses and, within a few days, our cell phone numbers. As a part of my healing from my first wife's passing, I had written our story and put it up on a website revolving around a quest to use a song I had written and sung at our wedding to raise funds to benefit breast cancer research. I shared this website and story with Rhonda. After reading through it, she was intrigued and suggested that we meet face-to-face. We set up a meeting at a restaurant roughly halfway between our homes for Friday, October 1. This was about one week after I initiated contact. I was still that impulsive guy, and Rhonda was beginning to see that maybe her prayers were being answered.

The few days before our meeting were filled with a flurry of e-mails and text messages and one phone call the night before. We both could tell that something special was happening. We were even counting down the hours starting three days before and shared a cautious excitement that God was in the middle of it all.

Now I am, by nature, a shy guy, slow to warm up to new situations and new people, but I had no qualms when I first saw Rhonda walking up to the restaurant where we shared a warm hug like old friends who hadn't seen each other for a while. I felt like I already knew her. The dinner conversation was somewhat forced because much of the time, my brain and mouth don't hook up very well together. After dinner, we went out to her car and listened to a CD of some songs I had recorded. When we had listened for a while, I asked Rhonda if I could pray for our new friendship. I maybe had trouble making conversation with a pretty lady I'd just met, but God had been working on me, and as we joined hands, I poured out my heart to Him, asking Him to guide and be in the midst of this new relationship. Unknowingly, this prayer had just fulfilled Rhonda's second "fleece," and I noticed that she didn't let go of my hand after the prayer. If anything, she was squeezing my hand even more tightly, seeing that God had just fulfilled both of her "fleeces." I turned to look at her eyes, and as they say, the rest is history. As I shared at our wedding a little over five months later (March 12, 2005), citing the old hymn, "Heaven Came Down," that His Glory came down and overwhelmed us. We knew that it was His Work, and that it was a done deal! Another "sign" of God's affirmation that we like to share was where I had put a limit of a fifty-mile radius for potential matches on the dating site. Rhonda's front door was forty-nine miles away from my front door. God was, indeed, all over the details.

Merging two households and five kids was not an easy task. Rhonda and kids left their new house (in June, at the end of the school semester. We like to say that, since we were married, we figured that it was okay to finally move in together), and we squeezed into my existing three-bedroom home. The kids were real troopers and all did their best to make it work. Stefanie had graduated high school and headed to Baylor University in Waco for the 2005 fall semester, thereby relieving some of the overcrowding. David had graduated in 2003 and was busy with his band and friends. Jordan and Julie were in high school, and Charlie was just entering middle school. Rhonda looked for a new teaching job, but we learned quickly that it would be better for her to be an at-home mom to manage the household and tend to the kids' needs and schedules.

In spite of the similarities of our dating site profiles, we definitely had some blending pains, most of them dealing with parenting styles and fitting everyone in. But we all made adjustments and settled into a good life. Rhonda and I were very thankful for the new start that God had given to us. It was so great being newlyweds! The two of us found some alone time away from the house by walking a three-mile greenbelt trail near our home multiple evenings each week. At one point, I suggested that we try to run some of the way, and I quickly learned that Rhonda had more grit and resolve than I did as she pushed herself to eventually jog the whole trail while I lagged behind and struggled to keep up with her. This "mind over matter," as she called it, this inner strength to rise to and meet the challenge would serve to give her the strength to keep going in the soon-to-be difficult months and years ahead. But for the time being, we enjoyed the time to ourselves as much as we could get it, including regular weekly date nights. We also got a kick out of the kids' response when we had our spontaneous moments of affection. All we had to do was say "recharge," and they all mysteriously disappeared.

After we'd been together about a year, I decided to quit the praise band. This precious group of souls had been a very dear and important part of my recovery and growth to prepare me for life with Rhonda, but I felt that I needed to attend with my new wife a Sunday school class that she had found. This loving, supportive, and wonderful group of believers quickly became a second family to us, and their love and acts of kindness would become a huge part of the support we would need to make it through the darker days ahead.

We also loved celebrating our anniversary each year with getaways—mostly to a cabin at a state park in Oklahoma where we would relax, walk, watch movies, and eat out when we wanted and more than we needed. Life was mostly wonderful as we grew together over the next few years, deeply breathing in the blessings of these times with hearts that overflowed. I'd forgotten how wonderful this life could be. God's Grace was over us, and Rhonda had become the best friend I'd ever had, and I'm pretty sure she felt the same about me. We were living our dreams and looking forward to many more wonderful years together.

As we went through the next few years, our blending was progressing well. The times when we could get the whole family together always went great as the kids were all gracious and accepting of each other. Stef was still at Baylor, enjoying the campus life. Jordan and Julie had both graduated high school and were taking their first steps into adulthood, while Charlie was making the most of high school, especially playing trumpet in the band. And oldest son David, after fulfilling a lifelong dream to experience Alaska and dog sledding, married his wonderful girlfriend Jillian in August 2007 in a time that brought great joy as well as some more blending opportunities to work through. Our amazing Lord brought us through it all triumphantly, and life was good!

But by early 2009, the clouds of suffering were moving silently and relentlessly toward us.

In spite of our walking/jogging routine, Rhonda had felt increasing tiredness for several months. When she went in February to see her primary care physician about it, her doctor told her, "We're not even going there. It's just your age." But Rhonda (who was forty-five at that time) knew that something was going on. She should have more energy for someone who jogs three miles multiple times a week. Then what had been an occasional shot of pain in her side started intensifying and being more constant. It came to the point where she decided she needed to try another doctor in the group for a second opinion. So she got an appointment for Friday, May 22, (Memorial Day weekend). A few minutes into the visit, the doctor told Rhonda that she needed an ultrasound ASAP to check out the area of her pain. He suspected that something was going on and that it was not good.

2009: Dark Clouds Moving In

May 10, 2009
Sunday School PRAISES and PRAYER REQUESTS

Scott & Rhonda
—Prayer request: trying to determine the source of Rhonda's frequent and severe abdominal pain.

May 23
update from Terry (SS teacher)

Prayer Request for Rhonda and Scott. They are in Baylor Garland hospital and will be until probably Monday (the 25th) at least. Rhonda has a blockage in her Gall Bladder. They have already done a scan and will do a scope tomorrow. If they are able to detect the blockage and get it out when doing the scope, they will. If not, she may be facing removal of her Gall Bladder. Please pray for comfort for Rhonda and strength to be able to heal quickly. Pray for Scott and his strength as well. As most of you are aware, the spouse in Scott's position often suffers as much. I know that our Heavenly Father will Bless them both. I pray that the Great Physician would touch them and Rhonda would begin to feel better even now.

Please say a prayer for them and the children.

May 24
Update from Scott to the SS class

Hi... I'm in Rhonda's email on the Baylor wifi network. Rhonda's bile duct is closed up, but we don't know why yet. Had a CT scan this afternoon, hopefully this will help give us more info. We will most likely be here for a few more days. We sure would have rather been in SS with you all this morning! Rhonda is feeling okay, just frustrated that we haven't gotten to the bottom of this yet. Thank you all for your prayers and sweet friendship!

May 26
The first "My Rhonda" e-mail to Scott's coworkers

All,

My wife Rhonda was admitted to the hospital on Friday afternoon after having sharp pain in her upper abdomen. After undergoing a myriad of tests and scans, they determined that a bile duct is pinched closed. The first attempt through endoscopy (through the mouth) to clear that up on Sunday was not successful. We are moving from the local Garland hospital to Baylor Dallas in a couple of hours. They will try to clear it up again there… probably tomorrow.

The hospital has wifi, so I'm able to log in at times, but will be largely unavailable most of the time. If you send an email, I'll reply as soon as I can. Quinn, Deborah, Bruce, and the team are there to help you with anything they can too… love my team!

So… we appreciate your prayers… this has gone on a lot longer than we thought it would. Rhonda has been made comfortable for the most part (no more morphine though please… too strong!) and is in good spirits. I will pass along updates as I'm able.

Thanks so much…

May 26 (evening)
My Rhonda update

What a day… we got transferred to Dallas early this afternoon and before we could catch our breath, they whisked her into the scope procedure. She was in for about 2 ½ hrs. They placed two stents to open the blockages and got biopsies of the pancreas. The lab results won't be ready until Thursday. The recovery was rough for a time, but she has now enjoyed some liquid dinner and is resting peacefully. We are hoping that maybe we get to go home tomorrow… but will see what they say.

God is good… all the time… Even in the midst of difficulties, He gives us Grace and sustains us… giving us the strength to face each trial… and the Peace from knowing that we are in the mighty Hands of our loving Heavenly Father. We trust all to Him.

Thank you again for your thoughts and prayers…

May 27
My Rhonda update

Well… not going home today. We saw the dr around noon, and he wants to wait until the lab results come in to decide whether we're through dealing with this thing or not. There is something going on with the pancreas… it's either inflammation or a tumor. Some of the cells were "funny looking." Rhonda's pain level is about the same today as it has been the last several days… still on clear liquids only. She is at peace that things will be okay.

Thanks again for your prayers and kind words… we know that we have your support and God's strength to get through all this.

May 28
My Rhonda update

Okay... we finally talked to the dr for a few minutes. He said that there were definitely 'funny looking' cells in the biopsy and he feels that they should be removed. So... we're looking at a surgery of some sort, but we won't know details until we talk to a surgeon.

It's only in the pancreas where the cells were found so nothing has spread.

Rhonda and I feel a great peace about all of this. It's not exactly what we wanted to hear, but since Rhonda's been dealing with this on and off for several months we feel that this was something maybe on the verge of becoming something much worse and we caught it at the right time. We can still see God's loving grace even in the midst of this news. We know that His Hand is over us still.

Thanks again for all of the warm thoughts and prayers... and for the BEAUTIFUL flower arrangement! Rhonda's eyes really lit up when she saw it... thanks so much! You all are great!

More news to come as we know it...

May 28
From Terry to SS class

Hello all. I wanted to give you an update on Rhonda and Scott. They are at Baylor Dallas in the Truett Building. Rhonda had another procedure to attempt to open the duct and to do a biopsy. Scott told me that the cells taken from the biopsy are not normal. There was not enough of the cells to determine with certainty what the cells are showing. So, they will be moving to a surgical floor in the Roberts

Building at Baylor Dallas. They are not sure when this move will take place. They will be talking to the surgeon about what is going on and their options. Scott and Rhonda are both tired and I am sure ready to be at home. Scott did say that they both have a peace at this time.

They feel like they have caught this at a good time and that they can prevent any further problems.

So say a prayer for them and the surgeon. Pray for a doctor that is a believer. One who knows how precious both Rhonda and Scott are. Pray for clarity and good medical decisions. Pray for the best possible outcome and that they both would be able to return back to life as normal as possible.

May 31
From Rhonda to SS class

We sure missed y'all this morning!! Scott cannot access email from the hospital because web-based email is prohibited. However, I thank you SO MUCH for the prayers, the visits, positive energy, etc. shared with us! I love challenges… and rising to them. We'll be doing our best to get this behind us as soon as possible. Thanks in advance for your continued prayers and support.

The kids will be here this evening so we can celebrate Julie's 20th birthday. Very exciting day! Have a blessed week!

May 31
My Rhonda update

Well… the scope dr came by early Friday (29th) evening to check on us and let us know that the final biopsy results had shown that the growth in the pancreas is indeed cancer. Even though we had suspected this, it was, of course, a shock to hear it. We had a couple of hours to let it sink in a bit before we finally got to see the surgeon.

This man really impressed us with his compassion and thoroughness… he had really put some thought into what would be the best way to handle this. He did tell us that there was a second 'mass', unrelated to the pancreas, but in the same general area. They don't know yet if it's cancerous or not. So… our next step is to get a full-body PET scan, which will identify any cancerous cells in this mass or that we may not yet be aware of. We won't be able to schedule this scan until Monday.

Pending the results of the scan, they will either do the surgery right away or put Rhonda through a round or two of chemo (4–6 wks) to shrink the cancer and then do the surgery. So we may not know until mid-week what the action plan is. I will keep you all informed as new info comes.

Rhonda is on a round-the-clock pain med pump and is comfortable most of the time. The last two nights she has slept like a baby. I've pretty much lived with her in the room… only been to the house a couple of times since all of this started 9 days ago. Today is daughter Julie's 20th birthday, and we're looking forward to a visit later with her, Stef and Charlie to celebrate (maybe even a small piece of cake!) Rhonda's mom is flying in Monday night to help out mainly with the kids and keep the house running smoothly.

After our initial shock, we have prayed and feel a great sense of peace in the midst of all this. This is where our spiritual "rubber meets the road"… do we really trust God or not? Rhonda is a fighter and is ready to rise to the challenge… so we will strive to live each day as a gift (as we already have been before all of this) and to meet this head-on with all of our strength… and then leave the results up to God. He has already brought us both through so much and we are so thankful for what he has given us. He holds our future in His hands… Doctors can do marvelous things with surgeries and drugs, but only God can truly heal… He is our Hope.

And we are most thankful to you all too… for the love, support and encouragement you so freely give us… for my terrific team who are wildly scrambling about to try and cover my work responsibilities… Thank you from the depths of our souls! May God richly Bless you all!

More later…

Responses

Clifton W

So sorry to hear about Rhonda. Please know that you all are in our prayers.

Dirk B

I cannot find words to express my pain but I know that it cannot compare to the emotions that you are feeling. I don't know what to do. I don't know what to say. Do I come see you? Do I leave you alone? All I want to do is puke. Words cannot express what I am feeling and I am so sorry that you are all being made to endure this. Please… Whatever you need… Whenever you need it… feel free to call on us. We are here and available for whatever support you may need no matter the sacrifice, 24/7/365. I don't know what to say. I feel helpless. This wasn't supposed to happen. I hurt for each and every one of you and our prayers and support are here and available for you. Please don't hesitate to ask if and when you have a need.

26

Please. We don't plan for what to do in times like this but, in all things, May GOD be glorified! I am sorry if what I have said so far is not the right thing to say but I just don't know what to say or how to say it. We love you all and are here for whatever you need.

Seriously… WHATEVER you need. Rhonda, are you o.k.? What can I do? What can I say? May God have mercy!!! Scott, I am sure that you have a support network of friends, but please feel free to call us for any reason at any time of day or night should you need to.

We are here for your family and are willing to help and support you no matter what is required. We mean that sincerely from the heart.

Roxzanne M

Scott, Cindy just sent me the news about Rhonda. I am so sorry to hear this news.

I know her mom is coming to help; however, if you guys need additional help let me know. Rely on your friends and family as much as possible. It will help you make it through this trying time.

Tell Rhonda hi, and that I will be praying for your whole family.

June 1
My Rhonda update

The PET scan was finished by early afternoon. The drs came to let us know the results this evening. Both the pancreas and the 2nd mass showed up as cancer "hot spots." All of the other organs were clean… meaning it has not metastasized… good news! We still haven't spoken with an oncologist, but they're thinking that it would be better to have 2–3 rounds of chemo before a surgery to help shrink the existing tumors. The surgeon used an analogy that doing surgery first would be like going after an ant hill with a shovel. You may dig up a bunch of ants, but a bunch are going to scatter around too. We don't want any nasty cells to be scattered around.

So… tomorrow they will perform another endoscope procedure (camera/tools through the mouth) to get a better biopsy of the cancer so they can get a more firm diagnosis of what type of cells we're fighting against. Then the oncologists will design the chemo treatment to knock down those tumors to prepare for surgery in maybe a couple of months. The surgeon also told us that they intend to use gene therapy after the surgery… actually taking a sample of the tumors and designing drugs that will specifically take them out.

Again… after some disappointment about having more than one place of concern, Rhonda and I prayed and we are ready to take this on and beat it. The docs impress us every time we speak with them… we feel very comfortable with their knowledge and skills… and with the knowledge that our God is with us to carry us every step of the way… every day… one day at a time. Today was a very busy… productive… good day.

And to top it off, Rhonda's mom and Stef came by late tonight on the way home from the airport. Maw-in-law is an ex cancer-care nurse and assertive care-giver. Our odds have just increased by a bunch! :)

God is good!

Thanks again for all of your love, prayers, and help.. you all are God's gift to us…

June 2
My Rhonda update

Rhonda had the scope/biopsy procedure this morning and the dr also performed another trick for her... it's called a "block." He actually 'blocked' the nerve that was sensing all the pain and essentially turned the pain off. She is now virtually pain-free for the first time in a long time... PTL!!! The 'block' should last many weeks... maybe months... hopefully until the cancer is gone and she doesn't need it any more.

The dr also gave us the preliminary results of the biopsy which was some long term I can't remember or pronounce. I asked him what that meant on the 'nasty' scale, and he said it was about halfway. Things are a little bit more involved than they had first thought... so they are recommending chemo AND radiation to start out.

While we were downstairs for the procedure, the cancer doctor came by our room during his rounds... so we missed him and haven't seen him yet today. So maybe tomorrow. No one has exactly told us when we would be able to go home just that it will be "soon." We have no information as far as what 'stage' we are at or what the treatment schedule will be... so... we will continue to wait.

Rhonda woke up early this morning with such a joy and euphoria at the goodness of God in our lives that she couldn't go back to sleep for hours. We both continue to live in the Peace that passes human understanding... refusing to look ahead at what the difficult experiences might be like and choosing to relish the days He has given us together... united as one with our Lord to battle this disease with all of our strength.

Also… Rhonda has asked Stefanie to create a "caringbridge" website to post updates for us. She jumped at the chance… and we feel this is a great outlet for her to share her thoughts and feelings too… good therapy for her. Here's the link…

www.caringbridge.org/visit/scrabblemom63

Once again… thank you so much for all of the prayers and well wishes… and esp to those who are running my work campaigns with all of the typos and bugs in them… God Bless your efforts to help a fella out!

June 2
From Rhonda to Debbie S

Hello Debbie,

Sure hope this finds you well. I'll keep this short as I'm in extreme need of rest.

Last week I was diagnosed with pancreatic cancer. We're at COMPLETE peace and VERY positive, but we also know we need prayer from everyone. We've been in the hospital since May 22. We will probably be going home this week to begin six weeks of out-patient chemo. After that there will be surgery, followed by more treatment.

One morning, as Scott and I awoke in the hospital, we both realized at the same time that our need of medical treatment was only a secondary reason we're here. We realize that being here will give us an avenue to reach someone while we're in these circumstances who would otherwise be unreachable… which is our primary reason for being here. Please pray that we will learn what it is He wants us to do to bring others to His kingdom. We have given God glory for all things as they happen in hopes that this will open a door for us to witness more.

My mom flew in last night and will be here as long as needed. What a blessing! Hope to see you at church on Sunday! We've missed greatly being there the past two weeks.

Again, we need prayer and as much positive energy as you can send our way. Thanks in advance for praying fervently for us. We love you and the family!

Debbie S's response

Dearest Rhonda,

I am lifting you up in prayer at this very moment: Heavenly Father, you alone are the giver of peace and comfort, and I thank you for giving both to Rhonda and Scott. I often notice the sweet way they sit together in church, and the way they are so attentive to one another. Lord, you brought them together for a glorious purpose, and that is so very evident in their lives, and the lives of their children. Your promise to us is not one of perfect days, but one of service that ultimately brings glory and honor to you. I praise you for the willingness of Rhonda and Scott to serve, and take this trial and use it to further your kingdom. I thank you that you have allowed our lives to cross paths, and that I now have the privilege of praying for them as they travel this road of uncertainty. One thing is most definitely certain… that you are in control Father, and we are sheltered in the wings of your almighty grace.

I pray, Lord, for strength in the days ahead; for many a comforting shoulder; for Scott as he supports his beautiful Rhonda; for the children as they watch their mother face the unknown; for Jordan, who is so very dear to my heart; for friends and family to be your hands and feet; and for the body of Christ to surround this precious family with love and support. God, you alone know our hearts, and you alone order our steps. May you carry Rhonda through this journey, and leave footprints that inspire others to follow in those steps. I ask all these things in your precious son's name. Amen

Rhonda, I will continue you to lift you up in the days ahead. Please know that I am only a phone call away, and would love to come and sit with you, visit, clean, take your son where ever he might need to go, bring dinner, anything. I sent Madison's announcement because you have been part of her life. And you have been a part of mine. I will be looking forward to seeing my favorite couple in church on Sunday.

Much love,
Debbie

June 4
My Rhonda update

Well the oncologist never made it to our hospital room, so the scope dr went ahead and discharged us late last night. We are now back home… exhausted and wrung out… but home. Rhonda called this morning and got an appt with the oncologist next Tuesday. So we won't have much news until then.

Some discomfort did start coming back last night, so they gave us a prescription for pain meds. She rested pretty comfortably overnight.

So now we start to get a look at the difficult road ahead… radiation… chemo… surgery… it will not be a picnic. We continue to be amazed at the outpouring of love and support from you all and so many others. We will take each day as God's gift and cherish the time we have together… and take on this challenge with every fiber of our being… relying on God for daily strength and leaving our troubled hearts in His loving care… knowing that His Love has saved us from far worse… that we know we will never be separated from His Love and that we will be more than conquerors through His saving grace.

June 4
My Rhonda update (expanded distribution)

Hi,

Rhonda and I have been absolutely overwhelmed by the outpouring of love and support. So much that I can't possibly keep up with responding to all of the inquiries and well-wishes. This email is a first attempt at consolidating our info updates about Rhonda and her battle with pancreatic cancer. The attached emails are what I've been sharing with friends at work. With this note, I'm including other friends and family. Please forward to others if you see they are not on my list. Thank you again for all of the support. Your prayers are precious to us.

Rhonda had a pretty good day today… mostly pain-free. She and I did attempt something 'normal' by making a quick grocery run and it was a bit too much for her. Tomorrow is her birthday and her mom is taking her to get a new hair-do. I know they'll have a blast. We do intend to go to church Sunday and look forward to bathing in the love of our wonderful SS class (Terry… pls forward these to the class for me… Thx!)

Again… our oncologist appt is for Tuesday afternoon. I will send an update after we've gotten more info there. Also be sure to check out Stefanie's updates and thoughts at www.caringbridge.org/visit/scrabblemom63

We feel your prayers and know that God will use this challenge to grow us and touch others. He always has a purpose greater than we could ever understand. We choose to trust Him with all.

God Bless!

Responses

Judy R
> Thanks for the update, Scott.
> My best to Rhonda!
> A spa/hair day sounds delightful.

Jim F
> Thanks for the info, Scott. Zelime and I prayed for you and Rhonda this morning.

Aunt Fran
> thanks for info on rhonda… have forward it on to family… naomi, marilu, sue, gary, lynn… lv to all… you are so very special..

Marylyn M

Scott, thank you for letting me know about Rhonda. Please give her a hug for me. I am so sorry to hear about her illness… if there is anything I can do, please let me know.

I called Doug and let him know about Rhonda. He is also just heart-broken that you two are having this challenge. I know that you both are very strong and your faith is even stronger. God will see you through this, He has been by your side during your courtship and marriage, raising a blended family and sees how much He's involved in all of your lives. We don't know why we are given these stumbling blocks but with the love you have for God, and He for you, you can get through this.

Love to both of you

D'Ann C

We were so sorry to hear that Rhonda was in the hospital. David forwarded some of your emails on Friday, so we know that she's home and doing better. I really enjoyed reading how God has blessed y'all with such faith! I really want to bring a meal over for y'all when it's a good time. I know that her mother is there, but she may need a break from cooking herself! Let me know. And, let me know if there's anything I can do now or in the future. We'll be praying.

*****

So the diagnosis was pancreatic cancer. It was not an easy thing to hear. I had some feelings of déjà vu as I remembered my first wife's diagnosis. Her fight had only lasted ten months. Rhonda's diagnosis was even more foreboding. Had I ever heard of anyone beating this? This is when our faith had to kick in. We are not like those who have no Hope. God does not promise us perfect health, but His perfect Love to hold us through all situations, all circumstances, all diagnoses. I was amazed (and always had been) at Rhonda's strength and faith. She's my hero. I asked God why it was her who was sick and not me. All I could discern as an "answer" is that I wouldn't be strong enough or have the courage to endure it. God knows us and allowed this nightmare into our lives so I could learn more about being a caregiver, to learn how to suffer with Grace and lend her my physical strength while I watched my most precious wife endure the suffering of this illness and the brutal treatments and procedures. I also had feelings of utter helplessness. I wanted to fix this, to make it all go away.

We had no sure knowledge of how it would turn out, but we knew that we would be together through it all, my Rhonda, me, and our Lord. From the beginning of Rhonda's hospitalization, I was determined to stay in her room with her day and night. And she wanted me there. We know that not all couples would want to be together 24/7, but we knew that we wanted to be. We learned to express this desire as "there's no place else I'd rather be" no matter where we were because we were together.

After we prayed and were able to turn all this over to Him, we had an amazing peace. What a gift that was! But there were to be many days ahead where there would be no peace, only desperate prayers to get through each day. God's strength is made perfect in our weakness. There would be ample opportunity to experience that in the coming weeks, months, and years.

We also had our amazing e-mail support group in our corner, consisting of friends from my workplace (I had some amazing Christian colleagues and managers who graciously allowed me to work remotely from hospital and home to be with my Rhonda. What a gift this was to us!), our Sunday School class, and other various friends and family—over fifty e-mail addresses in all. Many of these precious prayer warriors had had their own battles with cancer either personally or they had loved ones ill or who had even passed on from this devastating disease. These wonderful souls knew how to pray through adversity, and their love and encouragement would many times hold us up when we were ready to give up. God's people coming together is a mighty force for Help and Love and Hope.

And I also have to say that Rhonda's mother coming to stay with us sometimes for months at a time was the most wonderful gift from God to us. She just came in and took over the whole running of the household—kids, groceries, cooking, cleaning, everything. Hers was the most selfless act of service I had ever experienced, and it humbled me. At first I resisted: "I can handle this," but it didn't take long for me to see it was better for me to just step back and let her do it all. What an amazing woman and servant of God. What a blessing to our lives and family!

So as we were still learning about all this would demand from us, it was a great day when we finally had an attack plan in place, the first step in battling this monster and a plan to take our lives back.

*****

June 9
My Rhonda update

Finally… We have a plan…

Rhonda and I met with two drs today and have an approximate treatment schedule laid out. We saw the oncologist and radiation doctors to get each of their input on what Rhonda's treatment will entail. We told them we wanted to move on with this aggressively and they told us this is as aggressive as it gets. Yes!

Rhonda will have chemo and radiation simultaneously for 6 weeks. The chemo will actually be a continuous pump that she will carry with her… about the size of a small purse. She will just check in at the ofc once a week to get a fresh "fill-up" and to make sure she's doing ok. The radiation will be 5 days a week during the same time.

After the 6 weeks, they will wait another 4–6 weeks (while the nasty buggers are still shrinking and dying off) and then have another scan and set a date for a surgery to clean out the leftovers. We go back to the radiologist tomorrow to have a special CT scan so they can map the radiation points and get their equipment set up. We should also hear tomorrow from the surgeon to schedule a date/time to implant the chemo port.

All of this should be up and rolling within a week or so. We are excited to be moving forward with a plan to knock this stuff out and move on with our lives… hoping that all will be finished in time for the holidays. Rhonda hasn't felt real good for quite a while, and she's looking forward to getting past this and feeling better and having more energy than she has had in a long time.

Again.. we know this will not be a "walk in the park"… but we also know that our God's strength is perfected in our weaknesses… and He will carry us through this valley to the mountain top filled with light at the other end of this challenge. We feel confident in the abilities of those caring for Rhonda… and even more confident that our Lord will show us all great and mighty things through this time… and total victory when all is finished!

Thank you all again for your prayers and encouragement… we need your positive love to give God more channels of blessings for our strength to rise above this disease and then to declare all of the wondrous things He has done for us… and continues to do each and every day. He is our Hope and Peace.

I'll send out more info after we get things rolling along… may God Bless you all… as He has us!

Responses

Lynn B

Scott, thanks for the update. I am praying for you and Rhonda daily!

Usha A

I am glad to hear that the doctors have a good plan. May God give both of you strength to ride this out!

Good Luck!

Sylvia A

Good to hear the news, we will continue to pray that Rhonda and you may be uplifted during this time, and that God bless all those who will care for Rhonda during her journey so that they may be touched with God's mighty healing powers.

Marci E

Please know that your entire family is in my prayers. I am also praying for the doctors and any staff that will come in contact with Rhonda. In the name of Jesus!

Peggy A

Sounds like a good plan. Remember you will both continue to be in our prayers. You know I know how good it is to be a good fighter!

Tell Rhonda to put on her boxing gloves. She can beat this!

Jim F

Thanks for the report. You've made great progress. We'll keep praying.

June 14
My Rhonda update

Day One of the path to victory is coming... Thursday (18th)...

We will be at the hospital at 6 AM Monday to begin the process of getting Rhonda's chemo port. Tuesday and Wednesday are the days to finalize the alignments with the radiologist. And Thursday she gets the first treatment of radiation and the chemo pump hooked up and turned on. We are so ready to get this going and get it out of our lives!

We've learned some new and cool things about this chemo set-up. Since this is an ongoing infusion, the doses are smaller and so the side-effects are lessened... and... success rates are much higher. We really feel like we're benefiting from some cutting-edge technology here... God is watching over us.

Also... we did some research on the American Cancer Society website on Gene Therapy. The only article we found (dated 2005) stated that it was still "several years away" from being widely used... and here we are with the doctors telling us they planned on using it the very first time we met them... again... cutting edge... that we didn't even have to ask for... very cool!

So… here we go… finally going on the offensive to knock this stuff down and out. Rhonda is determined and I'm right there with her… by God's grace and strength… we can do this.

Thank you again for all of the prayers… support… encouragement and assistance. Maw-in-Law is back home in CA for now, but ready to come back whenever we may need her. Her strength and pretty much handling the house and the kids for 2 weeks allowed us to get things to a place where we feel we can manage things at the house fairly well. Thank God for Maw-in-Law! Rhonda's feeling pretty good as we finally have pain meds working consistently so PTL there too! We don't know yet what time the daily radiation treatments will be, but I will be driving her each day (thanks again to my wonderful team at work!). We are hoping for little in the way of side-effects and that Rhonda will actually start feeling better as the treatments do their job… even to the point of the reduction of pain meds.

We are ready for the battle and the Lord of Hosts is our Leader… our ultimate victory is in His Hands and we can almost taste it now that the counter-attack is starting soon. He is our confidence… in Him we will Trust.

Thank you again… you inspire and humble us with your love. We'll pass on more info as we know it… May God Bless!

Responses

Deborah M
    I am thinking of you and Rhonda.

Ronda G

Scott, it is always good to get your updates and hear how positive and united you and Rhonda are in all of this! It is especially good to hear your love for the Lord. That just jumps out of your notes and it's clear your faith is strong. I'm anxious to watch God's healing hands at work in Rhonda!! I fully expect a miracle!!

"Your faith has healed you. Go in peace." Luke 8:48

Aunt Naomi

Dear Scott, I so appreciate your news good and bad to keep us up to date. You are very fortunate to be on the cutting edge of cancer treatment where you are. We will be praying that all of that great treatment works... Keep in touch... Love you all

June 18
My Rhonda update

Well... they moved us up one day to yesterday and Day One is in the books! The radiation went fine but we had a bit of a rough start with the chemo... but Rhonda did great and things smoothed out quickly... we even did a major grocery run last night... and had a good night's sleep. The assault has started on those nasty buggers and... with God's help... we are going to clean them out!

All of the caregivers have been wonderful and understanding. God is also leading us to connect with others who are undergoing treatment. We met a 13-yr-old girl yesterday whose mom is undergoing radiation. We asked the girl how it was going and if she had any pointers since it was our first day. She really responded and wanted to share what her mom was feeling as a result of her treatment. We got to chat a bit with her mom too. I also met an older lady (while

Rhonda was having her treatment) who is really having a rough time and seemed to have no hope. She could barely shuffle down the hall. We want to try and reach out to her and tell her that we can always have Hope… that God is always there even in the dark valleys.

Thanks again for all of your support and prayers! And if you feel led… say a prayer for these others that we have met too… Thank you and God Bless!

Responses

Dirk B
Thanks for the updates. We have been praying for your family daily and are encouraged by your faith and your optimism. Again I say; if you need anything at all… do not hesitate to ask. I admire your strength in the Lord and you and your family are an encourage-ment to me and my family. Also, I expect that you will have a fabu-lous Father's Day. Furthermore please give Rhonda and your family our regards and deep felt support.

Marci E
Scott, thanks for keeping us updated. I will pray for the others you've mentioned. Prayer is so powerful. I'm glad I can pray for ya'll.
Remain strong and encouraged.

Sylvia A
Scott, we're all faithful in our good Lord that Rhonda is going to pull thru this journey and soon be on the road to recovery. I pray for her and your family daily, along with all the people in the world who are ill, hopeless or without medical care. We're the lucky ones who are blessed to have good Dr's and caregivers who help do God's work. I believe all the people we run into such as you have at the

hospital are all angels that God puts in our paths to both minister to, and to send us messages of hope and perseverance.

Please tell Rhonda she is in our daily thoughts and that we're here for anything you all need.

June 25
My Rhonda update

Hi… wanted to give you all an update to let you all know that things have been going pretty well as we mark one month into this challenging journey and the end of the first week of treatment. Rhonda's main challenge continues to be getting enough rest. She has never been a real 'nap-taker' person (one of the few areas where we differ!), so it's sometimes hard for her to give in and get rest when she needs it. She has gotten behind and needs some major rest to get her caught up again. The first "chemo refill" this week was another step that we had not experienced yet and we did have a bit of nausea and apprehension… but things went well. God continues to show us His goodness! Only five more weeks to go!

We did get a bit of a surprise this week. Our impression had always been that we would get the weekly chemo refills in the dr's ofc… but all their chairs were full this week, so for our first chemo refill, we got to go to the main "chemo suite." This is a huge waiting area surrounded by 3 or 4 large treatment areas. Here, we were again reminded that cancer is no respecter of persons. Rhonda said it looked like a 'lottery' to her… random people from all walks of life… age groups… ethnicities.

After checking in, we sat down next to an African-American lady… about our age… who clearly needed to just talk to someone.

Sandy has been in treatment since January, and is scheduled to go all the way to April 2010… with a surgery in the middle in August… for her breast cancer. She shared how she had lost her hair and eyebrows… her fingernails had turned dark… her skin had turned ashen gray and very dry… she is really having a tough go of it. Kinda puts a new perspective on Rhonda's 6 weeks of treatment. We are praying for her.

I also had a chance to chat with a Mr. Harvey… who thought he had a cold and found out it was lung cancer. He is in his 4th week of radiation treatment and has been losing weight because he just doesn't feel like eating. And then there's another lady, with two little girls, who bears the scars of brain cancer… we don't need to look very far to see how this awful disease touches so many.

As always… we will look to God for His strength to carry us through each day… each challenge… and each opportunity to reach out and touch another with His Love and Compassion. Thank you all again for your support and prayers… we need all you've got!

Please also remember the website that Stef is updating (more often than I am sending emails) at www.caringbridge.org/visit/scrabblemom63

God Bless!

Response

Lynn B
Scott, thanks for the update. I found it incredible the strength both you and Rhonda exhibit.

Let me know if there is anything I can do for you and your family.

Take Care!

Scott's response to Lynn B

We are so thankful and appreciative how you have allowed me to have so much flexibility in my work schedule so I can be with Rhonda during this time… this is a great gift to us! Several times Rhonda has looked at me and told me how much it means to her that I can be with her… taking care of appts and logisitics… keeping up with the kids… so she can focus on getting well. Thank you so much for giving me this time!

And… the root of our strength is a very real Christian faith based in the knowledge that God loves us without condition (even when we're not very lovable!)… and that He has a greater purpose that we may not understand in allowing this to happen to Rhonda. It's not something we would have freely chosen to go through, but we know that we can trust God to be with us through it all… and we try to always be aware that He has put us here not to feel sorry for ourselves… but to reach out to others with His Love. We naturally want to always focus on ourselves, but life is so much more fulfilling when we can make someone else's day a little brighter!

Thank you again… so much… for allowing me to be with Rhonda through this. It means more to us than words can say…

Other responses

Aunt Naomi

Dear Scott and Rhonda, Thank you again for the update. Sorry to hear of the upset when getting a refill. I understand how difficult it is to get her rest when she sees so much to be done. You have to learn to close your eyes to it and rest. Please take care of yourself.

Dirk B

Thanks for the update. We have been prayin' for you all. May God be glorified!

Trish M

HI guys! Thank you for opening your hearts to the other people undergoing treatment. People need people… and you are angels for walking hand in hand with the people you cross paths with.

Hugs

Sylvia A

Scott and Rhonda, we praise the Lord for helping you make it thru your first week of treatment and pray that His almighty arms continue to embrace you and hold you tightly each passing day so that you will soon be healed. I continue to keep you in my daily prayers as does my family and daughter.

Judy R

Glad the war is moving on in a positive manner. Seeing those other patients, what an eye-opener. Wretched disease.

July 4
My Rhonda update

Hello,

Well… 12 days down (only 3 more to halfway!) and Rhonda's been plugging away like a trooper! Still mainly suffering fatigue with some nausea at times… and that's about it. Terrific! This past week's chemo 'refill' was still a challenge for her, but she did much better and got through it just fine. We are so thankful for God's grace to us through this time... we know that the treatment could have her feeling much worse than it has. God is so good to us!

And... on Monday the 6th is our "big event"! We have tickets on the 10th row to see Paul Potts in concert, and then spend the night in a swanky hotel. We are so excited for this mini vacation break! If you don't know who Paul Potts is, he's the guy who told Simon Cowell that he planned on "singing a little opera" in Britain's "Got Talent" competition a couple of years ago, and then proceeded to blow their socks off... even Simon's! After winning the contest, he has put out 2 recordings and sold over 24 million copies worldwide. Rhonda and I are not opera fans at all, but Paul's genuineness and humility... and obvious talent... really struck a chord with us. We know that we'll be having a great time!

Back to the waiting room encounters... I got to listen to a guy's story on Thursday while waiting for radiation treatment. He had had cancer that was treated with a stem cell transplant back in 2005. All scans since then had been "clean." But in January, he hurt his upper arm and couldn't figure out why the pain wouldn't go away. Then he said that a bird had built a nest right near the front door of their house and that the mother started swooping down at him one day... seeing him as a threat to her nest. He waved his arm rapidly to fend off the attack and his arm broke... right where it had been hurt earlier. But it's not normal to have your arm break while you're waving your hand. They found a mass in his bone there... and two other spots on his other arm and leg. If that bird hadn't come at him... he may not have found out until much later. I told him that the Lord must have sent that bird... and he agreed! God is gracious even in our trials!

This guy's story touched me. While Rhonda and I were out on Saturday at the Christian book store, I found a bookmark to give him to celebrate his last day of treatment on Monday. It has a picture of an eagle (a bird, ya know?) in flight and quotes Joshua 1:9... "Be strong and courageous. Do not be terrified; do not be discouraged, for the Lord your God will be with you wherever you go." I can't wait to give him the bookmark! Life is so much better when we focus on God and others... and not ourselves!

This verse is great for anyone who's facing a difficult time... not just cancer patients... anyone. We find it a solid and affirming reminder that God is with us... even carrying us if needed... through this time where our lives have been taken over by Rhonda's illness.

While we allow Him to be in control of our thoughts and actions, we have no reason to fear. We can trust Him completely. His strength is made perfect in our weaknesses... and we all have plenty of those!

Thank you again for your prayers and support... it's so wonderful to see your faith and love at work on our behalf! Hope you all have a great holiday weekend! God Bless you all!

Paul Potts... here we come! :)

Responses

Trish M
    Have a GREAT time tonight!!!!

Brittany H
    Hope you two have a great time Scott!

July 10
My Rhonda update

Hello All…

Well… Day 17 of treatment today… and it's been a week of wonderful times… and also challenges.

The Paul Potts concert was everything we knew it would be… he is such a humble and regular guy… with an incredible voice! The music was beautiful and moving. We really felt blessed to be there! Earlier, we had killed some time by browsing around Northpark mall and ended up at Rhonda's favorite store… Coldwater Creek… where we did a little late birthday shopping for her. It was great to see her eyes light up with a new blouse and jacket to look forward to wearing! The hotel was really great too… very nice place!

However… through all of these wonderful things… Rhonda was dealing with severe nausea that robbed her of enjoying the time more fully. She couldn't eat. We weren't able to stay after the concert to meet Paul and get an autograph. The nausea finally passed overnight Monday, and she felt much better on Tuesday when we had a wonderful lunch with the people who are managing the rental of Rhonda's former home. And then Wednesday is our regular "date night"… so we went to dinner and a movie and just had the best time we'd had in weeks! PTL!

And yet again… all of this time Rhonda also had itching… virtually all over… and she was losing sleep and actually damaging her skin from all of the vigorous scratching. We talked to the docs about it and they decided to try a different pain med and also gave her a steroid pack to relieve the itching. So far, it has seemed to help. PTL!

Then yesterday the nausea started back again…

So… this is our life right now… good days and difficult days… wonderful moments and then just trying to get comfortable enough to get some rest. It will be great to get past the treatments and enjoy the month of rest before we embark on the next phase of a probable surgery and all that entails. We thank God for the good times… and we thank Him for bringing us through the difficult things… and we never forget the gifts that we receive from Him every day… family… friends… our church and SS family… a nice home… my job and incredible co-workers… food enough to gain weight on… and a place reserved for us in heaven. All things that we usually tend to take for granted… many things that can change or be taken away in an instant. Yes… our God is always good… and we will continue to trust in that goodness and strength for each day.

We know that this time in our lives will bring us to another dimension of our lives together… a time of growth and increased awareness of the wonderful life God has given us… a time of peace and rest.. and health. Our lives are in His Hands… and He is good.

Thank you all again for your love and encouragement! Please have a great weekend… and God Blessya!

Responses

Cathy G

Thank you for this most recent update. I was truly blessed by your thoughts and reflections on the recent events of Rhonda's illness. I am grateful that I had the opportunity to have some time with her last night and look forward to many more "Girls Night Outs" in the years ahead. I was just sharing with Greg this morning what a blessing Rhonda was to me during our year of dating and then preparations for marriage. That was a wonderful year but also an emotionally tough year for me in various areas of my life. Rhonda's encouragement through all of that helped me to stay focused on the Lord and wait for his timing in my life as well as Greg's. I will cherish those memories always.

You all continue to be in our prayers several times a day. We love you both!

Greg G

Thanks bro. It was good seeing you last night. I could tell Rhonda was having a tough time. I hope she's doing better.

Trish M

So sorry about the nausea. Know it's hard to work through it. Glad you enjoyed Paul Potts. Hugs to all of you!

Jim F

It was great to see you last night, Scott. We're praying not only for Rhonda, but for you as well.

Roxzanne M

Scott, you and Rhonda are such great witnesses for God.

When I had chemo, there was medicine I took when I was nauseous. Also, those red/white hard mints helped me a lot. Of course, you guys probably have information from Rhonda's mom that helps. Please keep in mind that I am not working, so I can help out. Scott, I really mean get with me if you need help.

I pray for you guys every night.

July 16
My Rhonda update

Greetings!

There's a light at the end of the tunnel! :)

Only one more chemo refill to endure… and two weeks from yesterday (the 29th) will be the last radiation treatment… and the day the chemo pack will be disconnected for Rhonda's month of rest and recovery… hallelujah and PTL!!!

We wanted to make that last day special… so we just made reservations for that one night at our Oklahoma getaway at Lake Murray… where we've spent our honeymoon… and every anniversary since… and we're really looking forward to a great time of relaxation to start the month of 'R & R'… PTL again!

And, after going through a couple of more hoops with the meds, Rhonda has had some pretty good days recently. The alternative pain med that they put her on really put her on edge emotionally… feeling very aggravated and tense. So we stopped that and went back to the good old morphine… and we now have a better med to deal with the itching… and to keep the nausea away… PTL!

Still… she needs a lot of rest. They asked us to switch to an earlier radiation time for these last couple of weeks to accommodate some extra time with a very difficult case. We were happy to comply, but it will take away the time for extra rest in the morning. I guess it'll just mean more afternoon naps. We will make it work!

Rhonda is also building a nice friendship with her radiation technicians… even sharing a few of her much-loved kakuro puzzles with one to share with her husband. And we always try to be a little bit of sunshine with those we encounter in the waiting rooms… attempting to share that we always can have some hope.

The kids are all doing well… Charlie and David both had bdays this week (now 15 and 25 respectively) and it was welcome to have the celebrations to serve as a distraction of the day-to-day treatments.

God has been so gracious to us! One of the nurses told us this week that this is the 'worst' they will be doing to Rhonda treatment-wise… and it made us realize how truly well things have gone for us to this point. We feel wrapped up in His Mighty Arms and know that we can Trust in Him whatever!

Again… we are so appreciative of our family and friends… so many prayers and well-wishes and hugs… and who want to reach out and help in any way they can… Thanks to you all… so much!

Yep… the light is getting brighter… and we are marching along and claiming our victory every day! God is soooooo good!

May God Bless you all richly!

Responses

Peggy A
Sounds great Scott. I'll continue to keep you all in my prayers.

Judy R
Yay!!! Light rocks. :)

Whew, big sigh of relief. Thanks for the excellent update!

Sylvia A

Scott and Rhonda, thanks for the update, I was just looking for an update the other day. God is truly miraculous and this will all be behind you soon and you'll be on the road to a speedy recovery. God bless you both, I continue to have you in my daily prayers.

Usha A

I'm glad that there is light at the end of the tunnel and Rhonda is handling it well. The combination of good treatment and the positive attitude that you both have will have positive results.

Please give my best to Rhonda.

Aunt Naomi

It is so encouraging to receive your emails and hear how well Rhonda is doing. I know that it is far from easy but God is faithful and is there for us. Keep up the good work, our love and prayers are with you.

July 27
My Rhonda update

Good Morning!

Three days of treatment left!

The last few days have been pretty good for Rhonda! We did have to switch to yet another pain med after the itching came back with a vengeance. She is now on a pain 'patch' that lasts for 3 days... but she has needed to supplement with another pill on occasion... just to make sure we stay on top of it. The new med does make it more difficult for her to relax, so more meds to help her sleep through the night and get the rest she needs.

But again… we are so thankful that this is the worst she is having to deal with!

We continue to reach out in the waiting rooms… meeting a whole new group of people when our radiation time got switched… including a young mother of 3 fighting cervical cancer. We hope to leave everyone we meet with a sense of hope and even a few laughs as we finish up our daily trips to the hospital. God is always with us… all of us… we just need to not be overwhelmed with our circumstances… but look to Him for His wonderful Peace! Rhonda has really been filled with that Peace recently… PTL!

The house was very quiet for a few days while Julie helped Stefanie to move back down to Waco to get ready to start her last year at Baylor. Charlie and I got his electronic 'robot car' thingy bday gift assembled (with Charlie learning to solder components on a circuit board… and he did very well!). It doesn't seem to be working quite right, but it was a fun experience for him! David and Jillian got a new dog… and Jordan is working out of town some and waiting for the Dallas firefighter interview process to start up… soon!

So… things are going well… Rhonda and I are looking forward to our one day celebration trip to Lake Murray on Wednesday… after the last radiation treatment and the chemo is unhooked! WhooHooo!

Thanks again for all of the love and support! We feel it! God has been very gracious to us to bless us with such wonderful family and friends!

Blessings to you!

Responses

Jim F

Praise the LORD for such a great report!

I pray that He will supply all that you and Rhonda need to see this through. Keep fighting the good fight of faith, Scott, as you have been doing so well. The battle belongs to the LORD!!!

Sylvia A

Scott and Rhonda, good to hear that the treatment is almost behind you now, and you can begin to look forward to your recovery soon. I continue to keep you in my prayers and include you in our intentions at mass on Sundays.

Enjoy yourselves this week at Lake Murray knowing that God is with you along with all the multitude of angels both here on earth and in heaven that have been sent your way to pray for you and uplift you!

August 2
My Rhonda update

Phase One is done!

What a week God has given us! So many opportunities to touch others in ways that only He could orchestrate…

Early Tuesday morning… our scheduled 2nd-to-last day of treatment… we got a call from Rhonda's radiation techs that the machine was down… probably for the day. Rhonda told him that we had another appt and had to be there anyways… and that we would check in while we were there on the chance it may be fixed. On the way, we discussed the possibility that, if we got put a day behind, we may be running back from our night at Lake Murray to get her last treatment... but left it up to God to see what happened. So... we got there and checked with the radiologist... not fixed yet, check back after our other appt... we did and they said it was fixed(!) and asked if we could wait another 20 minutes or so... no problem! In the course of waiting, we met this couple where the wife was in for a bone marrow transplant the very next day. They were from El Paso and had nobody in this area to be with them. I chatted with the husband after his wife went for treatment, and when Rhonda came back we told him that we would pray for them... he was so appreciative... and Rhonda got her treatment to keep us on schedule. If we'd been on our regular schedule, we wouldn't have met them. God is amazing!

In preparation for our last day of treatment, we had gone to a Christian bookstore and picked out some bookmarks to share with the techs and fellow patients. Rhonda also made some cookies (yum!) to share with her techs. On the bookmarks were scriptures we wanted to share. The ones we shared with the patients had Psalm 27:1... "The Lord is my light and my salvation... whom shall I fear? The Lord is the stronghold of my life... of whom shall I be afraid?"... and on the back we put our names and an email address. As we passed these out and tried to share a few words of encouragement... the moist eyes abounded... myself included. I'd love to share each person's story with you... but I'll just say that we were all touched... knowing that we shared a common struggle... and that we are never alone in that struggle. God is always with us... and it was great to share that with others who needed to hear it.

When we got to Lake Murray and checked in for our one-night-getaway... they put us into the exact room where we stayed for our honeymoon week... almost 4 1/2 yrs ago. That was special... God is so good! Rhonda didn't feel real great during our stay, but we both relished the time away and watched a couple of movies just to distract from all we'd been through and relax. Another couple of days would have been great, but we were thankful for what we were able to get!

So... Rhonda is still going through times of feeling great (which doesn't seem to last too long)... and times of exhaustion. It's difficult for her to sleep through the night... it seems she may be even having some 'minor' hallucinations from the strong pain meds. We go back on Tuesday for labs and will ask the dr then what we can do to help her. otherwise... we are on a four week time of rest and are working to regain some strength and stamina. I'm so proud... we've walked 2 miles for 3 evenings in a row... and plan to tonight too! With the rain showers we've had lately, the sunsets have been incredibly beautiful... yet another gift from God that we take for granted too often. We also got to share a group lunch with many of our friends from my work on Friday... and tried to express to them personally how much it's meant for me to be able to mainly work from home and be with Rhonda through this time... ya'll are a gift from God too... thank you all again!

The kids are doing well... Charlie starts marching band camp as a 10th grader tomorrow... we've been told that all of his transportation has been arranged... another gift from wonderful people reaching out to us during this time. Stef is working at a camp through her Waco church... Jordan is awaiting his 1st interview to be a Dallas firefighter... Julie is pursuing the possible careers of welding and perhaps being an oil rig 'roughneck'... and David and Jillian are approaching their 2nd wedding anniversary... my how the time does fly.

Thank you again... so much... for your prayers and love. We feel our strength increased through your caring and encouragement... and we thank our God for you all. The next scan will be around the last week of August... so we won't know how things are until then... but we know that we're in His Hands... and that we can trust Him... whatever.

Sorry this is such a 'windy' email... so much to share... :)

Thanks... and God Bless!

Responses

Greg G

Thanks brother for the update! You guys are an inspiration to a lot of people. Keep the faith.

Sylvia A

Scott and Rhonda, good to hear from you, I look forward to your updates, as they are so inspiring... even thru these emails, you are touching others in ways you may not realize, once again God's working thru you. I was out of the office last week so was disappointed I missed you as I had heard you would be in the office visiting.

We will continue to keep you in our daily prayers and petitions! Take care

P.S. keep those updates coming, we look forward to them... in the midst of our busy days they are a blessing!

August 11
My Rhonda update

Hello again,

August 24th...

That is the date of Rhonda's scan to determine how much of the nasty bugger is left after the treatments. After we get the results (a few days?), we'll know what the docs recommend next. Of course, we're praying that it's all gone and the docs will be amazed... but we will be ready for whatever transpires... knowing that our God will continue to be with us and keep us in the grasp of His Love.

So... Rhonda has had some really great days recently! We've walked nearly every evening for the past two weeks... most times for 2 miles... a couple times just a mile... and 3 out of the last 5 days for 3 miles! We are working to build the stamina and strength back after being knocked out of our regular routine for the past couple months. We are just having to take it slowly. Rhonda still feels pretty weak most of the time. It has still been a challenge to get a full night's rest, and the exhaustion magnifies everything difficult that she's working to overcome... still some nausea... still some extra 'twinges' of pain... and suffering some setbacks when she tries to do too much.

Still... all in all she can feel the strength slowly returning... which is very good... PTL! So we are waiting... trying to get as much strength back as possible to prepare for whatever follows.

Rhonda has swapped an email or two with the wife of a couple we met during treatment... John is being treated for throat cancer and has to be fed through a tube in his abdomen. We haven't heard from anyone else, but we are praying for them... the lady from the Corsicana nursing home... the lady who we met on our last day whose husband was just starting treatment for a reoccurrence... the lady from El Paso who received the bone marrow transplant... Sandy, who we met in our first chemo waiting room experience and has several more months of treatments... and others whom God has placed in our path during that time.

So many are touched by this disease... one lady I work with told me that her mother is in stage 4 breast cancer... another co-worker has an elementary-school aged nephew with cancer... it seems to be an accelerating epidemic that so drastically changes the lives involved. Rhonda and I had planned on going out and looking at new homes the weekend she ended up in the hospital. We're thinking now that we will aim for next spring to give us time to get completely past this... and we're ok with that... we trust in God's timing for every-thing. So we will wait... on the scan... and whatever may follow... and work and pray to stay in His perfect peace every day.

Thank you again for your prayers and encouragement. Our spirits are buoyed by your love and caring... you are God's gift to us.

God Bless!

Responses

Judy R
Thanks for the update! I was wondering what/when the next steps were. I'm rooting for the doctors to be amazed. :)

Aunt Naomi

Dear Scott and Rhonda. Your letters are very uplifting and encouraging.

August 23
My Rhonda update

Hi there,

Scan day is here…

Tomorrow we go to the hospital to get Rhonda's CT scan. This will tell us how well the treatments did their job. We're believing for a good result… but still anxious to see the outcome.

Again… this is a 'rubber meeting the road' moment for our faith. Do we really trust God? We know that we have no promise of what the result will be… but what we do know has been very encouraging. Rhonda has definitely been getting stronger. We walked 2 miles again this evening. That makes it something like 35–40 miles total in the past few weeks. She's had many more good days than rough ones… she's taken herself off all regular meds except the pain patch… only taking a supplemental med a few times in the last 2 weeks. This is all great news… PTL!

And yet… it's good ol' human nature to wonder… even worry about the future. The enemy of our souls never misses a chance to whisper some 'what if… ' to our heart. If we could package up the energy we use on wondering and worrying, we'd no longer have a dependence on foreign oil!

I see 'worrying' as a choice. Do I decide to affect today by the 'what ifs' of tomorrow? Do I make myself miserable worrying about something that 99.9% of the time never happens? And ultimately… do I trust God? As much as it is in my power… and the strength God gives me… I choose to not worry. I choose to dwell on what I know… to count my blessings… to focus on others… to leave tomorrow in God's able Hands. To live this day that He has given me to its fullest.

Rhonda and I are planning our future together… doing some work around the house here and there… and eventually moving to a home that we pick out together. This is our plan… God willing. We just need to get past tomorrow and whatever it holds for us… and then carry on with the wonderful life God has blessed us with. We will live each day in victory… and know that any challenges that arise we will not face alone. We have done well to get this far… relying on God's strength… and the prayers and support of you all when our own strength wavers. We know that we live a very blessed life.

Charlie and Stef start school tomorrow. Jordan found out this past week that he did not make the first cut to the interview process for firefighter, but they left open a door that he may be called in January. His current boss is happy to have him staying for now. David and Jillian continue working on their home… getting close to finishing some rooms… and have added two dogs to their family.

Thank you again for your love and support! It's so humbling to know that so many care. You are precious to our hearts. We will let you know the scan results soon… possibly even late tomorrow or Tuesday.

Also... please whisper a prayer for my Aunt Fran and cousin Cheryl... they are facing some difficult physical challenges. Thank you!

Thank you all... and God Bless!

Responses

Judy R

Best of luck with the scan!
I'll be thinking good thoughts.
Looking forward to hearing the good report. :)

Quinn W

Good luck today Scott!

Greg G

This is the big day bro. We are praying for you. Let us know if there is anything else that we can do.

Sylvia A

Scott and Rhonda—thank you for your inspirational words, once again, you can't imagine how you touch others with your words of faith, they are so empowering!

But I know that life is full of many tests, both wonderful and challenging, and it's all those that strengthen our faith and remind us that God is in control and He never lets us walk alone.

Not a day has passed that Rhonda and your family are not in my prayers or intentions. Continue your resolve to leave the healing to God and remember that only He is the healer who has and will continue to carry Rhonda in her journey wrapping her in His arms to keep her strong and bring her to a full recovery soon.

God bless

August 24
My Rhonda update

We got results!

The phrase I most remember hearing the doctor use... more than once was... 'very pleased'! He told us this afternoon (a mere couple hours after the scan) that there was extensive shrinkage of the tumors... that even the lymph node that was most swollen had 'normalized' in size. He had a big smile on his face. I don't think we could have gotten a better report unless God had chosen to intervene in a bigger way.

But... as the nurse had told us weeks ago... there is 'always a surgery'. So, even though the doctor couldn't tell us if there was truly any cancer left or not... he said we needed to do surgery to clean out the area and do biopsies and get clean margins. He told us there was scar tissue to be removed, presumably from the tumor dying off and shrinking. And also... that after surgery there would be another 6 months of chemo... a more 'conventional' chemo that would be administered in about 30 minutes per week. We don't know if additional radiation will be scheduled or not, but it was not mentioned today.

We tried to see the surgeon to get things moving there, but had to leave a msg to have him call us and schedule a consult. So we won't know a surgery date until that happens.

All in all… a very good day! We still have some time before all of this is over… but the first phase of treatment has been very successful… PTL! God has shown His grace and favor to us… again! We will continue to trust the end results to Him.

Oh… and we even ran into the mother of the young lady who is being treated for cervical cancer. We had just stepped outside and she waved us down from the other side of the courtyard. She told us that her daughter was having her last daily radiation treatment today. She was very excited because they have been driving from Greenville, TX every day… over 50 miles each way… ugh! She has a radiation implant that they hope will continue to shrink her tumor so they can eventually have surgery… and she's not due back for a test until November. We will continue to remember her and the others God brought across our path.

So… thanks again for your encouragement and love! We'll let you know when we have a date for surgery…

God is so good! :)

Responses

Jeff W

I am so happy for both of you for the good news! It is clear that God is using you and Rhonda and this experience to honor and glorify Him. Thank you for all of the updates. You guys are regularly in my thoughts and prayers.

Dina T

oh Scott. This is the best news ever! I am so elated that the doctor was pleased with the progress. I can't wait to share the news with the ladies from my bible study. I know they have been praying for Rhonda (and your whole family). Thank you for keeping us updated to date on Rhonda's progress. The power of prayer is an amazing thing and we will all continue with prayer and positive thoughts.

Clifton W

Praise the Lord for the encouraging report.

Jane B

Praise the Lord for the very positive report and for your communication and faithfulness in keeping us informed. We rejoice with you on today's reports and will continue to pray for you and for others to whom you are ministering.

Judy R

Excellent!!! That's the news I wanted to hear. YAY!!!

Trish M

AWESOME!!!!!! Hugs to all of you Scott!!!!! You guys are something else. God IS good!

Love ya!!!!

Cindy H

Praise God for the shrinkage of the tumors! I pray that the surgery to clean out the area is minimal and that the biopsies show no cancer cells and that Rhonda has a speedy recovery. I not only pray for no cancer cells, but that the need for more chemo will be eliminated and the peace of choosing not to do more chemo will be present.

Peggy A

So very happy to hear this news! Very happy! You will all continue to be in my prayers.

Sylvia A

Praise The Lord!

Drew C

Scott, what a GREAT report! PTL!!!

Aunt Naomi

I'm so happy for your good news. we can all use good news. Keep up the good work love you all.

September 1
My Rhonda update

Hello and God Bless!

The date is set… Sept. 21. This is the date the surgeon will remove the last stinkin' pieces of the dead and shriveled up tumor. From that date forward, we will be looking at this as something that has occurred in the past… from that date forward all that Rhonda will need is a time of rest to heal her body from the battle that's been wearing her down for maybe a year… maybe longer… from that day forward we will proclaim victory over this nasty disease and press to move forward with the wonderful plans that our Lord has already prepared for us. PTL!

On another very positive note, the surgeon is setting up appts and recommending us for 'gene therapy'. He mentioned this to us in a conversation with him many weeks ago, right after the diagnosis. We didn't understand exactly what it entailed, but knew that it must be wonderful! Well, this time he explained it to us. During the surgery, the 'gene team' will take the nasty tumor into their laboratory and start messing with its genetic make-up. They will 'mutate' some of the genes and create a vaccine (much like a flu vaccine) tailor-made just for Rhonda! When she receives this vaccine (not sure of the timeframe), her body's defense system will see these cells as an invasion and program her immune system to fight it… it's an anti-cancer shot! Pretty terrific, cutting edge stuff, eh? PTL!

Our visit with the surgeon was on Wed, the 26th… and it was not an easy appt. The dr was very up front about things… it is a long and difficult procedure… maybe up to 5 hours… followed by about a week in the hospital. Being confronted with the reality of the surgery was unsettling for us… with the weight of it still hanging around at times like a cloud that refuses to allow the sun to shine through for any prolonged time.

We had also hoped that the surgery would be in the next couple of weeks… so now we'll have to wait longer to get this over with. But… it is a set marker… a date that we can look forward to getting beyond and put it all of this behind us. The countdown is on!

So… while we wait for this date… we will continue to take each day as God gives it to us… to work to shoo away the cloud that wants to create anxiety and worry over such a procedure… to allow God's love and peace to penetrate and envelope us with the knowledge that we are never alone.

We also continue to be amazed at the love and support of our family and friends… at church… at work… and even over the internet from the other side of the world. Thank you again… so much!

Responses

Aunt Naomi

Dear Scott and Rhonda, Your news this week is exciting and scary. I'm so glad that you have met with the surgeons and, yes, it is scary to listen to all the possibilities that we just as soon not hear; but they have to tell you those things or they would be neglecting their duty. My prayers will be with you for a successful completion of the surgery and the following treatment. It is exciting to think of the results of all this to be completely free of the nasty cancer. I hope the rest of the family is doing well, My love to all of you Aunt Naomi

Jan R

Scott,

Thank you so much for forwarding all of your "My Rhonda" emails. After reading them, I can almost feel what you are feeling! You are very good at expressing your thoughts and your love for Rhonda is quite evident and comes through with clarity! This information will help us know how to pray for Rhonda, for you, for the surgeons & drs., and for the kids. We are truly blessed to be able to call you and Rhonda "friends".

Prayerfully,
Jan & Julius

*****

Earlier, Terry (our SS teacher) had prayed for us to have a Christian doctor. Our surgeon was Dr. Joseph Kuhn, an amazingly skilled doctor, a leader in his field, and a wonderful man of God. When we had our first appointment with him, Rhonda and I were reassured by the displays of awards and accolades we saw in the waiting area and exam rooms, but we were most impressed with and thankful for the Christian decor on display. We also brought a smile to his face when he came into the exam room. He was also a bariatric surgeon, and they had oversized chairs to accommodate these patients. Well, Rhonda and I saw them as cozy "love seats" and had snuggled into one of the chairs together while we waited. I think the nurse laughed out loud while the doctor raised his eyebrows and grinned. I think it gave him a pretty good picture that me and my Rhonda we were in this together. He then shared with us his take on his work: "What I do is mostly destructive—cutting, removing, etc. It is the Lord who does the healing and makes everything right again." We knew that our Lord had put Rhonda in this man's hands, who in turn prayed for God to guide those same hands. We were in the right place! Rhonda's surgery was to be what is known as the "whipple" procedure that is most often performed for pancreatic cancer patients. It is an extensive surgery and has a difficult recovery.

*****

September 15
My Rhonda update

Six more days until surgery...

We've been counting down the days... glad to have a 'break' from treatments and the like... but ready to get this done and put it behind us. Rhonda's been doing really well lately... she has given in to her body's need to get a lot of rest and is sleeping in later (after seeing Charlie off to school at 6:30), and taking more frequent naps... and feeling much better... PTL! We continue to walk nearly every evening and have logged 26 miles so far in Sept... PTL again! We know the walks are strengthening her for her recovery after the surgery.

Today we met with a lady in the Mary Crowley Cancer Research Ctr... the "gene team." We learned that the gene therapy is actually a clinical study... and Rhonda's been signed up as one of 200 participants. The surgeon's enthusiasm kinda led us to think that this was a 'sure thing'... the lady today described it as an "unproven treatment." But... we know that God has a reason for making this available to us... and we're taking it! The lady told us the ability of the lab to create a vaccine is not 100%, but then told us she knew of only one instance where they were not able to produce a vaccine. We also learned that, if they do produce a vaccine, it would be administered by injection on a monthly basis... we don't know how many months. We also learned that, since it is a "clinical study" there will be no costs incurred by us or our insurance for any of the work or possible treatment... it's all covered by the research grant... pretty cool!

So... we will see what benefit we may see from this... we won't know until about 6 months after the surgery. They actually have to get the cancer to grow in the lab so they can create the vaccine... and there may not be enough of the nasty stuff left to get it to grow in the lab (we have been praying for it all to be gone, ya know)... we will leave this up to the skilled technicians... and the Lord.

Rhonda's mom is coming in on Thursday... and staying for a month... or as long as we may need her around. Rhonda and I sure have some wonderful moms! Rhonda's brother will be coming also... maybe others too... we'll take all of the love and support we can get!

With each day... the roots of our peace about everything are deepening... it will be great to have this done and continue with our lives! We know that God has given us very skilled and caring care-givers to lead us through this maze of treatments and appts... but we also know that God is our Healer... the Great Physician... and ultimately it is He who will carry us through this challenge. We are so thankful for all that He has given us and done for us!... and at the amazing encouragement and love that we continue to receive from so many... Thank you all again!

We will get past this... learning anew that a gracious and awesome God loves us without condition... and that He uses our family and friends like you all to express that love in so many ways.

I won't have access to this email distribution from the hospital... we will be there at least a week... so I will count on those whom I am able to contact to spread the word on the wonderfully successful surgery that will happen on Monday... and don't forget the website...

www.caringbridge.org/visit/scrabblemom63

Every day brings us closer to the victory we will celebrate when this is all over... we know that God's Hand will continue to hold us each step of the way...

Thank you and God Bless...

Responses

Peggy A
My prayers will be with you - prayers to you both for Rhonda's upcoming surgery.

Sylvia A

We will continue to storm the Heavens with our prayers and ask our Heavenly Father to hold you close in his arms and bless the hands and work of all your caregivers so that you may make a quick recovery and soon be back at home with all your family and friends who are keeping vigil for you. God bless!

Amy C

We are praying and love you guys!

September 20
My Rhonda update

Tomorrow is the day...

Rhonda's surgery is scheduled from 12–5 PM tomorrow. We check in at 9 AM. This is it... the beginning of the end of this thing that has taken over our lives for the last few months. Let the healing begin!

Again... we are so thankful for the love, encouragement, prayers, generosity, and sacrifice given on our behalf... Thank you, thank you, thank you!

We also thank you in advance for your prayers for the surgeon and his team... for a smooth procedure... and a speedy and full recovery. We are so thankful for the expert care that Rhonda has received!

And we are most thankful for a loving Father in heaven who has orchestrated all of this love and care for us. We rest in the assurance that He is fully in control... and the fact that Rhonda (as well as the rest of us) is so very precious to Him. At times, the night… the darkness comes and tries to overwhelm us… but joy comes in the morning. Our joy is very near to its fullness. PTL!

Again… I will get the word out as I am able… your most timely information will most likely be the website www.caringbridge.org/visit/scrabblemom63 with many thanks to Stef for her wonderful updates. I will not have access to this email until we are home from the hospital… 7–8 days.

We are also very thankful to have Rhonda's mom here with us to help us through this time! She has virtually taken over the managing of the household and will be a tremendous help to us the next several weeks. Her gift of love and sacrifice is wonderful to us… Thanks Maw-in-Law! We love you so much!

And… we are very thankful to have reservations to our Oklahoma getaway for Oct 15–16 (courtesy of my mom!) to celebrate getting past this point and moving forward with our lives together! Thanks Mom! We love you so much!

We are so ready to put this behind us… tomorrow we start! PTL!

Thank you and God Bless!

Responses

Peggy A
I will be praying for Rhonda and look forward to wonderful results.

Ryan G

You know that you are both always in my prayers. Cara and I will probably come by once Rhonda is home and feeling better.

Quinn W

God bless you and keep you!

Julius R

We are praying for Rhonda today. Please tell her that we are doing that this morning and thinking of y'all.

Patti S

We love you dearly and our hearts are firmly with you today. Our prayers will be abundant. I know you will feel them.

Judy R

Thinking about you and Rhonda, fingers crossed, sending good vibes. Looking forward to a good result!

Sept 21
e-mail from Cathy G

Hi Rhonda and Scott,

Below are several excerpts from emails I have received from friends who are praying for you all today. (I sent out an email yesterday with pictures of you both and a picture of Rhonda and me. This really helped to make it more personal for those who haven't met you yet.)

Be encouraged!!

I will be praying for Rhonda, Scott, and all those who will be involved with her surgery. May God give her peace that passes all understanding, and may the doctors be skillful and alert to do all they need to do. Of course, we will pray for healing as well.

We'll be praying for you tomorrow as you both minister to Rhonda and Scott... Please keep us posted on how she comes through her surgery and let Scott know that he's in our prayers as well.

Rhonda is beautiful! I will pray for her and Scott.

Thanks for the reminder... we will be praying... it is great to have the picture to put a face with the name...

We will pray all day for Rhonda and her surgeons!! Please keep us posted!!!

Sept 21
Stefanie Caring Bridge post

SHE'S OUT.

The tumor was the size of a pea (she hates peas, by the way, so that probably reinforces her hatred of them). It is now gone. Her gall bladder was what was causing most of her problems (diseased, not cancerous), so that is now gone. They didn't take out any of her stomach or intestines, so that should help her recovery (my words not from anyone else, so don't quote that). She's in recovery now and everything has been really good so far. They will still do chemo to clean up things, so I'm not sure what that means, but my grandma did use the phrase "cancer-free" just now when talking to me over the phone, so that is AMAZING.

Praise the Lord.

Thank you guys so much for ALL of your prayers. Please continue to pray that she would be restored to full health and the cancer wouldn't dare show its face again in her body.

Additional Note from me: since her gallbladder was what was making her sick and pancreatic cancer is SO hard to diagnose, i wonder if they would have caught the cancer in time if her gallbladder had been normal… so I think we need to thank God right now for a diseased gall bladder for getting our attention!

Also, this is Scott's text to me: "Finished! Dr astounded! Tumor was size of a pea. Cancer free!" So now I've gotten the phrase cancer-free from the two people who were there and I'm thinking that the "clean-up" chemo is to kill any cancer that might possibly be left.

Sept 21
from SS teacher Terry C

Hello all. I have some very good news about Rhonda's surgery. The surgery lasted six and a half hours approximately. The tumor had shrunk from egg size when the doctors found it, to pea size. The lymph nodes that were involved were all tested as well as the rest of the lymph nodes in the area and all returned negative for cancer. The tumor was completely removed. There was not enough cancer left after the biopsy on the tumor to be able to generate the gene therapy that they told us about. The good news is the doctor said that she is cancer free. Praise God for answer to many prayers that have been lifted up about this. The doctor was amazed at what he found after he got in there. He said that he has never seen this type of result before. God truly touched her and has restored her body to be cancer free.

He also told us that her gall bladder was very ill and he removed it. This was causing infection throughout her body. So she no longer has that problem. They did not remove any of her stomach. They removed the stents from earlier and they also were causing some infection.

Rhonda still has a very serious recovery ahead of her. She has multiple tubes and drains. Please pray for God to continue to provide her healing and help her with the pain. Scott and Rhonda are both very thankful for the support, the prayers and everyone's love.

God is so good.

Responses

Ryan G
      That is the most excellent news EVER!

Judy R
      Sounds like a miracle has graced your life. Word on the street is that nasty tumor was only the size of a pea, and that the lymph nodes are clean. WOW!
      (dancin' in the streets!)

Jan R
      Praise the Lord! This is one of His many miracles! What wonderful news and another testament to the great Power of Prayer!

Patti S

Friends, I'm sure that you like me have been praising God all morning for this wonderful gift of healing he has bestowed on Rhonda and the joy of witnessing His miraculous power! I will carry this in my heart forever!

Greg G

Rhonda is Cancer Free!!!!!!!!!!!!!

Drew C

Wonderful, wonderful, wonderful I am rejoicing.

Sept 29
My Rhonda update

Hello Friends!

I'm hoping that you've already heard the incredible news of how the surgery went... after over 6 hours of operating, the surgeon came out and told us that he could find no trace of living cancer cells. This was confirmed to us again just last night when he came into Rhonda's room (we are still in the hospital) and told us the final pathology report showed no living cancer was to be found. It was all dead.

The surgeon also told us that he had NEVER seen results like this after just chemo/radiation... and then said that it must have been those prayers...

God has graciously and mercifully answered the prayers of his people... Wow and PTL!!!

And yes… we are still in the hospital. It was a major surgery and it takes time for everything to start working again. Rhonda will probably start on some liquid foods for the first time tomorrow, Wednesday. As she progresses with more solid foods with no issues, we will be released to go home… hopefully by the weekend.

Thank you all so much for the love, prayers, and support… and many thanks to those who are working above and beyond to cover for me while I'm out of the ofc… I have not left the hospital since we got here on 9/21. It has meant so much to Rhonda for me to be able to stay with her in the hospital. I still have to pinch myself to believe that there's no trace of cancer that they could find… God is so good! Please pass on the good news to those that may not be on this distribution… path to victory is coming… Thursday (18th)…

I will have more thoughts to share after we get home and this has all sunk in… and I get a chance to sleep for more than 2 consecutive hours… :)

God Bless you all for your amazing support!
Scott and Rhonda

*****

The surgery results were amazing and exhilarating to us! The doctors were astonished and scratching their collective heads. They had never experienced a result like this. Was it truly a miracle? We were ready to stake our claim to that! My joy was tempered somewhat by knowing that Rhonda's recovery would not be quick or easy. This procedure was a major surgery, and it broke my heart to see my Rhonda having to endure such suffering. But I was so thankful that the results were so wonderful so that after a time of healing, we could look forward to having our lives back!

*****

Oct 7
from SS teacher Terry C

Praises to God. Rhonda and Scott are on their way home from the hospital. I am sure that they are very happy to be returning home.

Response

Amy C
　Amen

Oct 7
My Rhonda update

Wow…

We just got home from the hospital about 3 hours ago… ready for our own home and bed after 16 days post surgery… and very thankful for what God has worked in our lives! Rhonda is comfortable for the most part… just needing to work back into a regular diet and shed a bunch of excess fluid she's retaining. The difficult part is over. We can now work to continue our lives together… post cancer.

Just to re-cap (or if you haven't heard yet)… The surgery couldn't have gone better. The egg-sized tumor was 'dead' and reduced to the size of a pea. All of the lymph nodes that had been involved were removed and were free of cancer. A week after surgery, the final pathology report showed absolutely no signs of any cancer. Anywhere. Dr. Kuhn has never seen a response to chemo/radiation like this before… and he's no "spring chicken." There was absolutely no tumor left to give to the gene therapy group, so Rhonda will not be receiving that treatment. It's not needed. She is cancer-free.

God has worked an incredible miracle of healing in Rhonda's body… wow!

So… the "war" has been won… the cancer is gone… defeated… but this was a very major surgery, and the recovery process has not been a picnic. Rhonda still will have a lengthy time healing from the wounds of the battle… she had some major reshuffling of her digestive system done. We were expecting 8 days in the hospital… not 16. It's been an exhausting couple of weeks.

But we definitely have a smile on our face… God has given us the victory.

So one more time… I need to say "Thank You" for all of the prayers and support. Our loving Heavenly Father has listened and granted our request. We give Him all the praise and glory. He is our Healer.

I may share more thoughts in a few days after catching up on some rest. We thank God for giving us you all as such a wonderful support group… we are humbled by your thoughts, time, and generosity.

God Bless you all…
Scott and Rhonda

Responses

Marci E

God is so awesome. I am so happy for you both. Thank you for taking the time to update us with the praise reports.

Linda S

Scott, this is such wonderful news! We are all smiling right along with you and Rhonda. What a happy day :)

Terry C

Scott, we rejoice in another step taken on the road to recovery. God is so merciful and gracious. Indeed, He is the one who heals. I thank God for the doctors and care providers that you both encounter through this. I believe he provided the right persons to help with this treatment. Both Rhonda and you need to rest, regain some strength and renew yourselves physically. We look forward to seeing you both soon. In Christ's Love

Suraya K

I am so happy for you and Rhonda. I hope she recovers all her strength and spirits soon. God is great and we are all thankful for His Mercy.

Theresa D-J

I just wanted to let you know that I have been following all your emails about Rhonda's treatment and am so happy to hear the good news that she is cancer free!

Patti S

Scott, we are so thankful that this ordeal is behind you and are mindful that the recovery process will be slow, but, praise Him!, complete!

It is hard to describe the joy that Rhonda's miracle brought to each of us including all the friends and co-worker we told about it. What a witness to his power and love!

To humbly thank Him, we all got on our knees in Sunday School to praise Him and pray for Rhonda's continued recovery.

Give Rhonda my love, mom and Jerry's too and once you catch your breath, please let us know if we can help… with anything

In His Love

Ryan G

Glad to hear that Rhonda is feeling better and you both are home.

Aunt Naomi

Dear Scott and Rhonda. we are so happy for your news. God is good, indeed! Undoubtedly, she has a lot of healing time coming.

Hopefully the worst of it is over and it is uphill from here. God bless all of you for the battle you have been through. I hope you can catch up your rest now and have some family time again.

Sherry W

Scott: So happy for the news about Rhonda's surgery… our Lord is truly amazing!

Oct 8
from Ronda G to coworkers (Scott back at work)

Thank you for contributing to the Smith fund. In addition to the flowers we sent to the hospital, we just presented Scott with this great snack basket and the remaining $240. Scott said the money will be very helpful to his Maw-in-Law who has been using some of her own funds to run the household.

I appreciate your generosity and know he does!!

Oct 18
to SS class from Scott

Our trip to Lake Murray was wonderful... but we stayed up too late watching movies and we had to take a day to recover and rest today. Tomorrow will be better. We missed seeing you all and look forward to the regular schedule of fellowshipping with you every week!

We are SO THANKFUL for everything Rhonda's mom has done for us this past month... we praise God for her gift of self-sacrifice and love to be here with us through this time... and we also thank Him for making Rhonda cancer-free! Georgya flies home tomorrow... we will miss her! Thank you for everything Georgya... you are the most awesome maw-in-law ever!

And Frances... we've officially made maw-in-law an honorary SS class member... please add her email to the class distribution...

Thanks!

Oct 23
My Rhonda—A New Approach to Treatment

Hello...

I hope that you all are doing well. Rhonda has continued to improve after her surgery little by little... sometimes having a day that is not so good... but overall getting stronger every day as we mark over 4 weeks since the surgery. The follow-up appt with the surgeon a couple of days ago went very well... everything is healing and progressing as expected.

We are still thankful to God and amazed at how "dead" the cancer cells were found... and so was our oncologist. He had never seen a result like this before. So he dug around some more with the pathology reports and consulted with his fellow doctors two different times... coming to a conclusion that we learned just this morning.

The initial cancer diagnosis was based on just a few cells gathered from an endoscopy biopsy and the location of the tumors. These cells were found to be 'consistent' with pancreatic cancer, and so that was what the treatment plan was based upon... and we saw that it was tremendously successful... a success that had never been seen before. So our oncologist checked and re-checked and... with his peers... concluded that this was not pancreatic cancer, but lymphoma.

So now they will treat things much differently... and we start on a whole new regimen of chemo a week from Monday (Nov. 2nd)... once every 3 weeks for 4–6 cycles. Today they also did a bone marrow biopsy... next Monday they do a heart scan... and then a PET scan (next week, but not yet scheduled).

The staff at the doctor's ofc had big smiles on their faces and very cheerfully saying "isn't this great news?"... while we sat there a bit shell-shocked... trying to take in all they had just told us. Their jovial mood was based on the cure rate of lymphoma vs. pancreatic cancer. Lymphoma has a 70–80% cure rate.

But we thought... based on the outcome of the surgery... that we were done with all of this.

So... Rhonda and I have re-grouped and worked to settle ourselves with this new reality... that we aren't finished with this stuff yet. The chemo this time will be much more "conventional"... with most probably heavier side-effects and hair loss. No picnic. But... we know that our Lord is still in control and has given us to these folks for the excellent care we've received to this point... we will continue to trust Him for strength and grace for this next phase. We know that we have been given no guarantees for anything except knowing that He is with us... and that will be enough.

Our attitude will continue to be one of prayer and hope... and we ask for you all to continue to stand with us as we step farther into this journey. Your love and support has humbled and amazed us. We thank God for you all.

We will share more news as we have it made available to us. Thank you again for your ongoing prayers! We are always in God's hands... and we will trust Him with the outcome.

God Bless you all!
Scott and Rhonda

Responses

Peggy A

Thank you Scott. I'm so sorry there is more to Rhonda's illness than you thought. But… it is true that lymphoma is so much more treatable than pancreatic so… you will be in my prayers.

Patti S

We love you and will hold you closely in prayer while you continue this journey.

Sherry W

You and Rhonda will continue to be in our prayers. Your testimonies in the Lord have been such a wonderful witness and continue to be.

We love you both.

God bless you in a special way this week.

Marylyn M

I just want to thank you for keeping us up-to-date on Rhonda. All-in-all, it sounds like good news. You both remain in my prayers.

Trish M

Wow! Forest Gump had it right…… life IS like a box of chocolates!!!?

We're all walking beside you guys Scott. Hang in there. You guys are an inspiration to all of us.

Hugs

Drew C

Scott, I am so sorry you're facing another round of treatment. It's so hard when you think you're finally DONE and then it's like you're back to square one. As you say, it is in God's hands and He has a plan. Praying for you bro.

Sylvia A

Scott and Rhonda, God is still with you along with all your earthly angels and friends. Keep trusting in Him as you have done, and you will continue to see His wonders working thru Rhonda. Take care and we will continue to pray for Rhonda's recovery and strength.

Cindy H

You and Rhonda and your entire family are continually in our prayers!

Linda S

Thanks for the update on Rhonda. Sorry to hear the latest diagnosis, I can only imagine what a shock that was to hear. We continue to pray for Rhonda and send her strength and good thoughts to aid in her healing.

Nov 3
My Rhonda—First Treatment and Still Thankful

Hello again… hope you all are doing well!

We got to have another visit with the nurse last week that did make us feel a bit better about Rhonda's new diagnosis. She told us that pancreatic cancer 'always comes back' and the prognosis of life expectancy is pretty much confined to five years or less. So the reason they were all so happy about the lymphoma diagnosis is that there's a very good chance Rhonda will be actually cured. We've decided we like that better too. :)

But we do still see the amazing success of the first treatment as God's gift to us. They could not have changed the diagnosis without the surgery of removing the dead stuff so it could be analyzed more. So we are very thankful to God for how this has come about!

The PET scan last week came back with some nodes under the chest muscle area showing some light activity… as in maybe something bad is trying to make a comeback there. But the doc is very confident that the chemo will take all of that out. He's still smiling! :) The area of the surgery was still impossible to read due to the massive amount of healing going on there. I'm sure that more scans will follow.

So Rhonda had her first dose of the new treatment yesterday. It was a long day of waiting rooms, but the infusion itself was not too bad and only took about an hour. After we got home, she was pretty much exhausted and rested well through the night. The only side effects she's experienced today were some stomach issues that she has handled like a trooper.

We had to go back for another appt this afternoon so Rhonda could get an injection to stimulate the building of white blood cells. Her low point of the treatment, as far as maximum weakness and such, is supposed to occur about 10 days after the treatment. She then has 10 days to rest and regain strength before we go through it all again.

One down… five to go.

Once again… thank you so much for your expressions of encouragement and gifts of caring. Every day we've had people reach out to us.

It's been wonderful to be surrounded by such a great group of people with such large hearts… you all are special to us!

We'll keep you posted on how things are going… thanks again!

Scott and Rhonda

Responses

Judy R
    <big sigh>
    Ok, only 5 left.
    Rhonda is a strong lady, and she's got a good partner.
    Sorry you have to suffer, but glad that there is a good result waiting at the end of this.
    <big sigh>

Linda S
    Thanks for the update. You and Rhonda are truly amazing, such an inspiration to all us with your strength and courage. :)

Trish M
    Definitely better diagnosis… but still not fun.
    Hang in there!
    Hug

Patti S
    We love you both and offer our most precious gift… prayer.

Cindy H
    Thank you so much for keeping me posted on how Rhonda is doing! Your family is constantly in mine and Bruce's prayers!

Debbie S

Hello there! I so appreciate this update. It lets me know specifically how to pray. May the God of all comfort fill you with his presence in the treatments and days ahead.

Ryan G

I am so glad to hear that Rhonda is doing well, at least as well as she can be. I wish that there was some way that she could be cured without all of the pain and exhaustion. I still pray for you two every night before I go to bed. I just wish that there was more that I could do. Please let Rhonda know that I am thinking about her.

Mom S

Bravo for Rhonda! Love you guys!

Nov 15
My Rhonda—Learning Curve

Hi,

I wanted to give you a quick update of how things are going for us...

Rhonda is going through the lowest point of her white blood cell count during this time (called 'nadir'). She is very weak, but is eating and drinking in very small portions. She should be feeling better in the next few days as she works to regain her strength. Her next treatment is a week from Monday (23rd).

As she went through the first couple of weeks after treatment, we saw some of the side effects that the literature had warned us about... mainly nausea and stomach upset. But, not being with her all the time, I wasn't cognizant of how much she was sick during the middle of last week. She was feeling pretty bad when we went to our appt on Thursday. They took one look at her and set her down with some IV fluids. She was getting dehydrated. We came back the next day and she received two more bags of fluids. The fluids helped her a lot… then the 'nadir' hit her and she's been pretty much resting around the clock the last two days.

I felt bad that I had let her get that dehydrated by not being aware enough… and definitely plan to stay on top of it from now on. We will learn as we go along and lean on the medical staff and God for wisdom as we tweak and adjust to make Rhonda as comfortable as possible. She also seems to be going through some withdrawal from her heavy-duty pain meds… but we think we have a handle on that now.

Also… Julie had her tonsils out on Wednesday so she's not been feeling real great either. Guess God figured I needed some more practice at being a caregiver… we are making it through each day and will be fine!

God will not put us through something without giving us the strength to do it. Rhonda is learning to rest as much as she needs it. These treatments are hard on her, but they will make her well and give us ultimate victory over this stuff. We WILL get there. And I am now in full caregiver/homemaker mode… it keeps me busy enough to stay out of trouble. :)

Thank you all again for your prayers and words of encouragement and support… we draw strength knowing that so many care…

Thanks and God Bless!
Scott and Rhonda

Responses

Debbie S

Our God has raised you up for such a time as this. You are both covered in prayer.

Marci E

Scott, I will remain prayerful. Your updates are such an inspiration. May God continue to keep, strengthen, enlighten and heal!

Linda S

Thanks for the update on how Rhonda is doing. Hoping her nausea improves quickly and her strength picks up real soon. Hoping also that Julie recovers quickly as well. She couldn't be in better hands. You are doing a great job as caretaker. :)

Pamela D

Thanks so much for including me on the emails and providing updates for us. Please tell her I'm thinking of you both and certainly praying for you.

Nov 16
My Rhonda update

Hello Again…

Just to let you know that I'm picking up Rhonda's mom from the airport later tonight… return date unknown. Rhonda had asked me to call her to see if she could come to help in a way that only a momma can. True to her nature… maw-in-law pretty much caught the first flight out of town. We welcome her love and knowledge… and strength of spirit… back to our home again.

Thank you all again…

Blessings,
Scott

Responses

Greg G

That's good news Scott. I'm glad she was able to come so quickly. I know you guys will be blessed by her visit. Tell her we said hello.

Tandy

Sometimes it takes the strength of our mothers to really help us get back on our feet. I know I thank the Lord for my mom every day that she is still living. Even though she is not here close, all I have to do is pick up the phone and call. She helped me most when I really needed it. I know that your mom will continue to be the blessing she needs to be for as long as she needs to be. Still in our prayers. Love ya.

Ryan G

Tell Rhonda that I understand completely. Sometimes you just need your mom. I hope that Rhonda is feeling better.

Marci E

What a blessing that her mom is available and can come. Praise Him! I'm sure this will be a blessing and help to everyone.

Aunt Naomi

Hi, I'm so sorry to hear that Rhonda has been feeling so poorly. My prayers are with you and her and the rest of the family.

Nov 22
My Rhonda—Learning Curve update

Hello All,

Well… today I need to give you a testimony to the power of a Mom's love. Last weekend Rhonda could not get out of bed… she was very weak and discouraged… to the point of wondering when she would every feel any better again. Today… we all went as a family to Sunday School… church… and then out to eat, at Rhonda's suggestion… at Pizza Hut. Rhonda said she felt 'strong'. Amazing.

I picked up Rhonda's mom at the airport just before midnight on Monday. Tuesday she started feeding Rhonda Blue Bell Milk Chocolate ice cream laced with protein powder… every hour… along with Gatorade and anything else she could get down her. We saw results almost immediately. Rhonda could barely get around the block the first couple of days. Yesterday, we walked 3/4 mile… and went out to eat with friends… and went Christmas shopping at two different stores. Wow. In the course of the week, Rhonda has had two full cartons of Blue Bell… and gained back 4 pounds. This after she had lost 30 pounds since the surgery 8 weeks ago. I told Maw-in-law they need to start the newest craze… the 'Blue Bell protein diet'. It'd be a sure-fire winner!

And now tomorrow is the 2nd chemo treatment… we believe we are ready to have a better go of it this time… it will be better.

We also had some med adjustments along the way, and will be asking to get back on the pain patch at the doctor's tomorrow. She had severe aches from the bone marrow/white blood cell stimulants that otc meds couldn't relieve, robbing her of the deep rest that she needs. After the dehydration issues last time, they gave us a prescription for a nausea patch to wear the week of chemo. We also look for that to help a lot this time around.

So... our hearts are very thankful to God and Rhonda's mom, Georgya, for her dropping everything in her own life in California to come and assist. I truly thought that I could handle it all... but I was wrong... and I'm afraid that Rhonda may have suffered more because I wouldn't give in to call for help. But God has this way of gently removing our pride when it gets in the way of His Work... and for this season in our lives... God is working wonderfully through Rhonda's mom to bring strength... and hope... back into her life and heart.

Thank you so much!

We praise God for His graciousness... and for moms for their special way of loving us... even when it includes a 'kick in the seat of the pants' to get us going again. How Awesome!

And continuing thanks to the rest of you for your unrelenting love and support...

And on a much sadder note... please pray for my dear Aunt Naomi and the rest of our family at the passing of her daughter Cheryl Friday night from cancer. Our love and God's is surrounding and holding up your souls as we say goodbye to such a great lady... Love you all so much!

Thank you all again... God Bless!
Scott and Rhonda

Responses

Clifton W

Thanks for the good report. I continue to keep Rhonda and you in my prayers.

Judy R

Um, Scott, fyi,

You can be the best husband in the world, but you can't be a mom, or a bucket of chocolate ice cream.

I think you're doing great. Rhonda would be completely lost without you.

Jan R

What an awesome mother! One of God's many many blessings! Praying for Rhonda and all of you!

Mom S

Hurray for Mom and Rhonda. Keep on keeping on. Love you guys.

Sherry W

Praise the Lord! You remain in our thoughts and prayers. I miss my mom for this very reason… I have such loving thoughts of times she came to the rescue to help me during times of sickness and much needed help when my girls were young.

God bless you, Scott and Rhonda. I pray you have a wonderful Thanksgiving.

Trish M

Don't beat yourself up Scott. You're doing GREAT!! There are just some things that aren't known to all and we learn by experience. Rhonda couldn't have a more attentive, loving, giving husband. You're both very lucky to have each other. I know when you sit down at the table Thursday you will be overcome by all that you have to be thankful for. You're my hero. I know how hard it is to walk in your shoes.

Patti S

We love you all. I know you will have a Blessed Thanksgiving!

Tandy

Just so you know, we love you and Rhonda dearly. Moms are so precious in time of need. I thank God for mine that she is still around to lend a helpful ear when I need it. Your mom in law is a special lady too and I am glad she will be able to get you through the rough times. We will pray that Rhonda will continue to be able to eat ice cream and drink adequate amounts of fluids.

Love ya

Ryan G

I am so glad to hear that Rhonda is feeling better. I think about her all the time. She has been a great source of strength during my whole recovery process. I tell myself all of the time how much more Rhonda deals with every day, and yet, she tries so hard to do everything she can to recover. Tapping into Rhonda's strength is what keeps me getting up and doing my exercises, walking on it even when I don't really want to. The doctors say that I am doing really well, and I feel that Rhonda's strength and everything that I have seen her go through is a big part of that. That... and I hear Cara in my head telling me to quit being such a wus. :) Please tell Rhonda that I am thinking about her.

Aunt Naomi

Dear Scott, I appreciate your letter with all of the information. My prayers are with you and Rhonda and the family. Your prayers and love are helping keep me going in this sad time for us. It doesn't seem real but unfortunately it is. There will be a gathering at the house the first Saturday in Dec. and we will say our goodbyes there. Chery is with the Lord and her daddy and your dad too and I have to be content with that. Love you all.

Marci E

I am always heartened after reading your updates. Thank u for being so willing to share. We overcome by our testimony. Yours is powerful and encouraging.

Dec 21
My Rhonda—3rd Cycle

Hi,

I've kinda slacked off a bit on sending these updates out… not wanting to inundate you with more of the same. We continue to take it a day at a time. Rhonda has had many days where she's felt pretty good… and then there's the 'yuck' days… and a few really rough days. Her mom is still with us… ready to stay as long as needed… not only taking care of Rhonda, but all of us… cooking, cleaning, laundering… amazing. I've started to tell people that I only need one pair of socks because when I put them in the laundry, they seem to be magically clean and ready to go the next day. We are so thankful for her tireless help! I no longer need to wonder how she made it raising 7 kids on her own… I'm privileged to see it in action!

Rhonda had her 3rd treatment a week ago… and it seems that the multiple nausea meds are helping somewhat… as she is not sick for as long as before. But we are also noticing a cumulative effect on her with the weakness and exhaustion being more intense and staying longer. She was not able to make it to church yesterday for the 1st time since her mom came… she was just too weak.

The doctor has told us that after the 4th treatment (January 4), they will wait a couple of weeks and do a scan to see where things stand… and make a determination at that point whether to continue with more treatments or not. So… by mid-January we should know about the effectiveness of the treatments. Going in, the doctors were telling us they could 'cure' this… so that's what we're looking for… in God's grace… and in hope and confidence in His goodness to us.

So now we get to celebrate Christmas this week with Rhonda's mom… for the first time as a blended family. It will be a special time to be shared. I love to see the Spirit of the season move in those around us… with toy and clothing drives and such. It is truly a magical time. This same Spirit is the root of our hope… the Spirit that gave birth to a child a little over 2,000 years ago… when a loving God decided to leave His majesty in heaven and become a man to live among us… to bring us hope… and eventually give himself to bring reconciliation between imperfect men and a perfect God.

It's Christmas all year 'round for us… His Spirit never leaves us to deal with things on our own. We are convinced of His goodness to us every day… His mercies are new every morning… Great is His faithfulness… to us. Rhonda's illness is not a picnic. We are not blind to its ramifications on our lives. But the life of Faith makes all things bearable because we know that we are not alone… not only through the love and support of you all and so many others… but because we know that Christ is born… Emmanuel… "God with us."

Thank you again so much for your continuing prayers for us. Our prayer for you is that the Spirit of the season may reside in your hearts all year long.

Thank you and God Bless as you enjoy the holiday… the season with your families and friends. We love you all.

Scott and Rhonda

Responses

Jan R
Scott, thank for that reminder of why we celebrate and that our Lord is with us all year long.
Much love

Jeff W
Thanks for the update. I had been thinking about you and Rhonda recently and your e-mails prompt my prayers. I so enjoy your wonderful writing. We are blessed beyond what we realize to be able to have a relationship with the God of the universe! I hope our group can get together some time next year when Rhonda is done with her chemo and your lives get back to something more "normal". Your faith is inspiring and a strong testimony.

Greg G
Thanks man!
We are praying for you guys. I know it's got to seem like this will never end, but try and take it one day at a time.

Cathy and I know that these trials are strengthening you guys, both individually and as a family.

Merry Christmas to you and yours Scott.

Aunt Naomi

Dear ones, I am so very grateful for your updates. We continue to pray for Rhonda's full recovery and send as much of our strength to you as we can spare. I love you all.

Trish M

Thanks for the update Scott. I'm praying that the chemo is doing exactly what it's supposed to. Hang in there. Sit back and realize the joys around you this Christmas. I know sometimes it's hard to see the forest for the trees…… but God is good and you guys will come out the other side just fine. Hugs to Rhonda too!!

Patti S

Scott. just had a chance to read this and I am so moved. Covering you with prayer…

this far... rely-
 support of you all when
 know that we live a very blessed life.

 start school tomorrow. Jordan found out this
 not make the first cut to the interview pro-
 door that he may be called
 him staying for now.
 close

2010: A Difficult Path to Healing

Jan 12, 2010
My Rhonda—Scans Scheduled

Hello,

Just a quick note to let you know that a heart and PET scan are scheduled for Rhonda this Friday the 15th. We are standing on the Rock of our faith that all will be well and cancer-free… but will accept anything less by trusting that our God will continue to be with us… just as He has all along. With the scans being on Friday, we may not get results until Monday.

Also… as of now… after seeing us through and performing a tremendous and sacrificial good work for all of us during the two months she's been here… Rhonda's mom is tentatively scheduled to fly home next Tuesday. She will not leave if we need her… but during this last treatment cycle, Rhonda has fared much better than with the previous three. We're thinking maybe we've turned a corner and are ready to head into the home stretch. She may have two more treatments, regardless of the scan results… but we're beginning to see the light at the end of the tunnel. PTL!

So… thank you again for your compassion and love… and for your continued prayers. I'll send a note as soon as we know results.

Thank you and God Bless!
Scott and Rhonda

Responses

Patti S
    A joy to pray for you all!

Roxzanne M

Scott, I am constantly thinking and praying for you guys. Don't forget, if you need any type of help, I am available. And, I mean any type of help.

I am so thankful that you and Rhonda have had the support of your mother-in-law. God has definitely been watching over you.

I don't know how Rhonda is doing in the hair department, but if she needs a good wig I have one.

I love you guys and will be here for you. Take care.

Ryan G

All I can say is that I certainly hope so. We all just want to see Rhonda better. I didn't know her before she got sick, but Cara always talked about how she was a little ray of sunshine. I know that Cara feels that Patti and Rhonda especially helped her through her heart-ache and pain. I will always be grateful to the group for seeing my best friend through such a horrible time, and we want to return the favor in any way that we can. Please give Rhonda my best.

Judy R

Wow! Getting to the end of treatments, feeling better, hope. Excellent!

Sylvia A

Scott, we will continued to storm the heavens with our daily prayers... Please keep us posted.

Drew C

Scott, thanks for the update. I'm really glad you're seeing light at the end of the tunnel; your tenacity and faith has been a great encouragement to me and I'm sure to many others. God is turning what was meant for evil into good!

Aunt Naomi

Dear Scott and Rhonda. It was so good to get your good news and we will trust in God that it will be followed by even better news. We all need good news! What a blessing Rhonda's mom has been for all of you. I know how much it means to you.

Remember I love you all and am praying for you

Jan 19
My Rhonda—Scan Results

Hi,

Well… we finally got results today… and the scan looked VERY good! PTL! The nodes under her pectoral area were no longer 'lit up', showing no cancer activity at all. Thank you Lord!!!

The area of the surgery was still difficult to read most probably because of the healing still taking place there… but… to be safe… the doctor wants to go ahead and do two more chemo treatments. We agree… let's put the hammer down and knock this stuff totally down and out!

So… the next treatment will be this next Monday the 25th… and then one more on Feb 15. And then we're done! Hallelujah!

However… we do have some major 'adjustments' for these last two treatments… Maw-in-Law is no longer here to take care of our every need. Rhonda drove her to the airport today to allow her to go back home after staying with us for over 2 months. We will never be able to fully thank her or tell her how much it meant to us to have her help during this time. She was a gift from God to us in our time of need, and it was so great to get to know her better and see her bond more strongly with all of the kids as we all shared a bunch of 'quality time' together. Thank you again… from the depths of our souls. We love you!

And thanks again to the rest of you for sticking by us and seeing us through… almost to the end now… very soon… and then 'new' life begins again as we move forward and beyond this stuff. Our God is so great and gracious to us!

God Bless!
Scott and Rhonda

Responses

Debbie S
    With tears of joy, I celebrate God's work in your lives. Please choose a night that would be good for me to bring dinner over next week.
    I am honored to serve.

Sandy L
    God told me you would need to celebrate!
    Congratulations our prayers were answered!

Roxzanne M
    Scott, if Rhonda needs help with anything, please call me. I have the time and I always want to help friends.

Sherry W
    Continue to lift you up in prayer… thank you, Jesus, for taking care of Rhonda and Scott.

Jan R

Thank you Lord for all the blessings! God will provide friends & family to help you - just let them know your needs!

Patti S

We love you both and pray for His grace on your family as you finish this journey.

Greg G

That's great news. Please let us know how we can pick up the slack. Cathy and I were praising the Lord this morning for yours and Rhonda's faith through all of this. You remember what God did with Job after he went through all his trials. So, watch out bro!

Peggy A

I'm so happy for you both. Thanks for sharing the wonderful news.

Denise A

Hi Scott!!

Kurt forwards me all your emails so I am up to date on Rhonda's status. PTL! I am so happy the scan came back clear! The kids pray for her every night at dinner and last night Jake was praying and said : "please help Rhonda Smith with her chemo" - I had added in "well I think we need to pray that her scan is clear and NO MORE CANCER IS PRESENT!!" Please tell her we think of her and pray for her and your family daily! Have a wonderful day! I can't wait to tell the kids tonight...

Sylvia A

PTL! God is very good and merciful. You're correct soon a new journey and life will begin, just in time for Easter. You'll see all the glory and abounding love God has for Rhonda and His children continue to reflect in all the beauty of the Easter Season. Please tell Rhonda I will continue to storm the heavens with daily prayers and thanks for all his blessings.

Feb 6
from SS teacher Terry C

Prayer request for Rhonda. Rhonda fell last evening and broke her ankle. She was just getting out of the shower and Scott was with her when she fell. They took her to Baylor Garland. Her blood counts are low because of the treatments and the doctors want to give her more blood. Scott and Rhonda would prefer to let the Oncologist handle this because he is aware of her treatments and where she is at in the treatment cycle. So please pray for her strength and healing. In Jesus Name.

Feb 8
My Rhonda—A New Challenge

Hello,

I just wanted to let you all know that we face a new twist in Rhonda's road to recovery...

During the the mid-cycle appt we had last Thursday, they told us that Rhonda's blood counts were 'impressively low'. They offered a transfusion, but were sure that they'd come back up in a few days... just like they had during the previous cycles... so we decided to wait it out. The next day Rhonda was actually feeling some better and wanted to get a shower before going to bed. The heat from the shower caused her to momentarily black out, and she fell… breaking her ankle… and most likely some bones in her foot too.

We spent a sleepless night in ER and then were assigned to a room to give her a transfusion. It was not a pleasant stay… sparing you too many details… the staff seemed to not understand our total picture… and seemed not to be listening to us… putting us through hoops and tests that we felt were not necessary… and we ended up checking ourselves out around noon.

I stopped and purchased a wheelchair on the way home as Rhonda has lost all mobility. I need to carry her wherever the chair won't fit. With God's strength, we did make it to Charlie's UIL trumpet solo competition (he got a '1') Saturday afternoon and to church yesterday.

Today we hope to get into the orthopedic dr and get a full cast put on (she has only a splint right now).

Of course… Rhonda's mom is ready to come, once again, to our rescue. We want to see if Rhonda will have any mobility once her cast is on… Maw-in-Law is strong… but I'm not sure she can carry Rhonda around like I have been. Knowing that she is willing and ready to be called upon is a comfort to us.

So… just as we were seeing the light at the end of the tunnel… this happens. The last treatment is on the schedule for a week from today. We know that somehow, somewhere God has a greater purpose in all of this… and that He will give us the strength for each day… just as He has through this whole ordeal. We will continue to trust Him because He loves us so much.

Your ongoing prayers and support are amazing and wonderful... precious to us and to God. We are strengthened by your love. Thank you... so much.

In Christ's Love and Grace,
Scott and Rhonda

Responses

Patti S

Dear Scott, Terry and I were talking about how "sick" we felt when we heard about Rhonda's fall... why does she have to suffer so. I'm sure this echoes the thoughts of so many of her friends and family. I don't know God's total and purpose in this, but I can tell you that Rhonda's strength and yours, to see you both at church yesterday... it awakened a new spot in my heart.

We love you all

Trish M

I'm so sorry scott. I know you probably feel like it just doesn't stop. Don't know if you're aware of the kneeling scooter devices they make, or if Rhonda is strong enough to maneuver on one, but something to think about... Hang in there. The prayers are non-stop for you guys from a lot of people.

Amy C

You have our prayers and sending lots of love your way. Both of you continue to amaze me!

Marci E

I am continuing to pray for you all. God is able to do anything but fail.

Clifton W

It is amazing how you manage to keep a "bright outlook" during all these trials. You and Rhonda continue to be in my prayers

Bruce W

May His healing hands touch Rhonda's body and cause complete recovery......... May her future be brighter than her yesterday... thinking of you all.

Feb 8
My Rhonda—Some Good News

Hi,

Well... we got into the doctor today... and he gave us the best news he could have given to anyone in Rhonda's situation. All of the damage (5 fractures) were on the outside of the ankle and at the base of the toes... but what the doctor checked for was ligament damage on the inside of the foot (which would've meant surgery)... and there was none! Thank you Lord for the little blessings!

They then put her in a boot and said that she could walk in it as soon as she felt she could put weight on the foot... and we're not there yet. But... this is about the best prognosis we could have hoped for. The doctor did tell us that chemo can double the amount of time needed for healing... so it's good that the last treatment is next Monday. We're looking at anywhere from 3 to 6 months for full healing... and hoping that she'll feel good enough to try walking soon.

So after learning all this... Rhonda and I spoke about it... and we've asked her mom to come out and assist again. We just feel this would be best for Rhonda... and help me with my work schedule...

and give the kids more direct attention than Rhonda or I are capable of giving right now. So… Maw-in-Law to the rescue… again! You are a true life-saver!

Thank you again for your prayers and kind words. We will get past this… with God's strength… and the love of our family and friends.

God Bless!
Scott and Rhonda

Responses

Sandy L

This is fantastic news. We are praying for you daily.
Please give Rhonda a big hug from us.
Love ya

Ryan G

That is wonderful news!

Cathy G

Thanks for the update, Scott, and for the good news! We know you all need some. It's also good to hear that Georgya is coming back. We look forward to seeing her.

Say hi to Rhonda for us, and know that we are praying for you all.

Patti S

So sorry about this latest trial. So glad that Georgya will be back! Praying!

Aunt Naomi

dear Ones, I was so sorry to hear of Rhonda's setback; it is hard to understand that she has to go through so much. i pray that things get easier for her at least they tell her she will heal, thank God for that. I was so relieved to hear that her tests came back good. How fortunate you are to have her mother to come in and help, what an angel. I love you all take care.

Tandy

This is great news. I know that it was a blow to you for this to happen. Will continue to keep her in my prayers. Love ya.

Jim F

I was very glad to learn that there was no ligament damage. Hang in there, bro.

Feb 17
My Rhonda—Chemo Treatments are Over!

Hello there… we are DONE!

The last treatment was infused on schedule on Monday. Now it is finished! Praise God! We are so thankful that God gave her the strength to endure so much… and so thankful for the support, love, encouragement, and generosity of our friends and family! We rode on the wings of your prayers to this successful completion… and can never find the words to thank you all enough! It's onward and upward from here! Wahoo!

Rhonda's blood counts were still very low, so they decided after treatment to have her come in for 3 units of blood on Tuesday. We were there most of the day and enjoyed more wonderful caregiving from the terrific staff at Baylor Dallas. Rhonda felt much stronger this morning and roamed around the house some on her crutches… but realized that the energy spent itself pretty quickly. It will come slowly at first, but she can now look forward to gaining more strength each day.

Now… if it weren't for that broken ankle… The impaired mobility is definitely going to slow down the feeling of coming back quickly. She won't be able to drive her new car until the boot is gone. Rhonda did let me talk her into getting her a 'leg scooter' that she can rest her bad leg on while scooting around. It will be much easier on her than crutches… and smaller than the wheelchair… a good first step to getting around on her own. She is so anxious to become more independent and I know is ready to work hard to get there.

Of course Maw-in-law has the household running smoothly… taking over the cooking, cleaning, laundering, trash, mail delivery, and keeping up with the kids. And in her spare time, she plays scrabble with Rhonda and Julie! Amazing! We are sooooo thankful for her help… again! She will be with us until March 19th… right after Rhonda and I get back from our annual anniversary trip to Oklahoma… our 5th anniversary! :)

So… now we start down the road to complete recovery… cancer-free! We are SO ready to put all of this behind us and move forward. God has been so gracious to us to bring us through each day's challenges… giving us opportunity to grow and bond in ways we wouldn't have been able to if every day had been without trouble. We know that we all have trouble at times in our lives… but we also know that God specializes in taking something difficult and making it into something beautiful… creating 'beauty from ashes'. We are so thankful for His goodness to us… and the hope of every new day!

That's the scoop for now... I'll send progress updates every so often as we climb back toward something akin to normalcy in our lives. Once again... many thanks to you all... we love and appreciate you so much!

May God Bless your lives as richly as He has ours! We will always give our thanks and praises to Him!

Scott and Rhonda

Responses

Penny F

I am so happy for you and Rhonda. The storm is over!!!! The two of you have overcome major trials and tribulations and your faith brought you through.

Thanks be to God!

Patti S

Bless your hearts and Praise God. Love to all!

Ryan G

That is so wonderful! Now the only way to go is up. Rhonda is going to continue to get stronger and feel better and then hopefully I will get to meet the Rhonda that Cara always talked about. My bet is that she is a lot of fun. If you all need anything, please let me know. Love you guys!

Usha A

I am so glad to hear the good news! I look forward to hearing more good news!

Amy C

This is so wonderful just made my day! So, so happy for you!!

Cindy H

Praise God! Your faith in God and constant yielding to His power and strength during such a difficult time is such a testimony to the rest of us! There were many days when I felt overwhelmed or defeated with life, I would think about all that Rhonda and your family has gone through, and it gave me strength and courage to endure what I was going through that day! Every day when I go down the road and pass by your neighborhood, I say a pray for you and Rhonda and the rest of the family.

Peggy A

I'm so glad she's done with her treatments. I will continue to pray for her strength to return.

Sherry W

What a wonderful e-mail... so glad that Rhonda is done with treatments. You have and will continue to be in my prayers.

In His Love

Mom S

What wonderful news. I bet you feel lighter than air with all that behind you. I am so thankful that you live so close to a wonderful cancer-medical center that you were able to stay in your own home most of the time.

*****

Yes... it was so great to get that last treatment behind us! It was a great pick-me-up after her fall. Yet even though the last chemo treatment had been administered, the nasty drugs were not yet finished wreaking their havoc with her.

*****

Feb 22
My Rhonda—Back in the Hospital

Well… a little setback here…

We went in for a post-chemo follow-up today and our oncologist has put Rhonda in the hospital. She was running a fever (which we've seen as typical during treatments)… but her white blood count was also very low… so… they want to keep her for a few days to be safe until they come back up.

So… I'm at the house gathering some stuff to camp out with her in her room for the rest of the week. We know that God has a purpose in all of this (Rhonda said "maybe we need to reach out to someone")… but we've really been working hard to get all of our wheels out of the ditch so we can put all of this behind us… so… not there yet.

We are SO thankful that maw-in-law is already here and handling the household and kids. She's been a lifesaver for us all!

Your continued prayers are so much appreciated! You've all been through all of this with us, and it means so much to us!

I'll let you know when we get home…

Thank you all again… God Blessya all!

Responses

Terry C

God Bless you both Scott. We will take you before the Throne and ask for a touch from the Masters hand. We love you guys.

Ryan G

Oh, Scott, I so want to go up there and be with her. I got sick, too, though. Just keep on reminding her that the worst is over and that we love her.

Patti S

Many prayers coming your way.

March 6
My Rhonda—Finally Home

Hello...

What a time it's been for us... for Rhonda. Thank you Lord for bringing her through it all...

When they put Rhonda in the hospital on Monday, 2/22, it was due to her white blood count being low and that she had a fever. They started her on massive antibiotics, but the fever would not go away... and she kept getting weaker. On Wednesday her hemoglobin counts dropped dramatically and they started her on 2 units of blood. But the nurse, Sonia, was very concerned because her fever remained... she was afraid Rhonda was going 'septic'... that her entire body was being poisoned by an infection. We thank God for her concerns. She requested that Rhonda be transferred to ICU... and when that didn't happen quickly enough for her, she called out their RRT (Rapid Response Team) which is reserved for the most urgent cases. We had 5 people in the room within minutes.

They hurriedly got Rhonda to ICU. She was so pale. They immediately ordered 4 more units of blood which they transfused using a high-pressure device that would tranfuse her as quickly as possible. They told me that I could not stay, so I had to leave her for a couple of hours. As I was walking out, one nurse told me that Rhonda was right on the edge... that she needed this blood desperately. I was numb as I left... wondering if she had the strength to pull through.

Friends Greg and Cathy were with me as we waited for them to let us know how Rhonda was doing. More angels sent by God to prop me up. Finally a nurse came out to tell me I could be with her. She again told us how close Rhonda had been to not having enough blood to survive. Some doctors thought she had massive internal bleeding, but there were none of the normal indications of that. As we talked, I felt sure that the chemo treatments had severely impaired her ability to make blood cells. Her bone marrow could not keep up with her need for blood. With the transfusions, she was stable at least for now.

They performed a scope procedure the next day to look for internal bleeding in her upper GI and stomach. What they found was a fungal infection in her esophagus (similar to 'thrush') which they started treating aggressively. This was the culprit causing her fever. They couldn't do anything for her white blood count, but gave her many units of platelets to help her body stop any bleeding that may be going on. Her red count was stable, so she just rested and tried to eat to gain some strength as they waited for her counts to come up.

The ICU rules did not allow me to stay with her 24/7 as I had been. I had to be out of the room during shift changes and could not spend the whole night in her room… although I could look in on her at times overnight. We found that the nurses had different interpretations of this, esp as they saw Rhonda was more relaxed when I could be with her. One nurse got chewed out by her boss, but stood by her decision to allow me to stay longer overnight. When I could not be with her, I wandered between waiting rooms and leaning back in my SUV seat… at best getting 3 or 4 hours of sleep a night.

By the weekend, we could tell she was doing better… although the counts were still low, the white count finally started to come up. They transfused still more platelets. Finally, on Monday the counts had come up enough to request a regular room for her… which we moved into at 10:00 that night. We felt like we were in some luxury hotel room after that trying time in ICU. I was so grateful for the chair that pulled out so I could lie down… I hadn't laid down at all the previous 5 nights.

Rhonda's appetite was picking up and she'd had no fever for 3 days. So, after another infusion of platelets, she was finally released on Wednesday night. We came home and gratefully crashed in our own bed… and slept for about 15 hours. Friday we went back to the doctor's to check her counts again. The platelets are still low. They told us if she has any bleeding at all to take her to the ER. We think we're gonna be alright.

So… of course… Rhonda is extremely weak and exhausted. She just needs rest and nourishment. Even as I was typing this message, I could feel the emotions and tears coming back… knowing that God had spared her and given her back to us to nurture back to health. And even as we languished in ICU, God sent us a reminder of how very blessed we are. An elderly lady came and knocked on our door one day. A minister from our church had come to visit and she found out we were from the same church. Her daughter has been in ICU since October… waiting for her second double-lung transplant. Her first transplant had been in Feb a year ago, and after doing well, she contracted TB and the lungs went into rejection… now needing another transplant. This elderly lady and her husband have been essentially living in the ICU waiting room… being with their daughter (she looked to be in her 30's) as she waits for another chance at a normal life. And another… one of the night nurses… not even 30 yet with 2 young children… recently had her second pacemaker implanted.

So many people have difficulties to deal with… how can we complain when things could be so much worse… when we have so much to be thankful for? We remind ourselves that the last scans were free of any cancer… that Rhonda has survived the terrible treatments… that all she needs is to regain her strength and have her ankle heal… and we can again look forward to a 'normal' life. This was again hammered home to us by the nurse yesterday during our ofc visit. She was excited because they need to help Rhonda regain health and strength for the next 30–40 years of her life. Most of their patients (for a pancreatic oncologist) live 5 years or less.

We are truly blessed.

The next weeks and months will not be easy as Rhonda will have to work hard to get back her mobility and strength… but we will accept the trial knowing that God has, in His great mercy, given us a good outcome. He is 'our strength and our song', and we will always give Him the thanks and praise He deserves.

We are also, again, so thankful and blown away by the love and support of so many... even those we have never met are sending prayers up on our behalf. And we thank God for listening and answering those prayers. And, of course, Maw-in-law came through in a big way... taking care of the needs of the kids and keeping the household humming along... I don't know what we'd have done without her. Another loving gift from our Heavenly Father!

We will get there... God and the love of our family and friends will carry us through! PTL!

God Bless!
Scott and Rhonda

Responses

Debbie S
And the Lord replied, "Well done my good and faithful servant"... that is what you have been to your family. God bless you Scott. And Rhonda will continue to be lifted up as will the entire family.

Patti S
We love you and we will continue to pray for healing strength, rest.

Linda S
Hi Scott—What a time you and Rhonda have had and what a relief you are home and can both rest finally in the comfort of home and with your loving family by your side. I can't imagine how I would be able to handle such an ordeal and with such grace. You

and Rhonda are truly extraordinary and an inspiration to all. I will continue to keep you both in my prayers.

Myra P

Praise the Lord! God is great and almighty. I will continue to pray for Rhonda's continuous recovery and for your whole family that God will continue to guide and bless all of you.

Please give my regards to Rhonda.

Take care.

Dana S

Wow. What an amazing story. I can't believe what all you and Rhonda have been through in the past couple of days (… weeks… months). It is so powerful to hear of the undying faith you have in our Lord. As I read your updates, they never fail to inspire me and reinforce how precious life is and how really blessed we are. My overwhelming stress and day-to-day problems are nothing in comparison to the trials you two are enduring… and yet, your head is held high and your eyes are always focused on the Lord. I'm so thankful for your beautiful ability to use your experiences as such an encouraging witness for Christ.

My prayers are with you and Rhonda.

Amy C

It's just so amazing how strong you both are, it truly blows me away. I feel guilty from time to time when I feel a little sad or just frustrated. I always seem to think about you. I then remind myself how strong you both are and I can do it. I believe in my heart God gives us friends like you to make us be stronger. Bless you both for being so awesome.

Scott's response to Amy C

I know that you all have much to deal with too... Aaron told me about Abbey's spider bite. I'm so glad it's getting better. Things like this I just see as "rubber meets the road" Christianity. Do I really trust? Do I really believe? I must... even though I don't understand. Otherwise, I may as well forget about God and just take back all of the worry and pressure and confusion that I try every day to give to Him. So each day I must decide to stay the course... He carries all of this much better than I ever could...

Your family is in our prayers too...

Amy C

Thanks very much Scott! Yes, it is so much easier to just give it all to Him. I so understand now how much better life is with the love He gives me each day and how much stronger I am!

*****

We were so close to losing Rhonda in this bout with a lack of blood in her system. I wasn't sure she'd be able to come out of it. It was very scary and numbing to be with her through all of the treatments and surgery and then be left wondering if all of the effort was for naught. The chemo drugs she had been receiving were designed to attack cells that propagate quickly like cancer cells and hair cells and the bone marrow cells, which exist to create and replenish blood cells. Rhonda had also lost almost a quarter of her body weight due to not being able to eat and was down to under 100 pounds. Most of the time, when she needed to be moved, I would stand her up and squat down to grab her around her upper legs (to protect the still tender tummy area) and just pick her straight up. She was light as a feather, and it was nice just holding her close. We affectionately called it "dancing," and it helped us to make some "lemonade" out of all of these "lemons" we'd been dealing with. But she would need fuel and calories and much time to start regaining her strength.

*****

March 14
My Rhonda—Step by Step

Hi All,

Just a quick note to let you know how Rhonda's doing and that we leave today for a short trip to celebrate our 5th anniversary (was on 3/12).

Rhonda's strength and just 'feeling good' has been very slow to return. She's had a couple of good days... and it then takes her a day or two... or even three... to rest up from doing even seemingly small things... like going to her dr appt (blood counts continue to improve... PTL!)... and eating a meal out for our anniversary... taking a shower... just ordinary, everyday things are still sapping her energy tremendously. The appetite also comes and goes (gone mostly)... which puts her in a 'catch 22'. It's a delicate and ever-changing balance to find out how much she can eat without overdoing it... but she needs to eat to regain her strength. We are finding that this is a time to just persevere and work to gain as we're able... a 'three steps forward, two steps back' kinda thing.

So... today we leave on our trip to Fort Worth. Three nights in a hotel to get away with mainly rest and movies on the agenda. We are really looking forward to it! If she feels up to it, we may try to visit with some old friends or see some sights in that area, but nothing is for certain. She still needs so much rest.. and nourishment as we can get it to agree with her.

The road back for Rhonda's strength and health is slow and even more arduous than we thought it would be... again compelling us to move forward slowly each day... even each hour as it comes... sometimes good... sometimes not so good. God is carrying us as we sometimes reach the end of our proverbial rope in wanting the strength and energy to come back... now.

But we know we will get there!

We had a great time of prayer last night... giving it all back to God... again... trying to keep our eyes on Him who is the Great Physician and Healer... who knows what we need before we do... who loves us as His own children. His mercies are new every morning... He has proven Himself faithful to us time and time again. Our strength is drawn from His.

I will be out of touch while we're away... getting back in town Wednesday evening. Thank you all again for your prayers and support... we still need and covet them. We love and appreciate you... so much!

God Bless!
Scott and Rhonda

Responses

Jane B
Be assured of our love, thoughts, and prayers. We love and value you and do pray for strength and healing!

I do so appreciate your including us in your reports and updates. With love

Mom S

Happy Anniversary! So glad you are able to get away for a while. Love you much.

Patti S

We will pray for a lovely, blessed time of rest, renewal and romance.

Aunt Naomi

Dear Scott and Rhonda, I'm sorry that I have not gotten back to you before this;

I want you to know that we are praising God every day for her recovery. That was a scary time for all of you. Our Chery went so quick, I can't believe it yet. God bless you all and he has! I hope that the few days away will do wonders for our Rhonda.

God bless all of you and he has! Love you

Apr 3
My Rhonda—Getting There

Hello,

It's been a few weeks since the last note, so I wanted to give you an update on how we're doing. We are definitely seeing some prog-ress... and a couple of more bumps... in these last few weeks.

During our wonderful anniversary trip, Rhonda learned that she could walk for short distances with the help of my hand and a cane. It was very uplifting for her to be able to get on her feet for the first time in six weeks! We pretty much stayed in our room and watched movies and snacked… going out to get a bite only once a day. To finish our trip, we rolled around the mall she had lived by before we met, and all in all, thoroughly enjoyed the time to ourselves for a few days!

Ten days later, Rhonda's mom went back home to CA (on Saturday the 27th). We are so thankful for her tremendous sacrifice and hard work to help us through these past several weeks! Her leaving us has given cause for both renewed determination to get this all behind us… and a bit of anxiety wondering how we'd all cope without her strength to hold us all up.

The lack of any real measurable progress for Rhonda over such an extended time of several weeks tried and tested our strength and faith. Many days we found ourselves exhausted and thankful just to get through the day… while pinning our hopes that tomorrow would be a better day. Sometimes it was, and sometimes not.

The low point hit on the day before Maw-in-Law left. We had planned on a family dinner out with all the kids who could make it (Stef couldn't make it from Waco). That day Rhonda was feeling a bit overwhelmed with things and we decided she should try a med that would help to pick her up… but it had the exact opposite effect. The emotional crash that followed gave an open door to let out all of the feelings of frustration and weariness of all that we'd been through in the last year.

I think it was good for her.

Although very weak and emotionally drained, she got through the dinner with her sheer determination… even insisting on using her cane (with much help) to walk. We didn't get home til almost 10 and had another of those exhausted prayers with hopeful thanks that the next day would be better. I had planned on taking Maw-in-Law to the airport myself since she had to be there by 7 AM… but Rhonda surprised us all by getting up and riding to the airport to see her off. We even stopped for breakfast on the way home. The following days still went back and forth some, but we could see that we were mostly moving forward. An amazing turnaround… PTL!

So… this last week we've all learned (again!) how to get by without Rhonda's mom. A physical therapist has been coming a couple times a week to help her gain strength, and she is now much more able to move around the house on her own… PTL again! We also see the hair starting to come back… another sign the chemo is wearing off. The appetite has even been picking up… we're getting there! We did have a bit of a scare this week when she got sick 3 days in a row… but then found out it was only the meds messing with her and are now getting past that too.

So… here we are at Easter weekend… a time that is precious to our Faith because it serves to remind us how great a price Jesus paid for us… because He loves us so much. Our lives have been forever changed by His selfless act of Love by laying His life down for us. But death could not hold Him down for long… because His Love and Power even transcend death. His glorious victory over death gives us Hope for each day… which, as we've been reminded of so often lately, is sometimes all we have to pull us through. And His 'mercies are new every morning'. Each day has the potential to bring forth both the wonderful and the tragic… but He is always with us… because He loves us so much. It's wonderful knowing that we're never alone.

Rhonda and I pray for your Easter weekend to be a wonderful time of family and love. We are so thankful for your encouragement, concern, prayers and love. Words could never say enough...

May God Bless you all richly!
Scott and Rhonda

Responses

Jeff W

Thanks for the update and the good word. I am very glad to hear that it sounds like Rhonda has turned a corner!

Your letters during Rhonda's sickness and you and Rhonda's faith during the whole ordeal have been a very strong testimony to God's sovereignty. I am blessed to know you as a brother.

Apr 21
My Rhonda—Getting There—update

Hi,

Just a quick note to let you all know that we have scans tomorrow (Thursday), and an appt on Friday to get the results. We are believing God for good results... but will always trust His will for us regardless. We also have an appt on Monday with the orthopedic to see if the boot is ready to come off. Although Rhonda's been doing much better at getting around... even walking on her own some... I think we'll be surprised if we're done with the boot because there's still a lot of tenderness there.

Otherwise... Rhonda is finally gaining strength... most days... and her hair is coming back with a vengeance... along with a better appetite… she's actually gained back some weight the last couple of weeks. PTL!!!

So… we'll let you all know how all the stuff comes out.

Thank you all again for your continuous prayers and encouragement… we are on the road to FULL recovery! :)

Thank you and God Bless!
Scott and Rhonda

Responses

Linda S

Wow, this is such wonderful news. There's a lot of positive progress, such a blessing. It's especially nice to hear Rhonda has her appetite back and is gaining strength. Each day sounds like it is getting better for her. Tell her I said hello and good luck with the scans today. :)

Jim F

Praise the Lord for His continued healing of Rhonda and for sustaining you throughout this ordeal. I really appreciate your status reports, Scott.

Tandy

God still is in control and He definitely has a plan. We are in His Hands Always.

Apr 23
My Rhonda—Scan Results

Dear Friends and Family,

It is with a most humble and thankful heart that I can now share with you the results of Rhonda's scan… all is clean… she is still cancer free!

Our loving and merciful God has poured out His grace and answered all of our prayers… and we give all thanks and praise to Him!

I don't really have enough brain power right now to put into words all of the feelings rolling around inside me right now… relief… tears of joy… humbled that He would do this for us… elation and exhaustion… all at the same time. Wow.

After sending out text messages to several people to spread the good word… the next thing we did was sit in the car… in the hospital parking garage… join hands, and give thanks to God… our Savior and Healer. Yes… the doctors and staff (most of them) were awesome… but we know in our heart of hearts where the work of healing came from… our Father in Heaven… PTL!!!

The doctor was so certain that we're cured that he told us we could get Rhonda's chemo port removed during our appt with the surgeon in a couple of weeks… yes! We had been told that they normally wait 6 months after treatment for that. Another gift… another sign to show us that all of the bad stuff is now behind us… PTL!!!

So… we will let this all sink in… we will immerse ourselves in the Goodness of the Lord… we will look forward to many, many more years of being together to do His work wherever He leads us… to do our best to live life to the fullest and share His goodness with the world.

Again… I am at a loss for words to thank you all for sharing this journey with us… for gladly helping us to bear this burden… for giving of yourselves through your love, encouragement, generosity and time… for all of this… and more… we thank you with all of our heart and soul… with all of our being. What an incredible support group we have had… you all are the BEST… THANK YOU!!!!!!!!!!!!!!!

Now you can share in our JOY! :)

So… next we visit the orthopedic on Monday… we still need healing in Rhonda's ankle and feet… we still need to build up strength and stamina… but the bad stuff is GONE! PTL!!!

Our God is an Awesome God!!!

God Bless you all!
Scott and Rhonda

Responses

Clifton W
I rejoice with you in this answer to prayer.

Debbie S
What an amazing testimony the Lord has given the two of you… the whole family. I am so happy to hear your news!

Sherry W

Praise Jesus! It's truly a miracle and I thank Him for it.

May the Lord continue to bless you both and be with Rhonda as she regains her strength and also that her ankle and foot gets better.

Jane B

Dear, dear Rhonda and Scott:

We thank the Lord for your wonderful report and thank you, too, for letting us share your journey. You and your family have certainly been in our thoughts and prayers throughout the ordeal, and your faith and spirit have been a blessing. We will continue to pray for your complete healing and renewed strength.

With blessings and love

Sandy L

Thank you Scott for sharing this totally awesome news! We are ecstatic with joy and excitement. That is the best news I have heard in a long time. I am praising the Lord!

Patti S

What a gift to be able to rejoice with you and Rhonda at this time. To know as you do that it was God who guided every step of the way. So relieved and happy for this wonderful news!

Tandy

God is indeed good. I am so thankful for the report. Love ya.

Roxzanne M

Scott, I am so happy and relieved. Here's a big hug from me, pass it onto Rhonda.

Pamela D

This side of heaven, you two will never know the impact of your testimony throughout your ordeal or how you have impacted me with your faith!! Love to you both and still praying with you.

Peggy A

Alleluiah! Tears of joy in my eyes!

Jan and Julius R

Scott, what glorious news! Our Lord is in the business of miracles & that's what we have here! Much love!

Jeff W

That is absolutely awesome news - you and Rhonda have experienced God's blessing in a special way! We do serve an awesome God!

Lynn B

This is truly wonderful news!

Trish M

Wow! My heart is so full and happy right now Scott!! You guys have been thru the most unbelievable journey... and I know it'll take a while for Rhonda to get her strength back, but YOU DID IT!!! You guys are an inspiration to many. Thank you for sharing your story with us and letting us be a part of this healing process. The prayers won't ever stop for you guys!

Hugs

Denise A

We are SO HAPPY for the great news!!!!!!!! We wish Rhonda a full and speedy recovery! The kids are still praying for her every night

at dinner and they were so thrilled to hear that she is cancer free!!!!!
PTL!

Have a wonderful day

Bruce W

Man...... PTL................. Our GOD answers prayers...

Usha A

That's great news! My best wishes to you and Rhonda!

Jim F

That's great news, Scott! Thanks for the wonderful report. Will
pray for complete and quick healing in Rhonda's ankle and feet.

Sylvia A

Praise the Lord. We know that God is the only healer and there
is definitely power in prayer. Please give Rhonda a big hug for me!

May 2
My Rhonda—Them Feet

All,

I just wanted to give you a quick update on our appt with the
orthopedic this past Monday. Rhonda's ankle is showing good signs
of progress... but she's going to need to keep the boot on for at least
another 6 weeks... until our next appt on June 7. Both of her feet are
still not right... broken bones, sprain, etc. She is able to walk on her
own... but it's a huge effort for her.

Well... we kinda expected it... but it was still a disappointment. This passing out in the shower thing has really put a crimp

in her recovery... and it seems like it was so preventable if I'd just grabbed her at the time instead of thinking so much... rats!

But... our faith tells us that God has a greater purpose in all things... that somehow out of this additional trial He will bring extra-special blessings for us... and those around us. So... we will choose... again... to trust Him through this portion of Rhonda's journey back to full recovery and full strength. He's already brought us through so much... how can we doubt Him now? His goodness to us causes our hearts to overflow with thankfulness!

And... the cavalry is coming too... Maw-in-law arrives on Tuesday for a couple of weeks so she can attend Stef's graduation from Baylor (go Stef!). It will be wonderful to have her with us again!

Thank you again for your love and support... for sharing our joy in the good news of Rhonda's battle and victory over cancer... and for sticking with us as we wait for full healing to come.

Have a great day... God Bless!
Scott and Rhonda

Response

Patti S
We love you all and it was so good to share a part of this Sunday with you.
Know it took effort on Rhonda's part and hope she soaked up rest this afternoon... pray for healing that astounds the Dr.'s.

June 7
My Rhonda—The Boot Comes Off

Hi,

We just had our appt with the orthopedic... and the bone is healed... she can take the boot off! PTL! The doc seemed kinda astonished that it had all healed... we just attribute it to all of the prayers that have gone up for Rhonda. Thank you so much... again!

Now... things are still tender... weak... and tight. That ankle hasn't moved much in 4 months... so it will take a while to get the strength and flexibility back... but... we crossed another important threshold in Rhonda's comeback from this last very tough year. So... overall speaking... we can see definite progress in her strength and appetite... but she still has a ways to go. She does have enough hair coming back now that she's just about ready to lose the hats too... it's too bloody hot for them now anyways! :)

So... the next scan should come around mid-July. We don't have an exact date yet. While we were at the hospital checking on this, we had a chance to go to visit the lady from our church who has been pretty much living in ICU waiting for a double-lung transplant. We are so glad we did. She has taken a turn for the worse and is probably in her last hours. We spoke for a few minutes with her mother trying to comfort her... but what do you say? We told her that we would continue to pray... and to try and find peace in knowing that God has a better place planned for all believers... on the other side... with Him in all His Glory. Please offer up a prayer for the May family.

Well... it's so wonderful to see that the terrible times and set-backs seem to be behind us. God has brought us through so much.

Every week we see a little progress… a bit more strength… eating more often… able to keep going a little bit longer than before. We praise God for His grace and mercy to bring Rhonda back to where we can all look forward to the future that He has so lovingly granted to us. This was driven home to us again as we visited the May family… their daughter won't be going home with them… but going home to be with Jesus. We know it will be a wonderful place to be… but we are also thankful that it was not our time yet.

We thank you again for your awesome love and support!

Responses

Peggy A

Great timing! I stopped by your office this afternoon to see how Rhonda was. Glad to hear she is progressing.

Patti S

Praise the Lord, indeed. I know that we all have experienced just an infinitesimal piece of your journey and cannot imagine the depths of the valleys and the heights of the joy as you are reaching an end to this walk, but our hearts and prayers have been steady and we rejoice in your faith and the miracle God has granted.

Jim F

Thanks for sharing the good news, Scott. I think of you and Rhonda often.

Quinn W

Scott this is awesome news! God is good!

Terry C

Scott, that is great news. Every day is one step further down the walk with the Lord. So glad to hear that Rhonda is continuing to improve. Love you guys. You will stay in my prayers.

Ryan G

Somebody is trying to make me cry this morning!!!! I was listening to the radio on the way to work and they did a bit with leukemia kids in the hospital. They had a day of beauty with facials, manicures, and make-up. Hearing one little girl's story just really had me tearing up. Then, you send this about the May family. It has me thinking that I need to make a trip down to Corpus to see my friend's kids (she passed away from cancer 3 1/2 years ago). I will continue to pray for you guys and the May family.

I posted on Rhonda's facebook that I can't wait until we get to go running together. :)

Love you

Sylvia A

I'm glad to hear that Rhonda's ankle is healing, once again God is the healer and is working miracles in your lives.

I'm so sorry to hear about the church parishioner whose daughter is ending her journey; I can only imagine how hard this must be for them. No parent should have to bear losing a child no matter what age.

Please tell Rhonda I said hello and that I continue to keep her in my daily prayers.

Linda S

Scott—What an uplifting email. Rhonda has made so much progress, I bet she's super glad to finally get that boot off. Sounds like she is well on her way and the two of you are so wonderful and kind.

I will continue to keep Rhonda in my prayers and also pray for the May family.

Sandy L

Yippee Hooray Praise the LORD!!!!!!!!!!!!!

Jane B

Thanks so much for including us in your "Rhonda Reports." They are such a blessing, and we do thank and praise God for His intervention, care, and healing. We think of you all often and do rejoice with you in Rhonda's progress.

With love and prayers

Jan R

Such wonderful news about Rhonda! We will pray for the May family.

Much love!

July 20
My Rhonda—Slow but Steady Progress

Hello,

Just wanted to give you an update on how things are going for us...

Rhonda has made some steady progress over the last several weeks. She is now able to drive the kids around town (in her new car!)... do some cooking, even laundry and household stuff... things she hasn't been able to do in months. Her appetite is much better than it has been... she's even put on a couple of pounds... And has actually walked up to a mile a couple of times. God has brought her so far from where she was!

But... the strength and endurance are still very slow in coming back. Her feet still feel like hunks of tingly flesh hanging off the end of her legs. She can't tell for sure where the bottom of her foot is unless she has shoes on. If she pushes herself to do more, it takes her 2 or 3 days to recover. This recovery is definitely going to be a process... taken over much time. And the last couple of days she's been through some more pain-drug withdrawal symptoms as we try to wean her off of them... her body just doesn't want to let go of that stuff!

Still... we are very thankful for how God continues to give strength and grace for each day... each challenge. Our faith has been strengthened through this all... we know that He will keep on bringing us along and taking care of us... just as He has been... from the beginning.

We've also finally gotten the next scans scheduled. The scan is on Wed, 7/28... with an oncologist appt the next day to get results. We will continue to trust God for good results!

And the best news for last... my Aunt Fran is turning 90 yrs "young" on the 24th... and Rhonda and I are taking a 4-day weekend and flying up to WI to help her celebrate! There will be a bunch of family there that I haven't seen in years... and that Rhonda's never met. We are so much looking forward to having a getaway and seeing these wonderful people that have been such a huge part of my childhood and life... and continue to inspire me today. Aunt Fran is amazing... she just wears us out with her schedule of cooking, cleaning, replacing floors, messing with storm windows, etc... and just underwent 6 weeks of radiation in Jan/Feb… and is still going strong. We praise God for her and the rest of those precious souls we'll get to spend time with very soon!

Yes… even in the midst of the tough days, God keeps on filling our cup abundantly and seeing us through it all. And we will keep on giving our thanks to Him who is more than able to keep us… until that day He calls us to be with Him.

And many, many continued thanks to you all too… for your love, support, encouragement and prayers. You all mean the world to us!

May God Bless you richly… as He has us…
Scott and Rhonda

Responses

Maw-in-law
Thank you so much, Scott for continuing to keep us updated. I still worry but not nearly so much. I, too am thanking God for His mercy in sparing Rhonda and the rest of us from losing her.
Much love and miss you guys,
Mom

Clifton W
Thanks for the update. Eph. 6:10 (Finally, be strong in the Lord and in the strength of His might.)

Sandy L
PTL

That is wonderful news. Thanks for sharing. I am so happy for all of you. Thanks again for keeping us informed and sharing this awesome news.

Jeff W

As always, thanks for the update. It is great to hear the progress Rhonda is making. You have both been through a remarkably tough time and your testimony for the Lord is awesome! Have a great trip.

Patti S

Thanks so much Scott. We love you both.

Lila C

How blessed we are, you would share about your precious Rhonda! I always want to know and have been educated, it is good for your healing to talk about her illness with those that care and we care, more than you could know! Scott I never know what to say and wanted to know everything you would share! You are so precious to share the better times first I was just thrilled about that progress. Scott this can't be easy, and yet I can hear how grateful you both are for Rhonda's progress! Time is so important for her!! I so wish I could be with her more as a girlfriend, but know you two know my circumstances, and most of all you know I love you both and care greatly!! Scott please take care of you. I am so happy to hear you will see your aunt! Thanks for sharing that too, such a dear and strong lady, I have said they are the strongest generation! Tell Rhonda, I love her. We are counting OUR blessings and try to keep our eyes fixed upon Jesus, not the suffering this world allows! You two are such an inspiration, such faith!

Thank you again, it means so much to be included in this very precious news about our Rhonda and Scott.

August 1
My Rhonda—Clean Scans!

Hi,

I am overjoyed to announce once again that the scans performed this past week served to confirm to us one more time that Rhonda is cancer-free… PTL!

Our Lord is so gracious to allow her to continue to heal and regain her strength… however slow that progress seems to be… all of the 'bad stuff' remains behind us! Yes!

We also had a wonderful visit with family up north as we gathered for my Aunt Fran's 90th bday last weekend. It was a really special time of connecting and re-connecting with family I hadn't seen in a looooong time. What wonderful people… what a treat it was for us! We're so thankful that God provided Rhonda and I the opportunity. I'm also looking today (back in TX) at the temperature difference in envy as I see 103 on my thermometer and that it's 78 in Milwaukee… ugh!

And one more bit of happy news to share… last Saturday Jordan called me early in the morning to let me know that he and his lovely girlfriend, Kathleen, had just gotten engaged at sunrise on a TX beach. What a romantic, eh? :) PTL again! We are so excited and happy for them. The big day will occur sometime in October, 2011… giving them plenty of time to iron out all of the details. We joyously look forward to having another terrific young lady added to our family! God is so good!

So… that's it for now… the next scan will be towards the end of the year. Rhonda will be starting with the 'Fit Steps' program (which was designed to help cancer patients build back their strength) this coming Thursday. We know it will take a lot of determination and hard work to get back to 'normal'… but the 'bad stuff' is behind us… and we know that she will continue to overcome with God's strength and the ongoing love and prayers of so many… Thank you so much… again!

Responses

Peggy A
　　Wonderful News! Yeaaaaaaaaa!

Jan R
　　The Lord has really blessed you both! We will need to draw on your wisdom & strength as we enter the next phase of Julius' journey with cancer.

Judy R
　　Excellent!!! Glad you have 100% good news to report. Thanks for the nice start to a Monday. :)

Amy C
　　That is just so awesome!!

Sylvia A
　　PTL! And congratulations on the soon to be addition to your family! :)

Dina T

Best news I've heard in a really long time Scott! So happy to hear that the scans came back clean... You and Rhonda have both been so strong through this whole ordeal. I know it was exhausting and trying... but the end result is awesome and miraculous! Life is such a gift and I think we often forget that... this has been such a reminder:) May God continue to bless you and your family.

Cindy H

Praise the Lord for this great news! I thank Him that Rhonda's scans were clear of cancer, and I am thrilled to hear about Jordan and Kathleen!

Sept 8
Rhonda—update from Scott to the SS class

Hi,

Just wanted to make you all aware...

Rhonda's been having occasional pains at the bottom right side of her ribcage the last several weeks. We thought it was just maybe scar tissue or something, but when we went to the oncologist for an appt today, he checked with the surgeon and they want to do a scope procedure... tomorrow morning if possible... to check it out. They think there may be a blockage in her duct.

The dr said it might be an ulcer or something... but this is the exact spot where everything started for her Memorial Day weekend last year. Rhonda is not worried... just wants to get rid of the pain.

I'll send out another note when we know more... but wanted you all to know.

Response

Vic C

Donna and I will be praying for both of you. We pray that the Lord will fill her with his strength and healing spirit. If you need us to help in any way let us know.

Praying for you

Sept 9
Rhonda—update from Scott to the SS class

Well... we just got home...

The scope dr told us he didn't really see anything out of the ordinary or of concern... great news... PTL! He also said he couldn't tell what is causing the pain. He took a culture of sample bacteria... saying that sometimes after surgery bacteria can build up and cause problems. We won't know those results until next week.

He thought everything looked really good... just some slight physical deformities caused by the surgery when everything was re-worked. In fact, instead of a handshake, he gave me a high-five... and said that everything looked 'great'! This is the same doctor we've had before (3 or 4 times before) and we remain completely impressed with his skill and knowledge. Another Godsend for us!

Bottom line... we wait to hear about the culture, and see where we go from there. We did get Rhonda back on the pain patch so she can relax… and heal more. I think it will help to increase her energy for more exercise to gain strength.

Thank you for your love and prayers…

Responses

Sandy L
> Fantastic News PTL!!!!
> Thank you soooooo much for keeping us updated!

Drew C
> PTL!!!! :)

Terry C
> Thanks Scott, good news indeed.

Vic C
> That's wonderful news!!! Keep us updated on Rhonda's condition.

Jim T
> Great news Scott - Thanks for sharing.

Pamela D
> Amen and Amen!

Rodger B
> The BEST tool a Christian has is FAITH in CHRIST and I believe you both are a great example of this incredible FAITH! I am so glad to hear that the pain is not serious, so ditto on the PTL!

Oct 9
My Rhonda—Turning a Corner

Hi,

Several folks have been asking about Rhonda's progress, so I figured that I'd send out an update on how things have been going. There's been a lot of back-and-forth... good days... not so good days. But it seems like we can now look back and see a time where things have been consistently improving... PTL!

As some of you may remember, about a month ago Rhonda's intermittent pain got to the point where our oncologist ordered an endoscopy to be done. We got the same wonderfully skilled dr who did the previous procedures to perform it and he found everything "looking great!"... he was really pleased for us and even gave me a high-five. :)

But that didn't answer our questions about Rhonda's pain. He also took a culture to test for excessive bacteria (which he said sometimes happens after surgery), and gave us a Rx for an antibiotic if the results warranted meds. We didn't want to fill the Rx unless we needed to... but had to wait several days for the results to come back. The tests came back clean. PTL again.. but it still wasn't an answer to her pains.

We did decide to go back on a low-level pain patch at this time... figuring that it would help her with the pains and she could get off of the pain meds when she was stronger. Being in pain or even the anticipation of pain was really sapping her strength.

About a week later, Rhonda unexpectedly came down with a fever… which climbed to 102 pretty quickly. It was a weekend, so I called the on-call dr to see what they thought we needed to do. I told the dr that we had the Rx for an antibiotic left from the scope dr… and she said to go ahead and fill it. Even before we could start the med, Rhonda's fever seemed to break… but she was really zapped. She ended up pretty much spending the next 4–5 days in bed.

And since that point… it seems that she now has more 'staying power'… having the strength to get through the day's activities (with rest in between tasks)… and not pay for it for the next three days. She's also learned that it's very important for her to get a good night's sleep, or she can hardly get out of bed the next day.

So… with Rhonda focusing on getting the rest she needs without pushing herself too far… she's had a pretty good time of it the last few weeks… a real PTL! And the pains do seem to be lessening… no more need for major pain meds when she feels it coming on. She's been to the gym a few times for stretching and walking… still walking around the neighborhood in the evening when we can… doing grocery runs (with Julie's help)… and has also been going to a chiropractor for about a month. She (a wonderful Christian lady) has been able to help Rhonda's feet start to get some feeling and strength back.

All in all… we are feeling much better about her progress and are seeing life returning to some sense of "normal." God has been so good to bring us through so much. When I think back, I'm amazed at all that Rhonda has been through this past 15 months… and that all of the bad stuff remains behind us! We are humbled to have our Lord heal Rhonda and continue to build her strength and health back day by day. The next scans will be the first week of December.

And thank you all, once again, for all of your love and support... prayers and generosity that have helped to carry us through this. We love you and thank God for you all.

May your cup overflow with God's richest blessings!
Scott and Rhonda

Responses

Peggy A

Thanks for the update. I think about how Rhonda is doing every time I see you. I'm glad she is doing better.

Patti S

One of my favorite moments this Sunday was watching Rhonda eat the rice that Charlie wouldn't eat...... and to notice the pink in her cheeks.

Trish M

Day at a time! Glad progress is being made!! Hugs to you guys.

Dec 5
My Rhonda—Scan Results

Howdy All,

Just wanted to send out a quick msg to those who hadn't yet heard... Rhonda had scans this past week and everything is still squeaky clean and beautiful... no signs of 'bad stuff' anywhere! PTL!!!

We are so thankful to our Lord for continuing to give us the grace to move forward and far away from this illness that has commanded so much of our attention… our resources… our lives… for the last 18 months. The love and support and encouragement we've received has been nothing short of amazing… God is so good! We really missed Maw-in-law esp at Thanksgiving… but Stouffers does make a pretty good lasagna! And next year will be much different with Rhonda continuing her 'comeback' to full strength.

Yet… she is still a bit frail right now… still fighting for the energy and strength to come back..but we know and can see that it's coming… one small step at a time. Every week we can see that she's able to push and do a bit more… yes… it's coming back!

We pray that you all had a wonderful Thanksgiving and are looking forward to the Christmas season… a season of Joy and miracles! We just came back from the annual Cherkosov (elderly pianist/violinist couple) concert with Rhonda's old church family in Ft. Worth. Such talented and humble people… it was wonderful! What a privilege and treat it was for us!

So… the doc said no more scans for 6 months (PTL again!)… and wants us to get more physical conditioning going. Rhonda's already got a plan that starts tomorrow. We know it won't be easy, but we will love the results! Thank you for your continued prayers!

Again… thank you so much for your love and support… and have a great Christmas season!

Love you all!
Scott and Rhonda

Responses

Peggy A

Yay! So happy for both of you.

Lila C

Precious Scott and Rhonda, I so appreciate these updates and the fact you would "share" with us. You both are such inspirations to us!!!

So happy to hear about your trip to Ft. Worth!!

I will be thinking about Rhonda (as I so often do) as she starts her plan tomorrow!

I love you both beyond words and it is very important to my heart that you know that. I thank God for the gift you are to my life…

I thank God for the squeaky clean.

Clifton W

Thanks for the good report. I still pray for Rhonda every day. I know it was quite an effort for yawl to come to our anniversary party, but we enjoyed having you very much.

Marci E

Wonderful news.

Sylvia A

Scott and Rhonda, PTL! God does work in mysterious ways and we all have to place our trust in Him to get us thru adversity. The two of you were chosen for a special reason I'm sure, to be testaments for us all of God's unconditional love for us all.

Linda S

Scott—This is such wonderful news. I'll keep Rhonda in my prayers while she continues to gain strength.

Dina T

Thanks for sharing this AWESOME news Scott & Rhonda! I continue to pray for good health and strength. Hope you and your family have a blessed Christmas this year.

Trish M

This is the best Christmas present any of us could get!!! Hugs to you guys and prayers for the strength Rhonda needs to improve her stamina. The hard part is over!

Dec 10
My Rhonda—Scan Results Update

Hello again,

Well… we found out today that the results we were given last week were not complete. We're not really sure why the dr told us "all looks great, seeya in 6 months" when he hadn't seen everything yet. Hmmmm. Bottom line is… there are some lymph nodes that are 'lighting up' on the PET scan… meaning the nodes show 'activity'.

The dr has consulted with his peers and has decided that they need to do a biopsy to see what this means. So… we are scheduled for this biopsy next Tuesday afternoon, the 14th… and hope to have results by Friday.

Rhonda woke up this morning feeling really great… better than she has in a long time. Got up at 6:00 to see Charlie off (like every other day)… then she and Julie ran some errands and did the weekly grocery run. Even tonight… she's made up some pancakes for the kids to have… It's been a good day! We look forward to many more in the days ahead…

But the call from the doc's did kinda put a damper on things… we trust that all is okay. We work hard through the exercising our Faith to not worry about things we have no control over… consciously choosing to take each day as it comes… being thankful for the abundant blessings that continuously overflow us… and meeting the challenges with all of the strength our Lord gives us.

Your prayers, love, and support have meant so much to us… words are not adequate to tell you how much you have been a help to us on this journey… but we're not there yet. Yet another chapter is unfolding before us. We don't yet know where it will lead… but we know, and trust, in the One who leads us. God is our Healer and Deliverer… He will continue to see us through to the other side of Rhonda's illness… and we will continue to trust… and follow… and rest in the Peace that only He can give.

We'll let you know as soon as we know results… hopefully by next weekend…

Thank you again… and may God Bless!
Scott and Rhonda

Responses

Usha A
I hope and pray that all will work out fine next week. I'm keeping my fingers crossed for both of you.

My best to Rhonda

Debbie S

You are a beautiful example of faith. You are both in my thoughts and prayers.

Marci E

You guys are in my prayers. We know that God can do anything but fail. We'll remain trustful of His grace, power and knowledge.

Trish M

Aaack! Yea, sure woulda been nice if he'd looked at everything before sending you guys on your way. It'll be okay though. Tell Rhonda good luck tomorrow and we'll wait to hear from you when they know what they're looking at.

Hugs!

Sylvia A

Scott and Rhonda, I know it goes without saying but keep the Faith. God is the healer and will continue to carry you thru this journey.

My family continues to keep you and your family in daily prayers and we know there is strength in prayer, and that one day soon Rhonda will be completely healed.

Our daughter Claudia gave birth to her son Julian Angel on Monday evening. Being present for his birth is a testament to God's mercy and overwhelming love for His own children. Baby and mom are doing great and will be staying at our house with the rest of their family thru Christmas. Among all the adversity we all sometimes face, we are reminded that we have so many blessings to be thankful for.

Thank you both for your encouraging words during our own journey of losing one grandchild and awaiting the arrival of our newest one.

Take care and may God continue to bless you all during this holiday season

Dec 18
My Rhonda—Biopsy Results

Hello,

Just wanted to send you all a quick note. We made several phone calls on Friday to run down the results and finally got the oncologist… and got the news that we did not want to hear… the lymphoma is back.

Good news is that it's in a very early stage… only in nodes, not in any vital area… and we already have an appt on Tuesday morning with a new dr who specializes in this area.

This was, of course, a real bummer for us to hear… but we know that God will continue to take care of us and see us through it…

Thank you again for your prayers and support… looks like we'll need them for a while longer…

I'll communicate more details after our Tuesday appt…

Thank you so much…
Scott and Rhonda

Responses

Donna and Vic C

We will continue to pray for Rhonda and you. It's just a good thing that Rhonda is a positive person & praying that she will continue to have faith for a positive recovery.

Peggy A

So sorry. Perhaps the new Dr. can eradicate the lymphoma for good. New medicines... all the time. Prayers continue to be with you.

Quinn W

Scott, I am soooo sorry to hear the news... I was praying for a different outcome. God is able... I will continue to lift Rhonda, and you and your family up in prayer. Take care...

Jim F

Scott, I am so sorry to hear this news, but we know very well that our God is bigger than any and every problem we have. Zelime and I will stand in faith with you and Rhonda.

Your brother forever

Sylvia A

Scott and Rhonda, my candles are already being lit as I write this, and we will continue to storm the heavens with our prayers that our loving God guides you in the path of those Dr's who will be blessed by Him to help do His work. God will restore Rhonda to health again, he must just have a few more missions for you to accomplish (perhaps in waiting rooms :<D).

Keep your faith strong and remember;

"He performs Miracles that cannot be fathomed and Miracles that cannot be counted." Job 9:10

In prayer

Linda S

Oh Scott, my heart just sunk. You and Rhonda are in my prayers.

Dina T

Hi Scott and Rhonda.

So sorry you guys have to go thru this again. I (and my bible study group) have never stopped praying for you… we'll just keep going.

God Bless.

Denise A

I just wanted to let you know that you both are in our daily prayers. The boys especially pray for you Rhonda every night at dinner.

Lila C

My Precious Rhonda and Scott,

I was with my granddaughter until late last night and came home to read these words. So, I sat here until later last night and thought about you both and then told the Lord "Lord, I don't have any, words to say that might show them my heart and care, and since this precious couple knows you so well Lord, I don't have the right "religious" words that talk about You Lord, our maker. And then just as I hurt enough because I wanted to write back, and be there for you both so very badly in exactly the right way, "our precious Jesus" told me in a clear clear Word, "Yes, you do know what to say, it is, I LOVE YOU BOTH." Scott and Rhonda He came to give us this love for one another and I know in one of the clearest ways ever, my heart is so pure for you both. This is God given. To love your brothers and sisters in Christ so very deeply, especially you. I see you as part my life and heart and thank you with all of my heart for sharing this life with me (us). I want to be here for you, and am trusting you to tell me when and if you need me. Nobody can know another couple's suffering or victory, I do plan on watching your victory in this. Again, only the words given to me I LOVE YOU BOTH!!

Always

Dec 21
My Rhonda—Biopsy results—update from Scott

Well...

We met with the new dr today and he told us the biopsy results were not conclusive. He said that the treatment approaches would vary greatly, so he wants us to schedule a procedure to fully remove the affected lymph node so they can be sure to get a clear biopsy and diagnose this thing correctly.

We agree!

So... we've got a call into the surgeon's ofc to see if he can squeeze us in before the end of the year. He is currently out on vacation, so it may be several days before we hear back.

So... we're planning on having a very merry Christmas with the kids and enjoy our time together! We'll mess with this stuff later (doc said there's no hurry). Rhonda's been feeling really good... and the Lord is in control!

And we hope you all will have a wonderful Christmas and holidays with your family too! Thank you again for your wonderful prayers and support!

We'll let you know more when we do…

Responses

Greg G

Amen brother! Great attitude!

Debbie S

sounds like a perfect plan!

Sally T

very frustrating medicine is not an exact science! You guys are in our prayers.

We are doing great and I know you guys will face whatever the drs. come up with

Patti S

We love you… enjoy every minute of this wonderful Christmas Season with the knowledge that the One that made it possible is fully in control.

Donna C

Thanks for the update! We will keep you all in our prayers… It's good to hear that you, Rhonda are feeling good, that's encouraging!

Jan R

I like your spirit—let's put all this cancer stuff aside and just enjoy the family & holidays! Praying for continued success for

Rhonda's treatment. I will be available in the coming year to help you & Rhonda as you need it!

Much love!

Judy R

Sounds like a great plan.

Sorry you have to face the medical regime again. Fingers crossed that it's easy. :)

Jim F

Very glad to hear that Rhonda feels good and that there is not an urgent problem. May your Christmas celebration be richly blessed.

Sylvia A

Scott and Rhonda, God is in control and He is the Healer that will restore your health.

Enjoy your holiday and time with your family, and may God bless you all,

"My hope comes from God, He alone is my rock and my salvation; He is my fortress. I will not be shaken." Psalm 63:5–6

Julie J

You and your family are still in my thoughts and prayers.

Jane B

Thank you for including us in your e-mail updates. We are thankful for your reports and are praying earnestly for Rhonda and all the family.

Love and blessings

2011: Nagging Side Effects but a Break from Treatments

January 1, 2011
My Rhonda—Biopsy Scheduled

Hello and Happy New Year!

The saga continues...

We got phone calls late in the day on Wednesday the 29th... they were going to fit us in for the biopsy early on the 31st... very early. We were to pre-admit the day before and then be at the hospital by 5:30 AM Friday. However, Wednesday night Rhonda got hit by a nasty bug that made her pretty sick for a couple of hours in the middle of the night. She felt some better the next morning, but was still weak and running some fever. So... I put a call into the surgeon to let them know... and they bumped us... all the way to January 10th for the biopsy.

After a great night's sleep on Thursday, Rhonda was feeling good and had a good day Friday... and another productive day today... we even got the Christmas tree and stuff put up.

So... now we wait some more... and enjoy each day as it comes... thankful for each day... and for this new year to look forward to getting this stuff behind us once and for all.

We pray that you will all have a great new year too! Thank you again for hanging with us through this seemingly unending ordeal.

One day... we will get there!

Responses

Maw-in-law
Happy New Year kids and I pray it is a great one.

Interestingly enough, I'm not as anxious over this time. Perhaps it's because you tell us that it is in the beginning stages. But my bags are packed (or can be quickly) and ready to move if you need me to.

Love you all so much,
Mom

Usha A
Happy New Year.

I hope and pray that this New Year brings you and your family good tidings!

Will keep my fingers crossed for you.

Take care

Sylvia A
Rhonda and Scott, Happy new Year to you and your family. May 2011 be one of renewed blessings, faith, health and happiness to you all.

Trish M
Yes, you will 'get there' soon!!! Hang in there and let's hope 2011 is a great year for the Smiths!!!!

D'Ann C
Praying for all of y'all tomorrow. Bundle up against the cold!

Jan 14
My Rhonda—Latest Results

Hello,

We met with the oncologist this morning to get results of the full lymph node biopsy that was performed on Monday. The biopsy itself went without a hitch. Rhonda was sore for a couple of days, but is now feeling almost no discomfort from it. PTL!

So.. this morning the dr told us that what we have is a 'low-grade' lymphoma… meaning non-aggressive and slow-moving. It's only in several of the lymph nodes. This type is currently not curable. But he also said that he's seen people have this condition for literally years with little or no change. So what he recommends (and we agree!) is to wait a few months and then do another scan to compare with this last one… and then see where we're at with this.

This was very welcome news to us! We are just fine with doing nothing further right now… no more poking or prodding or nasty drugs… and it will give Rhonda a chance to rest and strengthen some more. Then… around the first of April, we'll do another scan. The dr said that even if this appears to grow some by then… they have a very mild chemo treatment with almost no side-effects (and no port needed!) that we could try.

So… short of the miracle we've been praying for, that it would be totally gone… we feel like this is the best news we could have gotten today… PTL! The dr did also say that the lab was continuing to look at the biopsy (meaning it's not the 'final final' word), but he doesn't expect anything drastically different with the 'final final' results.

So… we wait… and grow stronger… and enjoy the life that God has given us!… looking forward to family time… Valentine's… and our anniversary in March. Life is good… and God's grace to us is even better!

God's Blessings to you all! Thank you and have a great weekend… we are! :)

Responses

Quinn W

Scott, grateful to God for the 'ok' news! Ya'll are so strong and your faith is unending. May God continue to bless and keep you both!

Deborah M

YEA… YEA…

Drew C

That's a great report Scott. Thanks for sharing. I pray Rhonda gets totally "clean" so y'all can move on. I'm glad you're getting a break of sorts and a chance to get away from all the medical stuff for a while. That must be so wearisome.

Suraya K

I am so happy that Rhonda will now have a chance to rest and grow stronger. Hopefully the scan in April will show no growth. You guys enjoy the days ahead. God has a plan and it's always for our good in the end.

Pam D

Sorry to hear that it is not gone but relieved to hear she does not have to go through any treatments right away. I will continue to pray that it will be gone by the next scan (we know he can do it).

Myra P

PTL! We will continue to pray for Rhonda's continuous healing. God bless you, Rhonda and your family.

Usha A

Thank you for the update. I am so glad to hear that it is slow moving and non-aggressive. Hopefully, you can put this behind you and Rhonda can get better.

Peggy A

Glad to hear the news that the lymphoma is low grade slow growing. :) You're still in prayers.

Billie M

Thanks for the update. This truly was good news. I can't wait to tell Mike.

Jan R

Wonderful news! God is so full of mercy!

Marci E

I will continue to keep Rhonda and your entire family in my prayers. It is evident God is at work and is putting good medical staff in your path.

Your strength and faith are wonderful to witness.

Lila C

Your update is so appreciated! We love you both dearly! One day at a time.

Mom S

You guys have sure had a stressful year dealing with all this. I guess all you can do is hang in there and keep praying. I hope you have been able to build your strength up Rhonda. You have sure been through a lot. Wish I could do something for you Rhonda to make it all better. Hang in there. Love you guys

Jan 20
My Rhonda—Blockage Fixed

Hi,

Just wanted to let you all know that we just had a little surprise taken care of today. On Monday we got a call from our scope dr's ofc saying that our appt had been set for Thursday… this morning. What was that? Our new oncologist had not discussed anything with us… but evidently some counts on Rhonda's last labs were off the charts and he had asked the scope dr to fit us in asap to check it out.

We didn't get the final story until today… after the procedure. It seems that at the site of the pancreatic surgery (where things had been rearranged and tied together), something had become swollen and covered up a duct, not allowing fluids to drain out. The scope dr said this was somewhat 'normal' after such a surgery… and it was tough going, but he got it opened back up and stretched it a bit so it would hopefully stay open. He did say that this could happen again, so it's something we'll need to keep an eye on.

We're also wondering if this has been the cause of Rhonda's occasional heavy pain that has hit her several times a week… it would be great if that goes away… we will see.

So… our second all-day outpatient procedure in 10 days… it's been a whirlwind. We're more than ready for that 3 months off the doc told us about last week… hopefully it starts now! We did manage to get our annual anniversary 'honeymoon' cabin scheduled at the same Oklahoma park we've been going to since our first honeymoon… and that will be great! We were surprised they still had some left… guess God knew that we needed it too! We are sooooooo looking forward to it! :)

Thank you again for your prayers and support… it really means a lot to us…

And hopefully there'll be nothing to report for a while!

Responses

Peggy A
  Oh my gosh. You guys deserve a break! Rhonda's poor body and all the stress for you. I'm continuing to keep you in my prayers.
  Hang in there.

Sylvia A
  So glad to hear things went well and that it was all taken care of!
  Let's pray this has been the cause of Rhonda's discomfort and that she now gains her strength to enjoy you're upcoming anniversary. :<D
  I continue to uplift you and keep you in my daily prayers.

Judy R

Wow, yeah, that would cause some heavy pain. Imagine, a break in the pain! That will be so nice.

Trish M

Oh that makes sense!! I sure hope that was the cause of the pain and it will be gone now!!! Hang in there!! So glad you will get away to OK on your anniversary!!

Jim F

I'm so sorry you had to deal with another all-day ordeal. It amazes me how you stay so upbeat. Obviously, you have the Holy Spirit within you!

Will pray for you and Rhonda.

Clifton W

I pray every day for yawl.

Feb 1

My Rhonda—Blockage fixed—update from Scott

Well… as the scope dr told us a couple of weeks ago… the "stretching-the-duct" fix may not be permanent. He was right. Rhonda was without pain for a couple of days and then it came back. And after going through some fever and chills… and unabated itch-ing… over the weekend… maybe we're finally gonna get this taken care of.

She had lab tests last week that did show the elevated enzyme levels again… and now they're finally recommending a stent to be placed in the pinched duct. We're hoping that this will take care of the need for pain meds… give her somewhat of an energy boost… and keep her out of the hospital for a while.

We are "penciled in" for early tomorrow afternoon with the scope dr (they can't confirm until in the morning because he's out of town). Of course… tomorrow is when the strongest cold front in 15 yrs is supposed to come in with rain, sleet, snow… and wind chills near zero. But we'll deal with it…

So… again… all prayers are appreciated… and we hope that this "broken record" will not need to be repeated again. God has brought us through so much… we're ready for a real breakthrough here… PTL!

We'll keep you posted on how it all goes… thank you so much for hanging in there with us!

God Bless… and keep safe and warm!

Responses

Donna C

Rhonda & Scott, we will pray that the procedure will go smoothly & will be a success. Be extra careful! Take care.

Sylvia A

So glad to hear from you both, I had you on my mind this am. We will continue to storm the heavens (and I'll keep lighting candles) that all goes as expected and that Rhonda will soon be pain free and soon on the road to recovery.

God bless

Linda S

Boy what a time Rhonda is having. I'll say a prayer that the doctors can give her some much needed relief. Be careful in that weather you're having.

Take care and say hello to Rhonda for me :)

Pam D

She is in my prayers. Please drive carefully if you get to go.

Debbie S

I hope you two are curled up by the fire and not out in these conditions. All updates are greatly appreciated and prayed over. God has a plan and your trust in your circumstances shines through. You are both a testimony to all.

Much love

Feb 1
My Rhonda—No Solution Yet

Well… after getting confirmation at 9:00 this morning… and after driving to downtown Dallas on icy roads… and after waiting until after 4:00 when they finally got Rhonda in the room… and after an hour-plus long procedure…

After all of that… the dr saw no need for a stent. He did some more "stretching" of the area… but everything was 'flowing along just great'. In short… he feels that this has not been the cause of the pain or high enzyme counts.

So he's referring us to a liver specialist… whom we will call 1st thing tomorrow and get an appt… possibly tomorrow, as he's expecting our call. Hopefully this dr will have some insight and help us get past this.

Rhonda's throat is pretty sore from today… but we did enjoy a stop at IHOP on the way home this evening. We didn't get the solution we had hoped for today… but we did eliminate another possible cause (I think Edison said something like that while working to invent the lightbulb)…

So… the quest continues for another day… another dr… but we are still being held by the hand by the same God and Savior who is the same yesterday, today… and forever. He will lead us to answers… and ultimately a final victory over all of this stuff!

Sorry about so many emails here lately… I'm trying to keep them short and to the point. Thank you again for standing with us in this battle… we appreciate you all so much!

More later as we learn more…

Responses

Penny F
    Stay strong. You and Rhonda are in my prayers.

Marci E
    Glad u reached your destination safely. We will continue to trust the Lord. God bless and keep you both.

Tandy
    It's just nice to know what is going on. Don't worry about the number of emails.

i am glad you are home safe and sound. Getting out in this mess was not easy I am sure. You all have a good week. See you Sunday. :-)

Linda S

Glad you were able to make your appointments yesterday despite the challenging weather conditions. I'm keeping you in my prayers Rhonda. I know that you guys will get to the bottom of this soon.

Take care and be extremely careful in this weather. :)

Pam D

Thanks for keeping us updated. I will continue to keep her in my prayers.

Vic C

Donna and I are remembering Rhonda and you in our prayers. We have been touched by the way Rhonda and you have dealt with adversity that you've had. The grace and strength that you have shown is an encouragement and inspiration to us. Our prayers are with you along with our hearts.

In Christ

Ryan G

Please don't apologize for the emails. I don't always respond, but I always appreciate knowing how she is doing.

Quinn W

Still in prayer for you both! Take care…

March 8
My Rhonda—The Specialist = More Tests

Hello,

It's been awhile since I've sent out any word on my Rhonda... so I wanted to send you all a note to let you know how things have been going. She continues to enjoy some REALLY good days... followed by sometimes multiple days of extreme fatigue. There doesn't seem to be much changing, but we do look back several weeks/months and see that she is slowly gaining strength. We are very thankful for every day and are looking forward especially to our anniversary weekend getaway this Friday through Tuesday... in our nice little quiet and rustic cabin in Oklahoma... and celebrating 6 years of being together... God surely has been good to us! PTL!

We've also been doing a lot of waiting... it sure takes a while to get into some dr's offices for a visit... ya know? We finally got to have an appt with the liver specialist this past Monday to explore why Rhonda's enzyme counts have not gone back to normal after her treatments (which ended on 2/15 of last year).

The first visit was somewhat encouraging... after some question and answer time (and dealing with a bit of a language barrier), the dr said he felt pretty sure that Rhonda does not have a disease of the liver... just possible inflammation/damage due to the treatments. That said... he ordered a full bevy of tests (so much that we had to have a lunch break in the middle of the labs being pulled so Rhonda's fluids could be replenished!)... which... we basically feel good about. We're glad he's taking the time to look at everything before discussing any possible treatments.

Rhonda will also have an ultrasound whenever they call and can fit us in. The dr's followup appt is in 3 wks. Hopefully we will get some enlightenment at that time.

So for now… we are excited and thankful to look forward past this very busy week to our cabin time this weekend… :)

Thank you all again for your inquiries about my Rhonda… and your continued prayers and encouragement. When we're tempted to whine about how all of this is continuing to drag out… dominating much of our lives, energy, and finances… we see several others in our circle of friends/family who are dealing with some very critical and much more urgent needs than ours… and so we pray for them… and keep on giving thanks to the One who gives us all grace and strength for each day… each challenge… and blessings too many to count… including you all!

I'll let you know what we find out as soon as we get results…

Thank you and God Bless!

Responses

Tandy H

Hang in there. You are such an inspiration to me… Hope that you really enjoy your weekend. Congratulations on the 6 years. Know they have been tough, but God has given you strength and wisdom through it all. Love you guys. :-)

Peggy A

Still sending love and prayers. Hope on the horizon for you guys – I pray.

Jane B

You ALL are precious to us! Have a wonderful trip and anniversary celebration.

Sylvia A

Congratulations on your upcoming anniversary! Enjoy your weekend and much deserved time away!

May God continue to pour his abundant love and blessings on your marriage and family.

God bless

Jan R

Thanks for the update—& for the blessings! Keep us posted!

Quinn W

Scott, I will continue to be in prayer. God Bless ya'll!

Jim T

Scott, Thanks for the update on Rhonda. I have been able to see her increase in strength and am thrilled to see that. Over and above that, I wanted to tell you how much of a witness you are to me when I see the way you and Rhonda interact… through your actions I can see things I need to do and should be doing. I feel very blessed and honored to consider you and Rhonda my friends.

God bless you both.

Patti S

hope the weekend is magic… praying always love Patti

March 28
My Rhonda—The Specialist = More Tests—update from Scott

Howdy,

Well…

We met with the specialist today and got some answers and some re-tests coming up. A couple of the results were just not in sync with each other, so he thinks they were skewed somehow and wants to re-do them. The good news is that there's no hurry. The enzyme counts are still up… and the only abnormality is a funky-looking biliary duct that he thinks may be a result of the surgery. The additional tests will confirm that for us. He did tell us again that he thinks the pain may be from the original surgery where something may be spasming… but that there was nothing he saw in the tests that would cause any pain like that. So… more tests coming in the next few weeks… but nothing bad seen in what's come back thus far… so PTL! :) We have a follow-up in about 6 wks… around the first week of May.

We also spoke to our oncologist nurse about Rhonda's next set of scans. She said it should've already been scheduled and was going to see if they could even get us in by Friday. When the labs are drawn for the scans, they will also do the specialist's tests at the same time… no double-whammy on getting poked and prodded… which makes Rhonda VERY happy! PTL! :)

So… today was a good day… no bad news… no needle sticks… and Rhonda and I really enjoyed a nice lunch together after it was all done! :)

We'll continue to keep you all posted as we get info and going along this path that we've been on these last two years. Rhonda has had a couple of real good days lately… and definitely more stamina. We'll take any progress that we can get! PTL!

Thank you again for all of your prayers, encouragement, love and support. It's much more tolerable knowing that we are not on this road alone…

Thank you and God Bless!

Responses

Jim F

Thanks for the report, Scott. I'm very happy to learn that it went well today.

Lila C

Thank you so much for the update, I have been talking with Rhonda via FB. I love you both dearly. So thankful you would update us as I WAIT to hear as I have always been so so grateful you would bless us to know about our dear dear Smiths.

Much love and care!!

Sylvia A

Scott and Rhonda, I agree, PTL!

We will continue to storm the heavens with our prayers and trust in God's tender love and mercy for us all.

In prayer

Quinn W

Glad to hear the positive news!

Maw-in-law

What a relief. I am seriously teary eyed over the news. I sometimes don't think I am aware just what a toll it has taken on me (It's definitely not about me and I'm very clear on that) but when my emotions come through after news like this, it makes me realize how I keep it under wraps even more than I know.

Thank you, and thank God,

Love you both,

Mom

Terry C

Thanks for the update Scott. Great news indeed. We will continue to pray for progress and good news from the tests.

Sandy L

Great news! I also know what you mean about walking the road alone, knowing that so many people are praying for my Sugar Bear makes a huge difference.

April 3
Stefanie Caring Bridge post from Rhonda e-mail

Two biopsies were done (one in December and one in January). The cancer is follicular NHL (non-Hodgkins lymphoma). It is very slow-growing and does not require treatment at this time. We are in "wait and watch" mode. There is not a cure for follicular NHL, but it is highly treatable. However, treatment won't begin until the cancer grows. Many people are in "wait and watch" mode for many years.

We are due for scans in early April, but insurance has initially denied payment for them, so they have been delayed until the doctor has a one-on-one with a doctor at the insurance company. At that point, we should be able to get them scheduled.

Lab tests show that the liver enzymes continue to stay about eight times above normal. Chemo causes this, but the enzyme numbers should be closer to normal by now as chemo ended over a year ago. We've been to a liver specialist who is in the process of troubleshooting the problem. At this time, nothing is conclusive. It is speculated that it has something to do with the surgery in 2009. He is in the process of trying to rule out infection in a biliary duct.

I remain on a pain patch that gets changed out once every three days for the abdominal pain. It is supplemented by pain meds as needed. The liver specialist thinks that this too is a side effect of the surgery in 2009.

Strength and endurance have steadily improved, especially these past six months or so. Some days I can get much accomplished; other days I still require much rest… but we don't have to look back too far to realize how far we've come.

I'm loving having hair again! It's been growing for a year now and is wavier/curlier than before but still the brunette "salt and pepper" look. Even when we start treatment again, I'll get to keep my hair so this is a major plus! The new treatment is not actually a chemo treatment, but the name of the new drug escapes me at the moment.

Another great note is that when the biopsy in January was done, enough of the node was removed to submit for a research study. It's possible they'll be able to make a vaccine for me. If this happens at all it could take up to a year. They did warn us that there might not be any benefit for us at all. Time will tell.

All is great! Scott and I walk short distances several times a week. Every now and then (several times a month) I get a mile done on the treadmill at the gym. Thanks for ALL THE PRAYERS!!

April 26
My Rhonda—Some Results

Hello,

Well we finally have some results from some of these tests! Last week we had some more labs for our oncologist and a CT scan... and everything looked good! The insurance company had twice denied the dr's request for a PET scan (just the same thing like we've been having since... forever it seems!) on the basis that 'studies do not show an improved outcome' by using the more expensive PET scan. So... we went with 'plan B', the CT. The results are from the oncologist. We have not yet heard anything from the specialist about his interpretation of the test results.

We did have an ofc appt with the oncologist before the CT scan... and the doc's jaw just about hit the floor when he saw how much stronger and healthier Rhonda looked compared to her last appt in January. He was grinning from ear-to-ear! We also told him how we are seeing slow but steady improvement in her strength and stamina, which he loved hearing too! He again went over the possible treatment options... when and if she needed any... that are much milder than what she went through a year ago... and that it's possible that she could maintain this same level s-l-o-w growth literally for several years or more... we'll go for that!

So... the CT we got was basically a 3D image of everything... and the only change was very minimal growth in the abdominal lymph nodes. No growth above the diaphragm, no spreading, no huge growth... and nothing that was of any concern to the dr... so he basically said... "seeya in July!" :)

Again... no more word from the liver dude yet... but when we see Rhonda improving like she is... we have no concerns... she's definitely getting stronger! We'll follow up with him soon...

So after getting this stuff behind us... this week we're purchasing tickets to go see our Moms and family in CA and NM around the 3rd week of June. Rhonda's mom has been needing a whole-family get-together... and we're happy to finally be able to oblige!

Thank you all again for your prayers, support, encouragement and love... it's great being able to share some good news with you all! And as we enjoyed the Easter season and the rebirth of hope it gives us in our faith... we know that even death and the grave have been defeated by our Lord and King. These old bodies are just decaying, temporary shelters for our souls as we long for the gift and reward of a new body in heaven one day... God's been so good to us!

We pray that you all enjoy His goodness too! God Bless!
Scott and Rhonda

Responses

Sandy L
Thanks for sharing the wonderful news!!!

Donna C
Always glad to hear good news. So happy that you will be able to go on a fun trip.

You both are a blessing to the class. We admire your courage and faith.

Have a great week!

Jim F

Thanks for the great report, Scott!

Clifton W

PTL for the good report. Rhonda continues to be part of my daily prayers.

Usha A

Please continue to share the good news. Have a great vacation in June.

Deborah M

What wonderful news.. WOW.

Peggy A

Yeaaaaaaaaa!

Trish M

Great news Scott!!! So glad everything is going the right direction! So sorry about the pet scan hassle. We went thru the same thing with Jim and I know many people in Greymatters support group who have to fight constantly with insurance about them. Should never be that way.

Anyway, so glad to hear this report. Hugs to you and Rhonda!

Sylvia A

Scott and Rhonda, PTL! God is certainly good to us and we will continue to keep the faith and pray that God continue to pour His blessings on each of you and your family.

God bless

May 15
My Rhonda—Some Results—update from Scott

Hi,

Just wanted to pass along some more good news!

We had an appt with the liver dr this past week... and the enzyme counts have returned to near-normal... PTL! No meds... no treatments... just all of our prayers! The dr just wants to check counts one more time (no ofc visit) in a few weeks... and then maybe have a follow-up... in November!

We are so thankful for God's mercy in answering our prayers... that there's nothing more to be concerned about... PTL! Rhonda has had some really good days recently... but if she pushes too hard, she can end up needing rest for the next 2–3 days. The strength and stamina are still very slow in coming back for her. We will just keep taking one day at a time... and enjoy the everyday blessings God has given us.

And thank you all again for your continuous prayers and well-wishes. We thank God for you every night in our prayers.

And even the Dallas weather has turned near-perfect! What a glorious evening it was for our walk! We'll take it while we can get it!

Please have a good week... God Bless!

Responses

Peggy A

So glad to hear the good news!

Donna C

PTL!!! Great News! We are so happy for you both...

Clifton W

Another PTL!!!

Sylvia A

PTL! God answers prayers in His own time. Have a blessed week.

Jim F

Thanks for sharing the wonderful news! Jesus rules!

Roxzanne M

Scott, you and Rhonda are such an inspiration to God. I am totally amazed at the intensity that you two witness to people. You definitely will bring people to the Lord. I am happy to hear such good news and will keep praying for your family's health and welfare. Take care and let me know if I can help in any way. Here is a big HUG from me.

Ryan G

That is fantastic news! I needed some good news!

Jan R

> Great news!

Judy R

> Whew! What a wonderful message. Thank you so much for sharing. I am celebrating for you.

Sandy L

> WONDERFUL WONDERFUL WONDERFUL… AWESOME NEWS!!!! I am sooooo excited!!!! PRAISE THE LORD!!!!!!

Marci E

> This is a blessed report. Thanks for the update. My continued prayers are with you all.

Denise A

> PTL!!!!!!!! I am so happy to hear the good news! Time to enjoy the summer together :)

Pamela D

> Yours is the best news since Easter Sunday! Still praying for you both.

Pam D

> That is GREAT news!

Greg G

> Great News!

July 17
My Rhonda—An Update

Hello,

I hope that you all are enjoying your summer and staying out of the heat… we've been at 100 or higher every day since July 2. I'm ready for fall!

So… we've had a couple of appts lately and I wanted to share that things with Rhonda are pretty much 'status quo'. And we'll take it! The doctors (surgeon and oncologist) thought that Rhonda looked great and stronger than she did before… and they see no need for any treatments… or even scans… at this time. PTL! Our next appts are in the fall, and we did request one more scan before the end of the year while the insurance is still at 100%… probably Nov or Dec.

In the meantime, Rhonda continues to gain strength and endurance… be it ever so slowly… which we are very thankful to see. Her lovely hair is growing and she's hoping it will be long enough for a pony-tail by the end of the year. :) The pains still come at times, tho probably not as often… but they can still "pack a punch"… so the pain meds will continue for now.

Our wonderful God did give Rhonda the strength to enjoy a 10-day vacation to CA and NM to have a precious visit with family. It was so great to get away and meet more of her terrific family… and spend a couple of quiet days with Mom in NM. We thank God for you and love you all!

So… our Lord continues to allow Rhonda to recover her strength… and stay away from treatments. She's really enjoyed the summer with more family time. It's just been too bloody hot to walk much… but we can work up a sweat just sitting in our living room these days!

Thank you all again for your never ending love and support! God is so good to place such wonderful friends and co-workers around us… you are all special to our hearts. Please enjoy the rest of your summer… and be safe and happy!

And may God continue to Bless!
Scott and Rhonda

Responses

Clifton W
Thanks for the update. I continue to remember Rhonda daily in my prayers and wondered how she was doing.

Dirk B
Thanks for the update. I'm keeping you in my prayers. Stay out of that bloody heat. Go have yourselves an In N Out burger and an ice cream shake.

Sylvia A
Scott and Rhonda, indeed PTL! I am very happy to hear Rhonda continues to make progress and gain her strength.
Enjoy the rest of the summer, hope your lovely family are all doing well.

Dina T

Great news Scott. I continue to pray for you, Rhonda and your whole family. You crack me up with the "can work up a sweat sitting in our living room"!

Pamela D

Wonderful! That goes for the great news and our God. Hugs to you both!

Deborah M

Wonderful... just wonderful

Greg G

Great news Scott. Thanks for the update, and say hello to the little lady for me.

Jan R

Wonderful gift from our Lord!

Suraya K

I am so happy for both you and Rhonda. Let's all pray that this good news continue and that she is completely recovered and healthy.

Oct 17
My Rhonda—An Update

Howdy,

Hope you all are enjoying the changing of the seasons! We've had enough of the 100-degree days around here... in fact... we have a cold front coming in tonight to knock the temps from the 90s today to the 70s tomorrow... YES!

Well, we had another appt with the oncologist on Friday and I wanted to let you all know how things are going for us… for Rhonda. Rhonda had an idea going into the appt that we weren't going to need to be going in as often next year… and the dr pretty much agreed with her! He does want to do one more CT scan in December… but no appts for another 6 months… and maybe a couple of years until the next scan! He also told us that there are well-documented cases of this stuff going into long-term remission… almost exactly what we've been praying for… permanent remission! We were very encouraged by the visit and the dr's plan to not do anything more unless the circumstances change dramatically… we agree! Right now, 'status quo' is good!

We've had another turn of events recently too. A couple of weeks before the appt, we had asked for a refill of her pain patch by phone… and somehow… it never got to our mailbox… even though the nurse called and told us she had mailed it. So… by the time we realized that we weren't going to get the refill… Rhonda had already started going into some withdrawal symptoms… edginess and restless legs mainly. So… after some prayer and thought, we figured that maybe God wanted her to get off of the pain patch. In the last 2 wks there's been only one incident of severe pain… and it was over in a few minutes. Still, the edginess is no fun… but we hope that it's nearly run its course. Getting off of the meds eventually is another step towards 'being normal'… and Rhonda is ready for that! The strength and stamina are still not coming back as quickly as we'd like… but we will get there eventually too!

So… thank you all again for your thoughts, encouragements, and prayers… it has been wonderful to know that we have so much support from so many! We love and appreciate you… and thank God for you!

May God Bless you all with the assurance of His Presence to be your hope and shield... as He has done for us... so abundantly!

ps—A couple of other recent/upcoming meaningful events in our family... Jordan and Kathleen were married in an incredibly beautiful celebration on Oct 1st... and Julie ships out with the Navy on Oct 26. Wow! We're so proud and happy for the terrific kids God has blessed us with!

Responses

Clifton W
Thanks for the good report.

Jan R
Such wonderful news! Praise our God!

Stefanie
thanks for the update! i told grandma the other day that i don't get info from mom (even after doc's appts) unless i specifically ask for specific details, but then she replied that mom had said the same about me! :) anyways, i just posted the update on the website.
let me know how she does w/o the patch. and maybe she'll be strong enough for a family walk by thanksgiving...

Suraya K
Hi Scott
Happy Birthday to you. May you be blessed with many more happy returns of this day.
This note is so good. I am so happy that Rhonda is doing well and improving day by day.

Both of you have been blessed with patience and the strength to endure. God has truly blessed you.

I wish you all the best and may Rhonda be free of this illness henceforth.

Sylvia A

Scott and Rhonda, so glad to hear the good news and that the Dr appt went so well.. I had been looking for an update in my mail box recently and always ask Peggy how ya are doing when I don't. Sounds like your whole family are doing well, God has certainly blessed your family and as I've always said, He has a special purpose for you both. take care and God bless

Pam D

That is GREAT news!

Dirk B

Thanks for the updates. I'll continue to pray for you, Rhonda, and your family. We are always here if you are in need of anything.

Dec 21
My Rhonda—Amazing Update!

Merry Christmas and Happy Holidays to All,

All we can say is "wow!"…

Well… Rhonda had scans yesterday… the nurse called with the results… and the affected lymph nodes are shrinking… as in moving towards going back to 'normal' size… which means the bad stuff that's been in them is going backwards… as in going away.

Wow! What an incredible holiday present!

Our wonderful Savior and Lord has heard our petitions and prayers and has had mercy on us... causing this "incurable" cancer to shrink back instead of staying "status quo"... or growing. We give all of our thanks and praise to Him... and for the support and love of so many who have stood with us during these last two years. We know all too well that things can change in an instant... in a heartbeat... in a breath... and we thank Him for granting this return of health to Rhonda. No more scans or dr appts are on our horizon... amazing!

Now... with this type of scan, all we can see is the size of the nodes. The PET scan would show us 'activity'... but the insurance company won't pay for those any more. So we'll take what we get here and see that shrinkage means... going away! And we've also been seeing the strength come back... being able to 'push' through busy days... more frequent and longer walks... less need for the meds... we're moving forward... PTL!

Yet our joy is still tempered with reality... having attended several funerals in the last few months... including longtime friend Steve Webb who passed from leukemia just before Thanksgiving... and wonderful sister-in-law Susan who passed away suddenly a week later. The gut-wrenching experience of losing friends and loved ones reminds us that our sovereign Lord does not always answer our prayers with healing and deliverance... and yet the 'ultimate' healing is going to be with Him... passing from this life to spend an eternity without pain or hurt. It is those of us who are left behind who must deal with the sharp pain of a severed relationship... missing our loved one's presence in our lives. And it is especially hard during the holidays... please send up more of your wonderful thoughts and prayers for those who are feeling the pain of loss this season.

And we also thank God for this season celebrating His wonderful plan… coming to join us on this earth as a little baby… living a life of example to us all… and ultimately giving His life to save us and give us an opportunity to believe… and become His adopted children. What an amazing Love!

So… please enjoy your time with family during this season… and thank you again for all you've meant to us with your unending support and love. We love you and thank God for you all!

God Bless!
Scott and Rhonda

Responses

Quinn W
Thank God Scott! That is great news! And a Merry Christmas it will be… :)

Peggy A
How wonderful!!!!!

Myra P
PTL! I'm so happy for Rhonda and your whole family. God is almighty and great! We will continue to pray for your family and Rhonda's continuous healing.
Have a Merry Christmas and a Happy New Year to all.
God bless you all.

Clifton W
PTL for Rhonda's progress.

Greg G

Great news my friend. Cathy and I are both overjoyed with the news.

Carolyn D

I celebrate with you!! God bless and have a joyous Christmas.

Jan R

I got tears in my eyes from reading your email! Yes, what a wonderful merciful God we have! You received the ultimate gift - the same one that the Lord mercifully gave to Julius - the gift of Life! All praise & honor be His!

Merry Christmas

Drew C

Great news Scott, what a long strange trip it has been for you two. What a great report for you guys at this wonderful time of the year!

Jeff W

That is awesome news, Scott! God Bless you and Rhonda. Have a wonderful holiday.

Lila C

We love you both, dearly. We will take all the good He has for us. This is an incredible holiday present. Our time is a present. Thank you for all of your precious words. This is life, it is real so we will know Him. Thank you for being our dear friends, true gifts.

Roxzanne M

Scott, I am so happy for you and Rhonda. I can't believe you sent this note today. On my way to work today, I thought I had better send you an email. I get home and you sent an email. You and Rhonda are such wonderful witnesses for God. I am so glad that he has wrapped his arms around Rhonda and he is producing good results. I hope you have a great Christmas and New Year. Give Rhonda a big hug from me and tell her that I pray for her every day. Love you guys and you deserve the best in life.

Usha A

This is definitely amazing news! My holiday wishes to you and your family!

Wishing you a Happy, Healthy and Peaceful New Year!

Dirk B

Thanking the Lord. Nothing is too hard for God.

Linda S

Such good news. Can't believe it's been two years. The two of you are such an inspiration to us all. Our family recently learned that my sister-in-law has been diagnosed with breast cancer. She started her first chemo session at 9:00 this morning.

I spent last week with her and I'm amazed how well she is handling it. Of course she has the emotions you would expect when faced with a serious illness. Reading your email was so uplifting. Your message of hope is just what I needed this morning. Thank you both!

Have a joyous Christmas!

Maw-in-law

Thank God for this news. It has made my Christmas & I know it has yours too.

Patti S

A Christmas blessing for sure. Our love to you all

Sylvia A

So glad to hear the news, what a blessing! We will continue to trust in our Lord's miracles.

The two of you are testaments to that and continue to be examples of trusting in God.

Take care and so sorry to hear about your other losses. Please stay in touch and may God continue to bless, happy new year!

March 26, 2012, Caring Bridge post from Stefanie

The latest labs look good! No scans until the end of year and mom's strength is slowly and steadily returning! She still has moments of intense pain, but can usually get the pain meds fairly quickly so it doesn't last too long. Mom and Scott go on walks again, a great sign of recovering energy! And they just celebrated their 7th anniversary, so yea!

*****

Our Lord was so good to us and had brought us through so much. This news of the lymph nodes shrinking was wonderful, an amazing relief to us all. When it comes, a cancer diagnosis just takes over your life. All energies and resources are consumed in taking up the battle. We were so thankful to able to move back into "normal" life the following year—church, work, kids—and in March 2013, the awesome gift of India, our first grandchild (courtesy of Jordan and Kat)! What a blessing to be at the hospital for her arrival, to hold her and get pictures. What an amazing miracle of God, the ability to bring new life into our troubled world! The appointments and scans continued to give us mostly good results.

*****

March 3, 2013
Caring Bridge post from Stefanie—Improvements

I haven't written in a while (ok, a year) because there hasn't been much cancer news on mom lately—yea!! In this case, no news IS good news. So now I will give you news but it is good so don't freak out. The last check-up went fine. Mom will continue to go to the doctor every four months, but there are no further plans for scans at this time.

Mom has been working out for thirty minutes each day, which has been really great for her. She's also taking her daily walks again. She has been for months, but I don't remember if I told you that or not. I talked to her on the phone today and she said her three mile walk now only takes an hour.

Mom has found a hobby that allows her to sit down (which she still needs to do on a regular basis) and benefits the family a great deal- crocheting. In recent months she has crocheted two baby blankets, a couple of scarves, and even a pair of house shoes! She enjoys learning how to make new things.

She is back to a mostly normal life again. She is driving and running errands and taking care of things once again. Like I said, my last post was a year ago and most of you (ok, all of you), know this already, but it is good news whether you know it already or not.

Take care.

And if things continue in this vein, I won't have to post anything on this website again for many more years. :)

Prayer Requests:
  Good lab results so scans won't be necessary.
  Improved strength.

*****

So we enjoyed the next two years of staying away from clinics and hospitals and such. We did have bit of an adventure in September 2013 where Rhonda's liver counts went extreme again, so much so that the liver specialist asked us to go to ER to have counts checked before we went out of town. Amazingly enough, the counts had corrected on their own, and we continued on our scheduled trip to Galveston for a wonderful week of relaxation and going down memory lane (Rhonda and I had both lived in the area in the early '70s). We truly had a great time!

At our Oklahoma getaway in March 2009

Eating out before Paul Potts concert July 2009

A special anniversary trip to Ft Worth March 2010

Some mall goofiness on our March 2010 trip

Rhonda and her amazing mom March 2010

On our wonderful trip for Aunt Fran's 90th birthday in July 2010

Our annual anniversary trip to a cabin in OK in March 2011

Attending a friend's wedding in January 2012

Always a good time for a hug and a selfie! January 2012

My Rhonda on our March 2012 anniversary trip to a cabin in OK

Life was good in June 2013!

My girl enjoying our wonderful trip to Galveston September 2013

The happy couple! Galveston September 2013

April 2014 before treatments for bone marrow transplant were to start

Sept 2014 Summoning strength for a smile with one
of the special caregivers after the transplant

Thanksgiving 2014 in the hospital waiting room with our beautiful family

A December 2015 visit with special hospital staff, and to deliver cookies!

Christmas 2015

Attending a dinner with former co-workers February 2017

2014: It's Back

In early 2014 Rhonda noticed a lump coming up on her neck. We didn't have any appointments scheduled, so we just watched it for a while even through our annual anniversary trip to the cabin in Oklahoma. The lump continued to grow and got to the point where it was too large and uncomfortable to ignore. So we went to see the oncologist. He wanted to biopsy the node, but it was so much "in the way" that we asked for it to be totally removed. So we saw our surgeon and set a date. It was, to say the least, unsettling to see this apparent return of the "bad stuff," but we were hoping that it was isolated and remembered the oncologist's description of a much more mild treatment. Stefanie posted an update for us…

*****

April 23, 2014
Stefanie Caring Bridge post—Surprise: Surgery

We have a surprise for you: Surgery! For the last couple of months, Mom's had less energy and more tiredness. Mom said she was fine; that no doctor visit was in order. But she has a swollen lymph node, so she went in today for a biopsy. Instead of doing the biopsy, though, they decided to go straight to surgery. Initially scheduled for Monday, they had a cancellation and moved the surgery up to… TOMORROW. On Thursday, April 24, 2014, at 10:00am, she will go in to surgery. Compared to her last surgery (a very stressful nine hours, for those of you just tuning in), this surgery will be short and sweet. No organs need removing, rearranging, or modifying this time. It should be over in about an hour. Scott will be with Mom for the recovery, which she will do at home and should only be a matter of days this time, not weeks.

Prayer Requests:

- No complications during the surgery.
- That everything else is good and there are no other hot spots causing problems.
- That anything else that does need to be fixed, would be discovered immediately and addressed promptly and efficiently.
- Quick and complete recovery and restoration to energy and strength once again.

Many thanks! We are always grateful for the prayers, support, and encouragement you've shown us over the years!

I will post my post-surgery update either during lunch or after school, depending on when I get the news. Check back tomorrow for the *good* news! Thanks again!

Responses

Peggy A
Sending prayers for quick recovery.

Sandy L
Maybe we can still do lunch on Monday! I'm praying for a speedy recovery! Love you all more than you will ever know!!!

Patti S
Just prayed for our dear friends. You each have our love and continued prayer.

Nancy P

Will be praying for you for a successful surgery and speedy recovery! Blessings to all of y'all!

Susan H

I'll be praying for short sweet and no complications. God will bless you with a quick and complete recovery.

Barbara C

Praying all goes well Rhonda!

Brenda S

We will be praying for you Rhonda! Many blessings sent to you & your Family! Expecting to hear good news tomorrow!

April 26
Caring Bridge post by Stefanie—Miraculous Timing

The surgery went very well, and mom is resting at home now. At this very moment, Julie and I are sitting with mom, enjoying a quiet afternoon. Well, Mom is enjoying the quiet afternoon, and Julie and I would be more than happy to run around yelling and dancing, but we know better. :) Mom is doing pretty well, taking it easy as she heals, but she still made mac'n'cheese for "the kiddos" today.

As is apparently normal in our family now, unexpected (and sometimes awful) things give way to miracles. As you'll recall, when Mom was first diagnosed with pancreatic cancer five years ago, it turned out that the intense pain that sent her to the emergency room in the first place was not a result of her cancer, but a diseased gallbladder. Had her gallbladder done its job and behaved well, the cancer might not have been discovered until it was too late. And now, tiredness, a swollen lymph node, and a surgery moved up due to someone else's cancellation, allowed the surgeons to remove the offending party as it was wrapping itself around Mom's carotid artery. Had they waited, it would have become even more entangled and been considerably more dangerous! The pain and soreness Mom feels now is a result of removing the lymph node from where it had been entangled in muscle and other neck "stuff" (clearly I'm going to be a doctor one day).

Although we are not fans of cancer, we are so incredibly thankful that it gets caught before it carries out the plans it intends.

The doctors said that the "initial tests are consistent with lymphoma" and we are awaiting additional tests with more data about what was and is going on, so I'll have another update for y'all in another week or two when that data comes in. Until then, please continue praying for renewed strength, comfort, and healing, and don't forget to thank God for his many blessings and miracles that keep my mom, and, you know, all of mankind, alive and moving forward.

Responses

Brenda S

Will continue to keep your Mom lifted in prayer. Thanks so much for the updates! God is good!

Susan H

Praise the Lord! It is so awesome how our God works to his glory in all things. I will continue to pray for his healing power on you and he will continue to strengthen you.

And to know the love of Christ, which passeth knowledge, that ye might be filled with all the fullness of God. Now unto him who is able to do exceeding abundantly above all that we ask or think, according to the power that worketh in us, Unto him be glory in the church by Christ Jesus throughout all ages, world without end. Amen. Eph 3:19 - 21

Mary B

I love this report! God is always in all the details of our lives-- praise His holy name! He is our Rapha! Will keep on praising and praying! Thank you for the updates! Love you all!!

Barbara C

Such a journey, and such a privilege to pray for Rhonda! Thank you for the update!

June 1, 2014
My Rhonda—It's Back

Hi,

We hope that you all and your families are doing well! Things have been humming along for us with no major trials or tribulations to deal with… until the last several weeks.

As many of you are aware, we've had a recent recurrence of Rhonda's lymphoma. In February, she noticed a growing lump on the right side of her neck. This had been coming and going for several months, but this time it kept getting bigger… to the point of being uncomfortable. Our oncologist recommended a biopsy before talking about treatment options, and instead of a needle biopsy, we decided to have it removed. The surgery was on April 24 and, after a series of delays, our oncologist finally got final pathology results this past Thursday... we met with him on Friday.

According to the lab results, the slow-growing lymphoma has "transformed" into a fast-growing strain. Normal treatment options in this situation call for aggressive chemotherapy for a few months followed up by bone marrow transplant (using Rhonda's own, cleaned up, marrow cells)... followed by one more dose of chemo. This regimen will be even more harsh than the treatment she had in '09–'10. Nothing fun to look forward to.

But first, we need to collect all of the info we can get. We are looking to have a full-body PET scan next week to show us if there is any more growing right now. Also, we will meet with a marrow transplant doctor to discuss that process... as well as a marrow biopsy to ensure it is not affected yet. After all this, we will meet with the oncologist again to lay out a plan.

At this time, there are no other externally visible evidences of growth... and Rhonda's feeling fine. She's still not back to 100% from what she's already been through these past several years, but is able to take 3-mile walks and pretty much function okay... but still not having the stamina she would like to have. In an interesting bit of trivia, we realized that Memorial Day weekend marked 5 years since her initial diagnosis.

So... in light of these developments... we are calling on our family and friends... our prayer warriors and support group... to join us in praying for wisdom, insight, strength, peace and healing as we face this new challenge. We have been doing extensive research to understand all we can about our foe... fully well knowing that everything that comes to us is being filtered by the love of our Lord and Savior Jesus Christ… and we rest in the hands of our Heavenly Father.

We thank you in advance for standing with us… again.

Scott and Rhonda

Responses

Lila C

My Scott and Rhonda, "yes" I say "My", you are a part of me, in spirit and mind and heart. I love you and am standing on the Rock with and for you. I love you with all my heart.

Pamela D

Thanks for letting us know what's going on and will continue to remember you all in my prayers.

Maw-in-law

I wasn't aware it is so aggressive. I'm heart sick. I will be standing by as in the past to do anything and everything that I can.

Praying and loving you both.

Sylvia A

Scott and Rhonda, we all know the power of Faith and prayer. God gave you the strength and endurance to face your journey the first time and He will grace you with even more of His love and mercy as you walk this journey. We will all be storming the heavens so that this journey is a gentle one and that God sends you His best angels to care for Rhonda and that all those who are part of her care team are blessed by Him so that they do His miraculous work of bringing Rhonda back to full health and recovery again.

I am on my way to church and will include Rhonda in my daily prayers and light a special candle for God to light your way with full confidence and faith knowing that this too shall pass and you will both be able to look back at this one day soon in full recovery and health.

God bless you and your family.

Sending you both a big hug

Roxzanne M

Scott, it has been a long time since I wrote to you, so I am happy you have kept me in the loop on Rhonda's health. I will pray for all of you.

Clifton W

Thanks for your detailed report on Rhonda. So sorry to learn that the cancer has returned. Be sure that you and she will continue to be in my prayers.

Bobbie O

I think you know how much you and your family mean to us. We will be praying for you and your family as well as for wisdom for the doctors and those doing the tests. As we well know cancer is a journey and one that God never intended for us to travel alone. Your family, friends and most important your God will be with you. God will take each step with you and at times will carry you when you are weak and tired. Know we love you and support you during this time.

D'Ann C

We will continue to pray for all of you.

Sandy L

Just wanted to let you know, I DID get it!

I was on and off my computer before you sent it.
I am praying for you both!
Please let me know if there is anything else I can do.
Love always

Mike M

We Love You Guys
I will continue to pray for you.

Greg G

Thanks Scott for the update. Cathy and I are lifting the both of you up. Man, I can't imagine how tough this must be on the both of you and your family. I'm trying to put myself in your shoes and think what I would do. For me it would be the ultimate test of my faith. I know I would want it one way, but would be afraid the Lord might want it another way. I think the Lord would understand that. He did when Jesus asked to have the cup taken from him, but then followed with "not my will but your will be done." All this to say that Cathy and I are praying for healing, but following that with, "not my will but your will be done."

Amy G

Scott, I am so sorry. I had no idea about her surgery in April. I will be praying for you guys as you navigate this yet again. But God is bigger and mightier than anything the enemy can throw our way. Prayed for you guys this morning and sending up prayers each time I think of you guys which is often.

Pam D

All of you are in my prayers.

Peggy A

I read your Caring Bridge last night and I am so sorry. My prayers will be with you constantly!!

Quinn W

Scott, as you know, I am already praying and lifting Rhonda up to God… Take care.

Marci E

I will be in prayer for and with you.

Jan D

Oh, Scott… I'm so sorry for this news. Praying for the best possible outcome for you two…

Drew C

Praying for you two bro!

Jane B

Dear, dear Rhonda and Scott,

You were on my mind just days ago, and I thanked the Lord again for touching Rhonda in answer to all the prayers years ago. I am so sorry to hear of the recurrence. Be assured of our love for you all and for continued prayers and faith!

Please keep us posted, and let us know if there is anything else we can do to help you.

With our love and concern,

Pastor and Jane, Sarah, and Susan

Ryan G

That's awful! Cara and I will definitely come see y'all soon. Please let Rhonda know we love her!

Debora B

I am so sorry to hear this news. Please know I will be praying for all of you.

Cari R

Matt and I are praying!

Marla L

Rhonda, don't know if you remember me or not but I will be praying for you! From church...

Terry W

my prayers are with you and your family, may the good Lord give you more good days than bad and hurry up and kick this sucker once and for all... or at least the next 50yrs... God bless

June 3
My Rhonda—It's Back—update from Scott

Howdy,

Just a quick update...

Rhonda had her PET scan today. The miracle we prayed for is that it would be totally clean! Friday we meet with the marrow doctor (and maybe the biopsy included). So... next week is probably when we get all of our info pulled together and meet with the oncologist again to lay out a plan. I would imagine that treatments would not start until the week after that.

I will let you know more info as we learn it ourselves...

Thank you again for your prayers!
Scott and Rhonda

Responses

Bobbie O
Thank you so much for the update. We are praying and will continue to do so.

Debbie S
Hello you two,
You are in my thoughts and prayers. I would imagine that you are quite weary of this path, Rhonda. My sister is dealing with long-term effects of multiple myeloma, and she is weary of the road, but she always has a smile. I know you do as well. God must have some great people who need your ministry, and I know you have used this trial as a blessing. I am praying for you.

Usha A
Hi Scott,
When your email popped up, I got very excited. I am dismayed to see not so positive news. I hope and pray that Rhonda will pull through just like she did before. She is a trooper and with you by her side and God's grace good things will happen.
I hope you are doing well and children are doing well.
My best wishes to Rhonda and God Bless.

Cathy G
We know that this is a very difficult time for you both and for the family and want you to be assured of our daily (sometimes hourly) prayers for you. Rhonda, I'm so blessed by your genuine and faithful friendship to me personally even in the midst of your own

pain. My prayer is that God will strengthen you and give you courage through this journey and ultimately heal your body of this disease.

We love you both and miss you!

Love and prayers

Donna C

As always, you are in our prayers!

Lamentations 3:22–25 It is of the LORD'S mercies that we are not consumed, because his compassions fail not. They are new every morning: great is thy faithfulness. The LORD is my portion, saith my soul; therefore will I hope in him. The LORD is good unto them that wait for him, to the soul that seeketh him.

In Christ

Karen B

Thanks for sharing, Scott. We are praying for all of you! We've added Rhonda to our Sunday School prayer list as well.

Patti S

You have our continued prayers and our love.

June 8
My Rhonda—Weekend Escape!

Hello,

Rhonda and I just got home after a wonderful weekend in downtown Dallas. I've lived in the area for almost 40 years, and still had not done much in the way of discovering the beauty and history in our own "backyard." So… Friday, after meeting the marrow transplant doctor, we drove into downtown to stay in a 'swanky' hotel corner-suite to escape reality for a couple of days... and thoroughly enjoyed ourselves with a lot of learning... a lot of walking... and a lot of eating! God is so gracious to us! :)

Btw... in that Friday dr appt... we learned Rhonda's scan results. Her last scan was in December 2010 and showed low-grade lymph node activity in several areas (actually considered "stage 3" at the time). The scan from last week showed that... all of that was gone... and the only activity was in the area around the biopsy surgery (right side of her neck). So... we are VERY thankful that the bad stuff is indeed isolated... and so some of the sense of urgency is relieved. :) PTL!!!

We also discussed possible scenarios for treatment... which included treatments that would not be as harsh as I had first feared... and the plan to consider donor marrow (instead of using just Rhonda's own) which would bring a potentially higher rate for ultimate success. It was an encouraging discussion.

More appts tomorrow (Monday)... and hopefully wrapping up the prep work this week so we can get this started... and finished! The sooner the better! The initial 4 treatments will take 3–4 days each time (inpatient or outpatient) and so will be more involved than the half-day infusions she had before.

Our weekend getaway was absolutely wonderful!... now we are ready to tackle this and get it behind us... hoping to finish all treatments by the end of the year.

Thank you again for your prayers and kind words... they are precious to us! More later... God Bless!

Scott and Rhonda

Responses

Sylvia A

Praise The Lord is exactly right! God is our healer and with Him all is possible...

We will continue to storm the heavens for Rhonda's journey to a full recovery. God bless.

Janet T

Although we missed you in Sunday school, I'm so glad you two got away for the weekend to just have time for yourselves.

I am so thankful that as you put it "the bad stuff is isolated". PTL!! God is good!!

Blessings and many prayers for you both

Julius R

Praise the Lord for He is Always Good.

Beverly K

This is such wonderful news. For both the get-away weekend with just the two of you and update from the doctors.

Peggy A

Sounds like things are a little bit more positive. I am so glad. Prayers still coming your way.

Mike M

Love you guys

Trish M

This is awesome news!!! So glad you guys got away to decompress. And the scan news is wonderful wonderful wonderful! (just call me Lawrence Welk! ha!) praying every day for the best possible outcome.

Bobbie O

The news sounds very encouraging. We will continue praying. Glad you had a wonderful weekend getaway.

Donna C

Wow, I love swanky hotels. What a wonderful escape for the both of you!

We missed you in class but understand about your get away...

Praying for the best outcome ever!

June 9
My Rhonda—Weekend Escape—update from Scott

Well... here we go...

We just got the news that Rhonda will have her marrow biopsy this Wednesday and then will be admitted to the hospital to start her first chemo treatments. She will be in the hospital around 4 days. When we spoke to the marrow doctor on Friday, we could tell he was leaning towards inpatient chemo treatments. It will be good that they will be able to keep an eye on her and so be more responsive to her needs. We are both surprised and thankful that we're getting started so soon... and are ready to beat this and get the whole thing behind us... with our Lord's Grace, Strength, Help, Healing, and Mercy.

These email updates may be less frequent while Rhonda is in treatment… my first responsibility is to take care of my girl. :)

Thank you again for your prayers and support

Responses

Greg G
>   Amen brother. Kick this thing in the you know what.
>   We are praying for you all.

Lila C
>   Terry and I love you both dearly. We stand on the Rock with you, every moment. Please let us know if there is anything we can do. I mean this. I truly believe she will be healed, and stronger than ever in His time… Please hug her for me now Scott.
>   You both have our hearts and prayers

Sylvia A
>   So glad Rhonda will get in-patient treatment, you're right that's best so that she receives extra care and will give you both the comfort and assurance you need during her treatment.
>   You take care of Rhonda and leave the storming of the heavens to us Prayer Warriors.
>   Please give Rhonda a hug for me.
>   God bless.

Jan R
>   Praying fervently for total healing!

Jeff W

Thank you for updating me. Rhonda, you and the doctors will definitely be in my prayers and thoughts! You are a good man-Rhonda is blessed to have you as a husband.

Billie M

Thanks for the update, Scott. We have been and will be praying!

Cathy G

Please know we are praying for you both during these days of treatment. We wish so much that we could be there as these treatments begin.

We love you both!

Bobbie O

I am thankful too. She is a fighter and has a wonderful attitude. She is an inspiration to me. Thank you so much for the update.

Carolyn D

I certainly do remember Rhonda daily in prayer. Please let me know if I can help your family in any other way. I really mean this so do not be bashful or hesitant in accepting my offer.

June 10
What a Great Group of Friends We Have!—from Scott to coworkers

Thank you so much to you all who made time in your busy schedules and came to the lunch today! It was so great to see Kurt's girls… and Melinda and sons there too! Special thanks to Pam for spearheading the effort to pull this all together and stay with it to make it happen. I know that there were several others who wanted to be there, but weren't able to… we are thankful to those too!

Rhonda was very touched… the hugs… the flowers… the words of encouragement… the generosity… and just "being there" for us as we move forward into the unsettling territory of more treatments. Just like you were 4–5 years ago when all of this first came upon us… you are a huge part of our support group! I will send emails/text msgs to let you all know how things go for us in these next several days.

We thank God for you all and cherish your prayers and friendship… and we pray for His Blessings to be poured over you and your families too.

Thank you again… you are awesome and wonderful!

Responses

Rhonda

Thanks to everyone for the amazing get-together yesterday! We thank you for your prayers, support and friendship!

Laurie R

Hello… just got caught up reading all of the recent journal postings… wanted you to know that I'm thinking about you and your family… keeping good thoughts.

June 13
post from Stefanie

I got to go see Mom last night, and it was good to see her doing so well. Since she didn't have chemo yesterday, she was looking pretty strong, had a positive spirit, and had some energy. The only pain she had while I was there was the same recurring pain she's had for the last five years as a result of her surgery. Apparently the numbers of something liver related were off, so they spent the day running tests to make sure she's ok before administering chemo. Since they missed yesterday's dose of chemo, they will be a day or two behind the schedule and will have to stay in the hospital a little longer. Counts were better today but still high, so they will see the doctor around noon today before moving any further.

I was very impressed with Baylor Dallas. First of all, the room was colorful, comfortable, and relaxing. The sofa folded flat as a bed and had drawers for guests' belongings underneath. With a refrigerator in the room and a microwave down the hall, and a workspace in the room, Scott can both eat and work as he lives in the hospital with Mom. Mom's hospital bed was also amazing- it has rollers inside the bed that move every 60 seconds, so she never gets uncomfortable sitting in the same spot all day and never feels the need to readjust. The nurses even came in during shift change to introduce the new nurse. What a wonderful environment for Mom and Scott to be in during this difficult time. Mom also has an IV in her arm- but it's a fancy three-pronged kind of IV. One needle into the arm, with three tubes sticking out (note: picc line). This awesome contraption allows the nurses to draw blood at the same time as administering medicine. Without any more needles. It's the little things that make a difference.

PRAYER REQUESTS: That whatever is going on with Mom's liver would be resolved, and for strength and healing as Mom goes through more chemo.

PRAISES: For great health insurance, for a great environment for this healing process, and for Mom's current strength and energy.

Responses

Marge B

Sounds like a very nice hospital setting. You are right - the little things can make a big difference. Lord, touch Rhonda's liver right now and give her the strength she needs. Continue to be with the family Lord! Amen

Trish M

Amen! thank you for the update. Your Mom and Scott are both amazing.

Penny B

Amen! Thanks Stef!

Wanda J

And thank you Lord for Scott, a husband that has been there for Rhonda not only through the good times but the bad! Thank you Scott for taking care of our girl!

Mom and Dad J

June 17
post from Stefanie

As with the last time Mom had cancer, Grandma is coming to Texas on a one-way ticket. Mom came home from the hospital today and is so nauseous and miserable, she's asked Grandma to come back. Mom had already prepared for this over the last couple of weeks: she has turned the spare room/ granddaughter's crib room into a guest room complete with a new bed and fresh bedding. I made the flight arrangements today and Grandma will arrive tomorrow evening. Please be in prayer for Mom's healing, mental and emotional comfort, and for Grandma, Scott, and the rest of us as we help Mom get through this difficult process.

Responses

Barbara C

Thank you for keeping us in the loop and giving us specific things we can pray about!!!

Moms make everything better! Praying the nausea will subside. Praying for sweet sleep. Praying for healing. Praying for the family.

Marge B

Praying Rhonda that you will have comfort and rest and able to enjoy your Mom's visit, too!

Wanda J

That is such a blessing that Grandma is coming! Nothing like a mom's love to heal the soul. We are praying for comfort, peace, rest and strength and please give her a very soft hug from us! Love to all! Momma and Dad J

We love you Rhonda

Ellen C

Stephanie, thank you so much for keeping all of us updated on your Mom. I have been praying for her every day since she got her first cancer and rest assured I will continue to pray for her and your family. Love that girl!!!

Petra R

Hi Stephanie: Thanks for taking the time to provide the update during this trying time. I'm sure it'll be a great comfort to all of you to have your grandmother in your home. I admire how you've shown such a positive attitude to date and I know your mother, grand-mother and family will rely on it in the coming days. I will pray for all of you. Lean on God. He will continue to guide and inspire you.

Merlene

Thanks for the update. I know Georgya will feel better being close to Rhonda and I know it will ease some of Rhonda's anxieties. I love you guys and you are ever in my prayers.

June 18
My Rhonda—Home at Last

Hi,

Just a quick update after the first series of treatments… it was a rough time for her. So glad it is over. Now we need to help her recover from it… and at Rhonda's request… her wonderful Mom has dropped everything in her own life to fly in and help out. She will be here this evening.

Please pray for comfort, strength, and that Rhonda's system will bounce back from 4 straight days of chemo. We are so thankful that God is always by our side… and for your prayers and support.

Thank you!

Responses

Suraya K

My Best wishes to Rhonda. I will always pray for her full recovery and happiness.

Trish M

Praying the worst blows over quickly. So sorry it hit her so hard. Glad her mom is coming. Take time for you too Scott!

Sylvia A

So glad to hear she's home now. May God's infinite love for her bring Rhonda back to feeling strong very soon.

God bless

Lupita O

Scott and Rhonda, GOD is with you, because HE LOVES YOU, so much, I will keep you on my prayers every day..

Clifton W

Praying.

Julius R

Praying for quick recovery.

Lila C

I just saw this, I have been waiting for news from you and Rhonda, almost every hour in many ways. I love you both so… I know Rhonda said she would wait until she really needed Georgya before asking her to come. I am glad you will have her great love and care. Scott if I can do anything please please let me know and also if she wants a short visit or you think she needs it please write to me. I have told Sunday school about your request to keep her immune system away from any chances. Scott I know you must be so very tired and I appreciate your update so much, I wait, until you can write again, this is a time for healing that I TRULY BELIEVE is coming, I mean this.

All my love and care and concern always

Karen B

So glad her mom is able to come. I know that will lift everyone's spirits!! Continuing to pray.

Bobbie O

Thank you so much for the update. Glad her mom is coming to stay with her. We are praying.

Donna C

Thanks so much for the update. I'm always thinking about her and praying for the both of you. I hate that she has to go through that.

I've been around family that's had treatments and it's no picnic!

We miss you both at church, but the sooner you both get this behind you, ya'll be back in no time! Praying for your request.

Onward Christian + Soldiers!

June 21
My Rhonda—Hanging in There

Hi again,

Just to let you all know how things are going…

We've been back to the dr's ofc 2 times since Rhonda was released from the hospital. The prep and trips totally exhausted her (even with the wheelchair) and she ended up having to lie down and get fluids each time. We go back again on Monday. At the house, she's been able to eat and drink pretty well but needs a lot of rest. But she has also has spurts of energy (like Friday night at midnight) where she can be active for a while… it just doesn't last long. Her white blood counts are almost non-existent, so we need to limit her exposure to people and use a mask when she is out of the house. Sadly… we won't be able to fellowship with our church family for the foreseeable future. By our unconfirmed calculation, her next treatment will start on July 3… so we have another almost 2 weeks to build her strength.

And… the hair was starting to go… so she and I got matching haircuts today. Her long, lovely hair will now be donated to 'Locks of Love'. In a few months, we know that she can grow it back again.

It's very hard at times to see her have to suffer through all this again… yet we do know that God is in control… and that He is good… and that 'all things will work together for the good of those who are called according to His purpose.' We thank Him for each day… for each moment of strength… for knowing that He cares even more for Rhonda than we do… and ask Him to carry her body through this time and into His Healing.

We are also thankful for Rhonda's mom's help and strength… and willingness to leave her life (and new husband) behind for a time to help us out. And we are thankful for your continuing love, prayers, and support.

God Bless
Scott and Rhonda

Responses

D'Ann C
Praying for y'all. I want to bring food over when her mother leaves or before if her mother needs a break.

Cathy G

Thank you so much for this recent update. Being so far away, we feel very disconnected from you both, and it helps to read your update and know how you are doing so we know how to pray. We will continue to pray for Rhonda's strength to increase during this time between treatments, and most of all, we are praying for her healing and that you will feel God's presence with you both during these difficult days.

Greg G

Praying for you guys. Pretty cool that you shaved your head. Way to honor your wife my friend.

Sylvia A

Please tell Rhonda that I have her and your family in my daily prayers. Your Faith, your family and your devotion to God will get you through this journey. Tell Rhonda short hair is in fashion, I'm sure she looks gorgeous.

God bless

Jim F

Thank you for this report, Scott. We are standing with you in faith.

Dale W

Thanks for the latest on updates. Kimberly and I are rejoicing with you on your continued healing. Please know that we are praying for you both and are trusting and serving a mighty and loving God for His strength and healing in the days ahead. Although you are not able to be with your church family, just know that we/ they are all praying and interceding on your behalf. Let us know if you need anything.

Mike M

We Love you guys and also pray for God's intervention.

Melinda H

Thanks for the update as always. We think of you often and are continuing to pray for strength and healing.

I'm doing something for Rhonda and would like to know some of her favorite snacks, scents, drink etc.

Please let me know if I can help in any way.

Hope to see you soon!

Clifton W

Thank you for the report. I can't imagine all the turmoil that you and Rhonda are going through. You are showing amazing courage. Our Sunday School study today was about giving a testimony. I used you as an example of staying true to the Lord during all you have and are going through. I have tried to come up with a Scripture to encourage you, but what keeps coming to mind is Psalm 23. I tell you once again that you and Rhonda are in my prayers daily.

Bobbie O

Thank you so much for the update. We will be praying for her strength to improve as she gets ready for the next treatment.

Give her our love.

Penny B

Stef... THANK YOU for the updates. I look for them because I know they will be here. My prayers continue. I hurt inside knowing that she is suffering through this treatment. I'm praying for her strength and for the family's strength. God Bless You All! I send my love and hugs! Thanks for taking such great care of her.

Petra R

Thanks for the update! Glad to hear Rhonda still has an appetite and is sleeping for strength. I'll pray that this continues through the treatments and her white blood count starts to increase. Rhonda, you & your family are real soldiers battling this fight. May the power of prayer refuel you each day and the knowledge that God's looking over you relieve you of worry.

With loving thoughts & prayers

Wanda J

We are sending love and prayers your way! We have asked God to heal, strengthen, uphold, and lift her up as only He can do!

We also pray for the family as you sit and watch her weaken with each treatment. We don't understand why such a wonderful Christian lady has to go through this but someday we will understand I guess. May God fill your home with peace, love, comfort and healing!

Love to all, Mom and Dad J

Susan H

I continue to hold you up in prayer. It saddens my heart that you are going through this again. God knows your strength and faithfulness to him. I do hope you are able to rest and find comfort in having your mother with you and all the prayers that are being lifted up to God on your behalf.

Psalms 40:1–5—I waited patiently for the Lord; and he inclined unto me, and heard my cry. He brought me up also out of a horrible pit, out of the miry clay, and set my feet upon a rock, and established my goings. And he hath put a new song in my mouth, even praise unto our God: many shall see it, and fear, and shall trust in the Lord. Blessed is that man that maketh the Lord his trust, and respecteth not the proud, nor such as turn aside to lies. Many, O Lord my God, are thy wonderful works which thou hast done, and thy thoughts which are to us-ward: they cannot be reckoned up in order unto thee: if I would declare and speak of them, they are more than can be numbered.

June 22
post from Stefanie—Fever

Mom was rushed to the hospital tonight with a high fever (which is super bad since chemo means she has zero white blood cells). After 1000mg of Tylenol, her fever went down to only 100, which is better but still bad, of course. Praise: Fever went down. Pray: that it keeps going down and STAYS down. She can't get through more chemo if she has no strength to start her out, and she can't fight aggressive cancer without the chemo. She's staying overnight and they'll be running tests. I'll update when I have more information.

Responses

Lourdes H
Sweet, sweet Rhonda. I was up for my usual nightly insomnia and wee morning scrabble. I frequently would catch you up at these times. Naturally, you weren't playing. So I check my emails and I read the update. I immediately got out of bed at 1:28am. I got on my knees and prayed sincerely for you, sweet girl. I prayed for your health and then prayed for myself so I could learn to be like you. All the best, dear friend.

Nancy P
PRAYING for Rhonda and all of you…!

June 24
My Rhonda—A Scare

Sunday afternoon Rhonda's mom had been monitoring her temps… and when she went over 104 she knew it was time to call the docs. They told us to get her right down to the hospital. Rhonda was going into sepsis. After a long night and tough day Monday (including a bad reaction to a transfusion), Rhonda's been pretty much fever free for the last 12 hours.

We are so thankful for our Lord and her mom for watching over my Rhonda… thank you Jesus.

Thank you again for all of your love and support. I'm heading back to the hospital soon… maybe she'll be released tonight or tomorrow. PTL!

Love you all…
Scott and Rhonda

Responses

Cathy G
We just prayed for you all, Scott, and will continue to do so throughout the day. We love you both!

Greg G
Man, that girl is a fighter! Thanks for the update. We are praying for all of you.

Sylvia A
Keeping you in prayer.

God bless

Debbie S

Praying for you both…

Denise A

Thank you for the update… prayers lifted…

Patti S

We love you

Karen B

Bless her heart. So glad her mom is able to be there with her. Is there anything we can do? I would be happy to prepare a meal and bring over after she gets home from the hospital.

Take care and let us know what you guys need.

Love y'all

Bobbie O

She has been on my mind so often. When I walk Peanut (our dog) I go in front of your home and pray for her. She is such a special person and has been a wonderful friend. Thank you for keeping us in the loop.

Trish M

Good grief! She just can't catch a break. Hang in there. Still praying for healing.

Quinn W

Oh No Scott! I was wondering how things were going. You and I hadn't spoken since earlier yesterday. I'll continue to pray.

June 26
post from Stefanie—Improving

Much like a roller coaster, Mom's fever has gone back and forth a lot this week. A transfusion of blood platelets was supposed to help, but she got a fever after that and it seemed that the platelets didn't "stick", but things have improved and her platelet count was up to 32 last time I checked. A healthy platelet count is anywhere between 100 and several thousand, so 32 is very low, but much higher than the 1 she has been at. They've been giving her stuff to keep her blood pressure up and being bed bound for so long has become really uncomfortable for Mom.

Praise: No more fever! More white blood cells (platelets).
Prayer: Comfort. Healing. Discernment on future course of treatment.

Thanks again for your continued support and prayers for Mom.

Responses

Barbara C
Some improvement is good! Continuing to pray and waiting for the blessing of total healing! Tell your mom hello and how much I admire her strength in the Lord.

Cari R
Continuing to keep her in our prayers & thoughts!

June 28
My Rhonda—Coming Back Slowly

Hi,

I'm home for just a little while to catch up on some things. Very quickly… Rhonda has been doing much better. No fever for the last 3 days… but her blood counts are recovering very slowly and the doctors don't want to release her until she's strong enough to fight off infection. Every day they tell us… ' one or two more days'. It's been almost a week. The most uncomfortable issue right now is trying to get rid of all of the extra fluids they've been pouring into her. She says she feels like she's 5 months pregnant. Also… with Rhonda being in the hospital so much of the time, there's not really been a true need to keep her Mom here… so we are flying her back to CA on Monday to be at home with her husband. As always, she'll be on standby should the need arise… Thanks Mom! :)

The next chemo cycle is scheduled to start on July 7.

So… that's where we're at now. I'm sorry that I don't have access to this email from the hospital… but thank you to all for your thoughts and prayers… cards and notes. We are never alone… our Savior is always at our side. We cling to this truth…

God Bless
Scott and Rhonda

Responses

Mike M
    We are here Scott.

Sylvia A

Just wanted to let you know I added Rhonda to the prayer intentions book today at church. We'll be praying that she makes it thru this next round of treatment with full force -remembering that God is the ultimate healer.

God bless

Greg G

Praying for strength for you both—physical/mental/spiritual.

July 3
My Rhonda—Finally Back Home

Family and Friends,

We are HOME!!! Thank God and PTL!!!

Rhonda and I are both on the edge of exhaustion, and are looking forward to a long weekend of quiet recovery. Her lingering fever kept us in the hospital for the last 12 days. We've spent 19 of the last 24 days in the hospital... ugh. In an act of grace by our doctor, the previously scheduled date for starting chemo cycle #2 on Monday the 7th has been pushed back a few days. We have an appt on Monday to assess how Rhonda is doing and possibly set the date for the next cycle.

The care of the nurses, etc. at the hospital was mostly amazing. The rooms are huge with a sofa-thing that folds into a bed... not the Hilton, but much more comfortable than on the floor crowded between Rhonda's bed and the wall like I've had before. We definitely went through some frustrating times... just when we thought Rhonda was starting to feel better, that old fever would come back and knock her down... and keep us from being discharged. The official cause of the hospital stay was defined as "neutropenic fever"... a fever that her body had no tools to fight back with after the knockdown of the first round of chemo.

So... the fever is now negligible... the blood counts are returning to normal (increasing her built-in defenses)... and we get a break before doing it all again. It's so good to be home... looking forward to an uninterrupted night's rest for the first time almost 2 weeks.

Thank you to you all again for your love, prayers and support! With you all and our Lord... we can never say we are facing this alone. We love and appreciate you all!

God Bless... and please enjoy a wonderful holiday weekend... we will! :)

Scott and Rhonda

Responses

Petra R

Happy to read the news that you're home! How thrilling for you and your family. Wishing you a safe and relaxing holiday weekend. May each day of rest make you stronger and ready to take on the next step in winning this battle. I will continue to pray for you and your family.

Debora B

I am so happy for you. Enjoy your 4th and know that your prayer warriors are standing in the gap for you.

Thank you Father for this blessing you have given to Rhonda and family. We give you all the praise!

Amen

Trish M

Wonderful news! Praying for continued improvement and a peaceful weekend to regain some strength.

Denise A

We are doing the happy dance for you guys! Have a great weekend :)

Mike M

Thanks for the update Scott.

We are here if you need us.

Billie M

This is most wonderful news! We have been and will continue to carry you to our Father's attention. He is:

Immanuel—God is with us

Elohei Mikkarov—God who is near

El Hanne'eman—The Faithful God

Elohei Ma'uzzi—God of my Strength

El Roi—God who sees me

El Chaiyai—The God of my life

El-Channun—The gracious God

El Sali—God of my strength, God my Rock

El Rachum—The God of compassion

El malei Rachamim—God full of mercy, all merciful God

El Yeshuati—The God of my salvation

Adonai Nissi—The LORD my miracle, The LORD my banner

Adonai Roph'ekha—The LORD who heals you, the LORD your healer

El Shaddai—The all sufficient God

Elohim—God (plural form of El in Genesis 1:1)

El—Might, Power, Strength

There is POWER in the name. I pray the names of God over you. Find comfort and strength in His name.

Love you guys

Jan R

So glad you are home & that fever is almost gone! We are praying & holding you both close to our hearts!

Blessings

Sylvia A

PTL is right, a big hug to Rhonda. And happy 4th to your entire family

Terry C

Rhonda and Scott, we think of you daily and pray for you every time God brings a thought of you to our minds. We love you and pray that God will strengthen you. May He even now provide what you need for the next step. May you find His grace sufficient for each day as it comes. I know you will and you will praise Him for it. We don't take the impact that this battle has on you both lightly. Our thoughts and prayers are with you always. May you both get some needed rest and renewal.

Your Brother in Christ

Donna C

I'm sure you both are more than happy to be back in the comfort of your own home! Praying for you both often.

Let us know if you need something other than prayers!

Hugs

Bobbie O

So thankful she is home. Hope and pray you both get plenty of rest. We are and will be continuing to pray.

Patti S

Love you dearly

July 6
My Rhonda—Mind Over Matter

Hi,

Just wanted to share quickly about how much we've relished being in our home and comfortable bed… with no interruptions to the wonderful rest for the last few days. God is good! Rhonda still ran a low-grade fever for a couple of days, but it seems to be completely gone now. PTL! She's been pretty weak but the time of rest has been very restorative for her.

We had talked about maybe making an appearance at Sunday School/church this week… but I didn't see how she would have the strength. And I didn't want the huge effort to be a setback for her before our dr appt on Monday. So… I was somewhat surprised when Rhonda informed me this morning that she felt strong enough to make a go of it. She was determined to do something 'normal'… to benefit not just herself... but also the kids.. and our church family... that she's still alive and kicking.

So... we got the wheelchair out... and the protective mask... and she did it. :)

It was 'mind over matter'. In tough times, Rhonda has used this phrase to push herself to do things that required more strength than she felt she had at the time. So today... we all witnessed that the 'old' Rhonda is still there... ready to fight and overcome the huge waves of physical and emotional trauma her body has been suffering. It is a wonderful thing to witness. I am so proud of her as my eyes well up with tears of thankfulness. It is a great day.

The sermon today was entitled 'Hope in Dark Times'. How appropriate. How amazing that our Lord leads us to words that we need at just the right time.

Thank you again for your love, support, and encouragement. The Lord is our Strength... as Rhonda shared with a friend this morning... 'His strength is made perfect in our weakness'. Our God is amazing. Thank you Lord Jesus!

Responses

Sylvia A

What a beautiful picture of the two of you.

I too have experienced going to church on a Sunday and the Sermon being very relevant to what I was experiencing at the time, and knowing God was talking to me!

Please tell Rhonda I lit a candle at church for her today and continue to keep her in my daily prayers.

Keep us posted on how Rhonda does on her next round.
God bless

Cathy G

Praise the Lord for a wonderful Sunday for you both! We miss you both so much and hope to see you soon. Know we continue to pray for you as you walk through all of this and the upcoming treatment.

Love and prayers

Bobbie O

PTL. She definitely is a fighter and as they told Gary that is half the battle. We pray for you all daily and know God has a plan through this. Yes the message was great yesterday and uplifting. Please let us know what the doctor says.

Mike M

Praise the Lord.

Peggy A

Wonderful report Scott. Prayers still coming.

Greg G

Good stuff. Wow, "Hope in Dark Times" huh? You guys are bringing light to those so-called "dark times." Just know that. You are a testimony to all of us.

Lila C

Rhonda and Scott you are the greatest example of being "one" in marriage, I will probably ever know. Seeing you on Sunday gave us all a clearer picture of Christ's love. I told everyone "Rhonda loves us all so much" Thank you with all my heart for being who you are and loving us as you do. I didn't see you in church until later in the sermon. Touched and stronger just to see you and yes Scott the sermon was perfect and I almost didn't go. I believe with all my heart God set our marriages and friendships in place. I am clearly able to share with you, He has placed on my heart over and over, the plan you have for Rhonda's healing will all be exactly right. I know you already know that, I just wanted to affirm how He has placed this on my heart, clearly. Scott thank you so much for sharing the news about "your" Rhonda, I realize how blessed we are you would do that and as I said when I began, I need you to know how much I love you both and care about your life together and Rhonda's healing.

Pamela D
    Beautiful shot!! Love to you both!

July 8
My Rhonda—Round 2

Hello,

After another 4 hour appt at the dr's ofc this afternoon, we finally learned that Rhonda is being admitted tomorrow (Wednesday) afternoon for her second round of chemo treatment. One blood test about kidney function is concerning the dr, so it may be a new batch of drugs this time… and only 3 days in the hospital. We will see how it all works out.

Today was the closest we've had to 'normal' in a while… I went into the ofc for several hours and Rhonda felt strong enough to be up and around some, although it really taxed her. It will be good to get one more good night's rest at the house… good for us both.

Also… the dr told us that it is possible that this will be the last chemo before the actual marrow transplant process. He also said the transplant process consists of some heavy chemo. We're still learning what it all means… but we're all for shortening the process if possible! PTL!

So… we will be in the hospital for the next few days… but maybe home by the weekend. That would be wonderful!

Thank you again for the love, support, generosity… and mostly the prayers to our Heavenly Father. We know that He is listening!

God Bless!
Scott and Rhonda

Responses

Lila C
Oh my I was writing when you were Scott. You both are on my mind and in my heart throughout every day, and night and your keeping us updated, is a great blessing. Thank you with all my heart for letting us know. Standing on the promises of God "our" Father. We are tossed and turned but we will stand.
I love you so…

Usha A
Praying for a speedy recovery… Best wishes and lots of love.

Mike M
Hang in there Scott.
We are praying for you guys.

Jim F

Praying for you!

Bobbie O

Will be praying for you both. Pray this round won't be as hard on her. Yes, it will be wonderful if they can do the marrow transplant process sooner. Pray she is home by the weekend. Love you all.

Denise A

Thank you for the updates. Our love and prayers for you both. Please let us know if we can do anything:)

Suraya K

My Prayers are with Rhonda. May it all pass quickly and she emerges well and energized.

July 10
from Rhonda to Scott's coworkers

Thank you so much to you and your colleagues for the beautiful card and very generous gift! We are continuously amazed at how people reach out to us. We are very blessed! We got great news today: one of my brothers is an exact match to be a marrow donor! Great day!!

Thanks again for the generous gift!

Response

Pam D

You and Scott are very special to us and have shown so much support to each of us as things have happened in our lives. We hope we can show you by our small ways of support how much you both mean to us. Watching you and Scott work through the things in your own lives is a shining example for others.

That is awesome news!

I am praying that this round is not as rough as the last one.

July 12
My Rhonda—Home!

Hi,

Just wanted to let you all know that we are back home after the second chemo regimen. For the first day and a half, Rhonda was just cruising through it all with no side effects… but then they hit yesterday. Still, they were much milder than the first treatment. The biggest thing now is to rest and recover.

And please pray for 'NO FEVER'… we do not want to go back to the hospital for another several days again. We are going to the clinic tomorrow for a white cell booster… and then hoping to have an appt with the dr on Tuesday.

We also found out a couple of days ago that Rhonda's brother is a 'perfect match' for her bone marrow. This is great! The dr is still not settled on using donor marrow due to the increased risks to Rhonda… he may use Rhonda's own marrow. We may find that out… and a possible schedule… at our appt this week.

Thank you again for the prayers and support! We feel them… our Lord is good!

Take care and God Bless!
Scott and Rhonda

Responses

Debora B (in response to Stefanie's post)

Isn't it just like our Saviour to answer prayers (your uncle before he was born) for your Mom's future (her need in 2014).

I am glad she feels this round was easier on her. Will still be lifting her up to the Father.

Bobbie O

So thankful she is home. Will be praying.

Sylvia A

Praying for Rhonda's rest at home and no fever.

Denise A

PTL! Give her our love!!

Lila C

I have been watching and so grateful for this update. I know now to pray for no fever. I love you both greatly. We are blessed, you would write Scott.

Hugs and great love

Mike M

Hang in there buddy.

Greg G

No Fever. We are on it.

Pam D

So glad to hear this time is going a little easier!

Quinn W

Hi Scott… so glad that the 2nd round went better. I will continue to pray.

July 16
My Rhonda—Doctor Visit

Hi,

Just to let you know how the Dr visit went yesterday. He wants to run a couple of more tests, including a PET scan and another check of Rhonda's marrow, before deciding whether to use donor marrow for the transplant. He seems to be leaning towards using Rhonda's own marrow to lessen the risk factors for her, but needs to do these tests to know if it's the best option. The tests should be next week sometime.

Rhonda has been doing okay. This last chemo treatment was different from the previous, so we are learning each day how it affects her. She is needing lots of rest… but there is NO fever… and we are very thankful for that! PTL! :)

Thank you for sharing this journey with us… between your love and prayers… and God's mercy and strength… we will persevere.

God Bless!
Scott and Rhonda

Responses

Lupita O

I'm so happy to hear this news, we still praying for you!!

Bobbie O

So thankful she doesn't have any fever. Will be praying for all of you.

Lila C

You have our hearts and our prayers, I am standing for her healing.

I love you Rhonda and Scott, I am grateful you update us, it's so hard not to know.

Standing on the promises.

LOVE and HUGS to you both.

I woke up early, praying for you and Rhonda. We thank you for always praying for us. I am humbled by your care for others. I appreciate this update. I am so grateful Rhonda doesn't have a fever.

July 26
My Rhonda—A Busy Week

Hi there,

We are looking forward to a quiet weekend after running back and forth to the clinic/hospital 5 times in the last 8 days. It always hits about a week after the chemo treatments… all of her blood counts take a nose dive… so every 30-min appt for 'labs' turned into several hours as they had to administer transfusions, etc.

Yet all in all… Rhonda has had a pretty good week. She even managed to cook up some pancakes for Charlie one day… but paid for it the next. This coming Tuesday is the big 'workup' day. We'll be at medical offices all day for a battery of tests to make sure Rhonda is ready to move into the transplant process. We start with a PET scan at 7AM... and finish with the marrow biopsy scheduled at 3PM. Test results should be complete by the end of the week... and then we'll know.

In the meantime... we're working on building strength... and rest. :)

Thank you for your encouragement and support... and mainly prayers! We've made it this time without going into the high fever that had her in the hospital for almost 2 weeks before... thank you Lord for answering our prayers! He is Faithful!

Take care... and God Bless!
Scott and Rhonda

Responses

Carolyn D
Thanks so much on keeping us updated on Rhonda. I continue to lift you and Rhonda up in prayer—just like I pray for my family. Always thankful for life and strength for today!

Lila C
Thank you so much for your update! You are so right, He is Faithful! I love you both and wait for any news every day. Standing on the promises!

Patti S
Thanks Scott for being so faithful to keep us updated. We love you both and are praying for our sweet Rhonda...

Sylvia A

Sending prayers your way.

Bobbie O

Thank you for the update. Been praying and will continue to do so as you all continue this journey. Thankful she didn't have the high fever and the other issues from the last chemo.

Peggy A

I was thinking about you over the weekend. Keep up that strength. Still keeping you in my thoughts and prayers!

Myra P

We will keep on praying for Rhonda and your family.
God bless!

*****

While Rhonda was enduring these treatments and all that went with them, we were shocked and hugely saddened by the sudden passing of our beloved surgeon, Dr. Kuhn. He had performed the initial "whipple" procedure back in 2009 and also the surgery to remove the enlarged lymph node in April. As we were calling in for lab results from the procedure, we learned that Dr. Kuhn's father had become ill and passed away in May. The next thing we heard was that Dr. Kuhn himself had passed on July 27 after the onset of a sudden and serious illness with complications that he could not overcome. This man was so special to our hearts. It was quite a blow to us, but we were forced to focus on Rhonda's own battle. Cancer and its treatments are like that—they take precedence over everything else in your life. Even so, our hearts went out to his family and the many who were impacted by this tragic loss (even our current bone marrow transplant doctor had had a procedure performed by Dr. Kuhn). Dr. Kuhn was a skilled physician and a great man of God. He will be sorely missed.

*****

August 11
My Rhonda—Results… Moving Forward

Hello,

The last couple of weeks have been spent in resting and as much normalcy as we could grab. We did have a few bouts with fever (incl last night), but thankfully the temps always went down within 12 hours… so no unscheduled trips to the hospital. PTL!

So… Rhonda just got an email from our transplant doctor's nurse. Basically… the tests came back with good results, so they're going to use Rhonda's own marrow cells for the transplant. We have a consult with the dr on the 19th… and pre-work happening rapidly thereafter… and into the hospital on the 29th to do 6 days of chemo, and then the transplant around Sept 6th. We may be in the hospital up to 4 weeks. So we hope this will all be finished by the end of September when we can be done with it and once again focus on long-term recovery… and October 1 being the 10th anniversary of our first date! :)

It is both good… and kinda scary… to finally get this news. We can't finish and put this behind us until we start, so it's good to have an idea of the upcoming schedule. But… we know it will not be an easy road. We will really be leaning on our Lord for strength… and are confident that He will provide whatever we need to do this.

Thank you for your continuing concern, love, and support!
Scott and Rhonda

Responses

Quinn W

Scott, thank you for the update! I am praying for speedy recovery and that this process goes exceedingly well.

Cathy G

Thank you, for the update, Scott. Please be assured of our prayers and love to you both.

Greg G

Thanks man for the update. We are praying for you guys. I know it's tough.

Stefanie

Wow, so good news and hopefully a swift recovery.

Jim F

Thanks so much for keeping us informed.

I remember when you told our Reunion Group about your first date with Rhonda… how excited you were. It does not seem like that happened ten years ago.

Yes, the Lord absolutely, positively will see you through this time. Whatever you need, He will provide. Love you

Donna C

Great news! So happy for you both to get the show on the road.. What a journey you both have had and to come!

Still in our prayers,

Love and God Bless

Lynn B

Thanks again for the update! Great news regarding marrow cells!

Bobbie O

Thank you for the update. We will be praying for her and you as you continue on this journey. Know you are anxious to get this behind you and start the process of recovery.

Suraya K

Thank you for the update Scott. Give my fond regards to Rhonda and she continues to be in my prayers. All Good wishes to both of you.

Mike M

Praying…
If there is anything we can do please ask.
We love you guys.

Terry C

You are in our hearts, thoughts, and prayers. Love you guys and look forward to your recovery and return to health.
Your brother in Christ.

August 13
post from Stefanie—Transplant Time

You can tell that things with Mom are going well when there are fewer posts on here. When things are constantly changing or her health is deteriorating, then I'm on here all the time, passing along the changes, prayer requests, and praises. When things go back to normal, there's not so much "news to report" and I go back to tackling my always super long to-do list.

So Mom has been doing VERY well since her last batch of chemo. With the severe response she had had before, the docs changed the chemical in the chemo, and she responded much better. Mom was less nauseous, less sick, and her fevers were low and short-lasting. She has still needed much rest and has to be careful not to overdo it on her high energy days, but it is clear she has recovered much better this time. We're happy not only that's doing better, but because she will need to retain her strength in order to keep going through more batches of chemo during this round. When I went to visit her last week, she was even standing and she and Scott were going out for date night. They are such party animals!

Mom's bone marrow tested well, so we will be able to use her own marrow for the transplant.

Next week, Mom and Scott will meet with the doctor, do their pre-transplant stuff, start six days (wow!) of chemo on August 29, and then she'll have the transplant on September 6. Recovery time after bone marrow transplant could mean that she's in the hospital for up to four weeks. September will be a big month for Mom, and if she can get released before the end of the month, maybe we'll play that song about good things happening when September ends.

Praises: Minimal fevers and no more emergency hospital visits or issues. Standing and walking and strength, oh, my!

Prayer Requests: Continued strength and energy. Not-awful response to six days of chemo. Encouragement through six days of chemo. Smooth and straightforward transplant with no complications. Comfort while living in the hospital- again. And, no more cancer. That's always a good prayer request.

Peace and Love to you all.

Responses

Barbara C

So happy to hear the news of being able to use your own marrow for the transplant! Excellent! I will be praying for your recovery time to come and go quickly and uneventful.

Sandy L

Thanks so much for the update! I am praising the Lord for the good news!!! Still praying!

Nancy H

Sounds exciting! Marvelous that she is so strong going into this!

Vicky S

Thanks for the update Stefanie -- will pray continually for her and all of your family!

August 29
My Rhonda—Into the Hospital… Day -8

Hello,

Well… today is the day… we'll be heading to the hospital shortly to begin the transplant process. We had appts for 8 consecutive days to "mobilize" and "harvest" Rhonda's clean stem cells. The

Dr's were shooting for 5 million cells and they got 6.4 million in only 2 days of harvesting... PTL for that! So now we've had a couple of days to rest and get ready.

The "-8" in the subject line means that we are 8 days out from transplant... with that being "day 0"... and every day after that referred to as a "+" day... even up to day "+365" and beyond. They also refer to this day... Sept 6... as Rhonda's 'new' birthday. After one year, she will have all of her childhood vaccinations again, because the transplant will wipe her current immune system clean.

So... the 6 days of chemo start tomorrow... then 1 day of rest before transplant... followed by at least 2–3 weeks of hospital recovery.

We thank you all again for your support and encouragement... but even more we covet your prayers as we begin the process. The Lord Himself... and the prayers of His saints... will carry us through this valley and into His Healing... and more blessings than we could ever fathom.

May God Bless you all... we know that several of you all are facing stiff challenges in your lives as well... and our prayers will be with you as yours are with us... and together, with our Lord's strength, grace, and mercy... we shall overcome.

We love you all,
Scott and Rhonda

Responses

Melinda H

Thanks for the update. I think of you and Rhonda often. Missed seeing you at the office the last time I was there. We are still praying for you and Rhonda and you are still on our church prayer list.

Please keep me posted and let me know if I can help ya'll out in any way.

Sylvia A

Scott and Rhonda, please know that you are in my daily prayers each day along with all my other petitions. God is good and never gives us more than we can handle. Please keep us posted and may God bless you each thru this journey to a quick recovery.

Greg G

Dear Lord-we first praise you, and give you all the honor and the glory. We pray this day for Scott and Rhonda. We pray that your will be done in this situation. That you will work through the doctors and guide them, and that you will give strength and peace to both Scott, Rhonda, and their family. Thank you Lord for your faithfulness.

In Jesus name we pray!

Mike M

Love you guys.

I pray that the Lord comforts and strengthens you both.

Bobbie O

We are praying. Thanks for the update. One of my favorite verses that has helped me through some dark times is IS 41:10. Do not be afraid for I am with you. Do not be discouraged for I am your

God. I will strengthen you and help you. I will uplift you with my righteous right hand. May He give you both peace as you travel this hard journey. Know many are praying and we love you.

Patti S

Praying always, you have our love. We will be counting down with you in our hearts. Love P & J

Denise A

Our love and prayers to you both!!

Donna C

We are praying! I'm always thinking of her and her journey and how blessed she is to have you in her life to help her through this.

You both are a wonderful couple.

Peggy A

Prayers are with you!

Sept 4
My Rhonda… Day -2

Hi,

Just a quick update…

Rhonda just received her last dose of 6 days of chemo. The main challenges have been lack of deep sleep (a combination of insomnia and overnight sleep interruptions by staff) and meds that have kept her emotions on edge. Early this morning (like 3 AM), she also had a fever and nausea come on… peaking close to 101. The doctors are running tests, but keeping her on her schedule… a day of rest tomorrow… and transplant on Saturday.

We were surprised and blessed by a visit from our transplant Dr the other night at 9 PM… he overrode the "rounding" dr's opinion and ordered transfusions and sleep meds for her. Unfortunately, the transfusions kept her from getting into a deep sleep… and then the fever hit. It's amazing how difficult it is to get good rest at the hospital… you'd think it would be a priority to support good health.

We're almost there… but the recovery is going to be a chore too… so please keep the prayers going. We will make it through… with God's help… and the prayers of the saints.

Thank you… God Bless,
Scott and Rhonda

Responses

Deborah M
thank you so much for the update.

Bobbie O
We have been praying for her. Thank you for the update. Pray all goes well with the transplant and she will be on the road to a strong recovery.

Kurt A
Scott, is there anything you need? Denise was asking what we could do to help?

Cathy G

Thank you for the update, Scott. Please let Rhonda know we are back, and when she is able, would love to stop by if only for a few minutes. We'll do and wear whatever we have to as we know her immune system is non-existent. If she isn't up to it, please be assured of our continued prayers. We love you both!

Greg G

Cathy and I are praying for you guys. Praying for God's supernatural peace and strength through all of this.

Lupita O

Everything will be fine, because we are praying for you, and GOD, is holding you in his blessing hands.

Lila C

I have wanted to hear from you so badly! Thank you so much for this update. I only know to worship knowing the blood of Jesus is our hope and stand in His love for you and Rhonda and stand we all will, with great love and faith. I love you both so very much. Scott I will have some time off soon, am I able to come for 5 minutes? I want to see her so badly. No worries if you must say no, but please let me know. I can't tell you how many times I have started down there. I have not felt that was best for her. But now I want to at least ask.

Patti S

Praying always for our dear friends.

Terry C

Praying always for you guys. Scott, is there "anything" we can do? Let us know. Love you guys.

Donna C

We are praying that all is going well with the transplant today. Hope that she was able to get some rest yesterday after all that went on with her prior to this day.

Praying for good rest for recovery! My sister, Debbie is also praying for Rhonda. (*note from Scott—Debbie was going through breast cancer treatment at this time*)

Patti S

Hi Scott, When you have a moment, could you send us Rhonda's address at Baylor? We would like to send cards, notes etc.

We were talking about how helpless we feel to help Rhonda right now… and how prayer is our most perfect gift… but we are hoping some cards will cheer her sweet heart.

You have our love

Sept 6
My Rhonda—Transplant Complete!

Hello,

It is finished… PTL!!! The whole process took about an hour. Four nurses came into our room to massage and relax her, thaw the stem cells (8 bags), and slowly inject them into Rhonda's central line. The preservative has an odor and caused some nausea, but she did great! I'm so thankful and proud of Rhonda for persevering through all of this… it is not a fun time.

From here… all efforts will be to make her comfortable, and get the rest and nutrition she needs to recover.

Thank you for your prayers and encouraging words. Our Lord is faithful and has given Rhonda the strength to keep going through it all... and we can now see a crack of light at the end of this tunnel... PTL!

btw... I also made reservations today for a few days at our OK getaway near the end of October... and praying that it will work out for us to be there.

God Bless!
Scott and Rhonda

Responses

Jim F

Thank you very much for this report. The Lord has given dear Rhonda the strength to endure a very long ordeal. Now may she recover quickly and fully.

Your friendship has meant so much to me over the years.

Julius R

PTL for sure.

Greg G

PTL indeed Scott. Keep fighting.

Hey if you will allow us Cathy and I would like to pay for those days in OK. That would really bless us. Just let us know what the amount is. Please tell Rhonda how proud we are of her as well.

Maw-in-law

I'm in awe. I have no words to describe how I'm feeling.

Don & I would like to be there the day she comes home if she would like that. Lmk.

Love & continued prayers
Mom & Dad

Usha A

Praying for speedy recovery! God Bless!

Clifton W

Thanks for keeping me informed. I praise the Lord for the progress that Rhonda is making and for how you are standing strong through it all. I continue to pray.

Denise A

YEAH! We are so glad everything went well. Tell her we are praying for her and love her!!

Sylvia A

PTL please tell Rhonda we send a big hug! Will continue to uplift you both.

Lila C

My dearest friends, I am praising God and sending you love and joy. I know this is trial few people face, and difficult beyond words. You will be going on your getaway and many more. After time to recover and gain strength, Rhonda will finally be well.

Thank you with all my heart for sharing.

I love you both with all my heart!

Patti S

Rhonda has shown amazing grace and strength through this hard time. An example to all of us. We will pray for a strong recovery and that you will be able to enjoy that trip to Oklahoma!

Jan R

Praise God! Praying for swift recovery!

Bobbie O

So thankful things went well. We are praying for all of you. Glad you made reservations for your place in OK. That will give her something to look forward to. Thank you so much for the update.

Myra P

PTL! We are very happy that the transplant was complete and Rhonda is doing good.

We will continue to pray for her immediate recovery.

God bless!

Pam D

That is awesome news!

Sept 10
My Rhonda—Through the Valley

Hi,

Well… this is the tough time of getting through the lowest days of the chemo side effects. We are at day "+4" after the transplant and her new immune system has not had time to kick in yet. Throat/GI soreness has her on major pain meds and makes her not able to eat so she is on iv nutrition. Fever that spikes at over 101 at times... this is the valley. It may be another week before she starts to feel better.

Rhonda is hanging tough... she knows it will get better. We know that the light at the end of this darkness is still there. We know that our Savior is carrying her through all this... that these days shall soon pass... and better days are coming.

Thank you again so much for your support and love. We really covet your prayers at this time. We will get there... after just a few more days of this valley. Our Lord is faithful.

God Bless,
Scott and Rhonda

Responses

Denise A
　　How long is she expected to be in the hospital? We would like to send flowers but I'm not sure that's allowed?
　　(*note from Scott: Flowers are not allowed in the cancer hospital*)

Pam D
　　She may be feeling very weak but it sure sounds like she is amazingly strong!

Sylvia A
　　In my prayers every day.
　　Bless you.

Suraya K

I am praying for Rhonda and for your family through this major test. BY God's Grace and Mercy she will get better. It may be slow but it is certain God Will keep her safe.

My fond regards to both of you.

Cathy G

We were just thinking of and praying for you all this morning. I feel so disconnected from my dear friend and want to do something to encourage her. Can she have flowers in her room? Also, what hospital are you all in? I know we can visit her room, but we'd like to plan to at least leave you all some encouragement. :)

Please give Rhonda a special hug for me and assure her of my love and prayers – Hang on to Jesus, Rhonda! He will carry you through.

Love and prayers

Donna C

Thank you for keeping us updated on Rhonda's progress. She is putting up a tough fight all due to her strength in Christ! We think of the both of you daily with prayer.

Please tell her hi for us and for putting up a good fight! We can't wait for you both to return to church!

Love and God Bless

Lila C

Thank you Scott. I wish there were perfect words for you and Rhonda to let you know how deeply I care, how much others care. I am praying and standing. I love you both so very much…

Soon she will be able to walk out of this valley with you, her loving husband. As you say, you will get there. I am praying that she has great comfort and peace, Dear Lord, please hold Rhonda and Scott in your arms, more than ever before. Father we need Your complete healing for Rhonda now. Please Lord stop this pain, allow Rhonda to eat and be strong for Your Glory. Only You Father understand this, we are standing on Your promises. We come to You as little children. Father as your children, we need Your hand of love to bring Rhonda out of this valley.

> I love you Rhonda and Scott.
> Scott please kiss her on the cheek from me,
> Thank you, I wait for any news

Bobbie O

Thank you for the update. I know this is hard on her. We are praying and will continue to do so. Tell her when she feels like a visit I will bring her the gift I got her to go with her new gray hat. Love all of you.

Drew C

Praying for you both Scott. The Lord has focused me lately on Ps 23, particularly "His rod and staff comfort me." Comfort in the Greek means the Lords deepest empathy surrounds you now as you walk with Him next to you through the valley of the shadow. The light isn't far off my friend; soon you shall see it.

Love you brother

Maw-in-law

You expressed kind of how I was feeling this morning. This is the lowest point and it is uphill from this day forth. We are continuing to pray.

Sending oceans of love your way. If you guys need us, just say the word. Seriously, we will be there in an instant.

Mom & Dad

Peggy A

I keep praying for continued strength…

Patti S

This is all hard to hear but yours and Rhonda's testimony even during these dark times is uplifting. Your faith is glorious and it encourages everyone who comes in contact with you. Love and prayers

Sept 14
My Rhonda—Getting Closer

Hi,

Just wanted to let you all know that we've seen some improvement in Rhonda's symptoms the last few days. They finally gave her steroids for her fever… in fact a huge dose 48 hrs ago… that have completely taken her fever away. PTL! And then this morning we saw the first increase in the level of her white blood count… which means her transplanted cells are "engrafting"… and that healing for her throat, etc will not be far behind… PTLx2!!! She is still on the iv feeding, but is actually having hunger… yet another step in the right direction.

The staff here at the hospital, for the most part, have been amazing. One young nurse, Christina, actually prayed with Rhonda a couple of times and she and Rhonda shared several hugs… and I think they may end up being Facebook buddies too! :)

So… our wonderful Lord has lifted our spirits by answering our prayers in His great mercy… and even sending new precious souls to bless our lives. The compassion of our Savior is never-ending… not because we deserve anything good at all… but because He has always loved… all of us… with the unfathomable depths of His great love… and we give to Him all of our thanks.

And, of course, we also give thanks for our wonderful support group. It is so precious to us that you continue to stand with us through it all.

We love you all…
God Bless!
Scott and Rhonda

Responses

Julius R

Scott and Rhonda, thanks for the update and PTL indeed. God is good. Thank you Lord.

Sylvia A

Hi Scott, so glad to hear that Rhonda is making progress. I continue to keep Rhonda and your family in my daily prayers. God is the healer and will carry Rhonda thru this journey as he has done before.

God bless

Donna C

Awesome news and very encouraging! This is what we like to hear!

We appreciate you taking the time to update us to inform us how God is working in your lives.

Please let us know what we can do if you need anything.

God Bless and love to you both!

Peggy A

Hunger… yayyyy! So glad to hear good news.

Greg G

Great news. Keep it coming. Scott, let us know if there is anything we can do at your home (water plants, pick up the paper, take care of the yard… etc., or if we can bring you anything to the hospital (food, paper, books… etc.)

Clifton W

Looks like prayer is working. Keep up your good spirits.

Denise A

Great news!!!

Cathy G

Thank you so much for the update. I have moments during the week when Rhonda will come to my mind in a very strong manner, and last night was one of those. I asked Greg if he had heard from you, and he said not since the last update. So, we spent time in prayer for you and Rhonda last night – we pray regularly, but this was above that. Rhonda was heavy on my heart. Please give her a hug for me.

Bobbie O

What wonderful news. Tell her I love her and I am continually praying.

Jane B

Thank you for the update and positive report. You are in our prayers!

Sept 16
My Rhonda—Not There Yet

Hi,

Just wanted to give another quick update. After the counts started coming up the other day, we thought that we were almost home free. However, we got a mean reminder that the chemo side effects were not through with her yet. Rhonda has been very nauseous and ill the last few days... and feeling pretty miserable.

She is hanging tough, but we're wondering how much longer this will go on. On the positive side, her throat/GI tract are feeling much better... but she still can't eat due to the nausea. Also, her counts are rapidly improving each day. The drs are saying this means that the transplant is working and she'll be eligible for discharge as soon as she feels better and can eat and take her meds. PTL!

So... these last few days have been somewhat of a setback in our thinking... but we know the nasty stuff's days are numbered.. and life will be more comfortable again soon.

Thank you again for the prayers... our Lord is listening and will work all this out according to His perfect will and timing.

God Bless!
Scott and Rhonda

Responses

Lila C

Just looked at my e-mail only to see if you had written, and here you are! I AM SO SORRY, Rhonda has to be so very sick, as she comes to her complete healing. It is heart breaking. I love you both so much and miss you badly. I know this is going to get better soon and she will eat, and feel like a new woman. Scott I hope you are eating, please keep your strength. We love you and I will pray steadfast for this horrible time in this time of pure healing, as Rhonda's precious body and mind, go forward with life and your next trip together. God has many more happy times ahead for you as a couple, as "one" You are such a beautiful example of the love He gives us. Thank you with all my heart for being our true Christian friends. I just wish I could do more… Hug her for me Scott, hug him for me Rhonda.

With great love and care,
STANDING

Bobbie O

Thank you for the update. Sorry she isn't feeling well but hopefully that will pass soon and she can start eating. We will continue praying.

Lupita O

I'm so happy to hear, the last and difficult days is going to be behind, and better and bright days will be coming full of blessings to celebrate!!!

Greg G

Hang in there Scott. I know this must seem like it will never end. I am praying God gives you wisdom and strength through this.

Terry C

Scott, pray for you both. I pray that God helps Rhonda physically tolerate all of the treatments and that she would gain strength. And I pray for your strength and ability to continue to help her through all of this. I pray for protection for both of you. We all love you guys and look forward to the Lord healing and renewing physical health.

Your brother in Christ our Lord and Savior.

Give your sweet bride a hug or kiss for me!

Sept 21
My Rhonda—Still Not There Yet

Hello,

We are at "day + 16"… over 2 weeks since the transplant… starting our 4th week in the hospital. Friday they moved us to another room to free up space in the transplant unit. We are still waiting for the nausea to go away completely. She has times of feeling pretty good… starting to eat a few bites… and then it comes back. The dr yesterday told us it could be another week or so.

So… we continue to wait it out… knowing we will go home soon… but that day continues to be a moving target. So we also continue to pray for strength for each day… sometimes each moment… to get through this time and enter into the promise of much better days ahead.

Thank you so much for your prayers… words and cards of encouragement… and offers to help out. We know that our Lord will always give ear to the pleas of His people… and will answer according to His purpose and timing. His purposes with us here are not yet complete... but one day... soon... they will be.

Please enjoy your worship services today... and dear Lord help us to lift up our eyes to see what you want us to see around us... perhaps an opportunity to encourage others... perhaps a hand that needs to be held... perhaps taking the time to listen to someone who needs to know that someone cares. We are so blessed to have so many standing with us through this.

May God Bless you all for your willingness to share this journey with us.. Thank you for putting perfect Love into action... :)
Scott and Rhonda

Responses

Melinda H
So good to hear from you. We continue to think and pray for you and Rhonda often. May God continue to pour out his blessings upon you.

Patti S
No words Scott... your beautiful faith ministers to me... Give Rhonda my love

Maw-in-law
We are both there willing and able to help. Say the word and we'll be on the next flight out. We want to be there when we can be of most help. We are so concerned, worried, and yet trusting that this will soon be behind all of us... especially Rhonda. My heart is heavy... I'm her mother and it hurts to see her so sick. I am hopeful

and anxiously awaiting bright news. Have a blessed day and know that Dad and I love you so much.

Mike M

We love and pray for you guys

Lila C

Thank you as always for any update! I can't imagine how badly Rhonda must feel!! I am so sorry. They probably have no idea how much she has already been through. This time though the suffering is for healing. Please tell Rhonda we stopped Charlie today in church and he speaks of this time being the way to complete healing for you both as "one". Charlie is precious and looks so much like Rhonda. I pray he could feel how positive we are Rhonda will get there and feel wonderful, in His time. I love you both with all my heart.

Donna C

We are so happy about the progress! Nausea is no fun at all! Praying that will just go away and praying the next week or so will go by fast for you with awesome improvement so both of you can go home! We are anxious to see you both back in church..

Love in Christ

Bobbie O

We pray for her daily and pray she will get to come home soon. Tell her I love her and look forward to our chats when she gets home.

Amy G

Thanks for the updates, I continue to lift ya'll up in prayer.

Nita S

Thanks for the update. Sorry she is still feelin' poorly.

Love and prayers

Jake A (*Kurt/Denise A's young son*)

I just wanted to say I am so inspired by you and Mrs. Rhonda. To see how you both are so firm in the Lord just makes me stronger in my walk as well. I'll be praying for you both.

Marc A (*Kurt/Denise A's teenage son*)

Hello sir, hope you are doing well. I just wanted to let you know that I think you are great inspiration by setting an example of God's path for us and that you didn't blame him. I hope Mrs. Rhonda is doing well and I will be praying for her, and our family prays for her too. I know it's hard right now, but God is amazing and will always be there for you. Have a great day sir.

PS: (By the way Hebrews 4:12 is my favorite verse)

Sept 28
post from Stefanie—More Time

As we all know, one of Mom's favorite things is to chill out in the hospital. So it's a great thing she's getting so much of it, right? Yesterday marked 75 days in the hospital since June. Today was day 76. She might hit 80 by the weekend. The docs suspect some of her past issues (liver, whipple surgery, etc) have been causing her fevers, so she'll have a scope to check things out and hopefully fix the problem. *sigh* More time in the hospital. Please keep Mom in your prayers as she continues to deal with this fatigue, lack of platelets, high fevers, and everything else that keeps knocking her back down. We're praying for healing, health, and comfort. I'm waiting to hear back from Scott to find out how we can bring them some sunshine and happiness, and I'll be sure to pass on the word as soon as I know.

Responses

Lourdes H

Okay Rhonda. Your vacation at Club Medical is over. Time to go home. Tell your platelets and your liver to get a grip! We all need you healthy already. Missing you much. I am getting a huge Scrabble-ego as I am finding it hard to lose. Once you're well and playing again that will all change I'm sure. Take care. Looking forward to seeing you well again

Petra R

Hi Stephanie: Thank you for taking the time to post an update on your mom. This must be very trying on your entire family. What a marathon! Hopefully you're soon to see the finish line and triumphantly finish. Everyone in your family deserves a medal for hanging in there and staying hopeful. I pray that the doctors can identify the underlying cause for the fevers and find a solution that will turn this around, so your mom can spend the holidays at home. Praying for your family, so you can continue to be the sunshine that lights up your mom's spirits. Most of all, praying for Rhonda's body to heal and for Rhonda to stay mentally and emotionally strong.

Thinking of you

Sandy L

Stefanie

Thank you soooo much for this update. I had no idea she had been in the hospital that many days. I miss her so much! Please tell her I Love her and I continue to pray for her and Scott and all of your family. I really want to help any way possible. I will be watching for your next update. You are AWESOME!!!!!

Marilou H

Aunt Naomi and I are sending lots of love and prayers especially for Rhonda, as well as the family. We love you so much. Keep up the good fight Rhonda, you are truly an amazing woman! Love your cousin, Marilou

Oct 2
My Rhonda—Time to Go Home :)

Going Home... what a beautiful thought!

An endoscopy on Monday revealed an ulcer in Rhonda's esophagus... an after-effect of the chemo. This has been the major source of her pain... and inability to eat... it was good to find out exactly what it was, and then take measures to help it heal.

So... when she told the dr this morning that she could finally eat a bit... he jumped on it and said 'discharge tomorrow'... and we heartily agree!

Rhonda is still a ways from a complete recovery of her systems and strength... but her counts are strong and we were reminded strongly by the dr yesterday that the transplant was a success and prognosis is great... PTL!

It will be so amazing to be in our own home... our own bed... to rest without interruption. We are so thankful to our Lord and you all for standing with us though this whole ordeal... including these last 35 days in the hospital.

Going home... God is good!

Thank you again… and God's Blessings to you and yours!
Scott and Rhonda

Responses

Maw-in-law

What amazing news. Tears in our eyes. PTL from this end, Don said. Do you need us to come out. If you do decide you'd like help, we will hop a plane and be out there. Wow. So thankful.

Thank you for sharing fabulous news.

Love you guys.

Mom & Dad

Greg G

You guys are warriors. PTL indeed.

Usha A

Good to hear that Rhonda is going home. I am sure once she is home recovery will be faster.

God Bless!

Lila C

Dearest Friends, all day long, while I was working I thought about Rhonda and Scott, and prayed for you!! I am so thankful for your update and you are finally coming home. This is the best news! I am so sorry Rhonda is still weak and will pray specifically for this horrible ulcer and weakness. This will take time for you, 35 days is a long time and yet I know it will be awhile before Rhonda is strong and not suffering. But is so much closer. Nobody can understand all the suffering you have both endured. It's in His timing and yet so hard. I have felt so badly I have not been at her bedside, please forgive me. I love you both with all my heart and thank God with all my heart for Rhonda's healing. I stand in love through Christ. Your faith in Christ and love for others is precious and gives us all strength to stand. I thank you again for sharing this life with us. Please know every day we come home and say "is there a message from Scott?" Here you are and we are thankful beyond words you are coming home!!!

Great love and standing

Sylvia A
Keeping you in daily prayer. And we all know God answers all prayers in time.

Prayers to you all.

Peggy A
AMEN! So happy to hear the news!

Linda S
Great news Scott :)

Bobbie O
PTL. I am so thankful for both of you. Looking forward to seeing her when she is up to visitors. We will continue to pray.

Clifton W
Sounds like good news. I am saying a prayer for yawl right now.

Pam D
That is AWESOME news!!

Denise A
PTL!! We are so happy to hear this news! Can we send her some flowers now :)

October 3
My Rhonda—Fever

Well… I guess the Lord's time for us here in the hospital is still not yet complete. Rhonda woke with fever and chills this morning… her temp was over 101 the last time they checked it.

So… they've done a chest xray and are doing other tests to see what may be going on. She has had a history of running these fevers that last for a day or so and then go away… and no real reason found for it. We will see if this is the same thing…

This is definitely a disappointment for us… yesterday evening everything seemed to be going so well… she was eating normal and we were so looking forward to going home.

But not yet… our Lord's timing is not our own…

I will keep you updated… thank you for your continued prayers…

Scott and Rhonda

Responses

Pamela D
Still praying and believing with you and for all of you

Myra P
We will continue to pray for your family and Rhonda's immediate healing.

Jim F
Hang in there, Bro.

Denise A
So sorry :(Praying…

Peggy A
:(

Lila C
Just got home, thank you as always for the update. Please let us know asap about Rhonda's temperature. I am so sorry, I know you are ready for your beds and beautiful home. Scott I know it has to be so hard. You want to be home for good, and I believe with all my heart it will be! SO blessed you speak of God's timing, such beautiful faith.
Standing.
I love you both dearly!!!

Bobbie O
Thank you for letting us know. Know you were disappointed. Hope she gets to come home soon. We will keep praying.

Oct 9
My Rhonda—Home Where We Belong

And on the 41st day… we went home.

Rhonda was finally discharged this Wednesday. She had started feeling better… able to swallow and eat… and no fevers… by this past Sunday night. The dr's were a bit more careful this time in declaring her "ready to go"… and it was even a bit dicey on Wednesday as we had to wait for one last transfusion before we could leave.

When we got home we were pretty much exhausted… enjoying some quiet time to relax… no interruptions… just time together. And our own bed felt like heaven… amazing… and we quickly collapsed into the deepest sleep we've had in a while… and we're ready for some more. It will take some time to recover.

Thank you Jesus for bringing Rhonda through such a time as this… even up to the last day we were able to touch people with our story… the special relationship that He has blessed us with. We know… that not all wives (or husbands) would want to room together in a hospital room for 6 weeks… but we can both say… "there's no place else I'd rather be"… because we were together.

The multiple follow-up appts start tomorrow… it will keep us busy, but we will be able to go home after each one. PTL!

Thank you so much… so much for the prayers and encouragement… and for my incredible co-workers and mgrs. at the office for working with me to allow me to be with my Rhonda… our gratitude cannot be expressed by words… but… thank you again!

God is faithful… His mercies are new every morning… great is Your Faithfulness, O' Lord. Great is Your Faithfulness!

May God bless you all abundantly, as He has… in His unending kindness and mercy… blessed us.

With overflowing hearts,
Scott and Rhonda

Responses

Lila C
I love you both with all my heart.

Sylvia A
Praised Be Our Lord.

Greg G
Cathy and I praise the Lord for giving you both the strength and the perseverance to endure this… test, this trial… I don't really know what you would call it, but I do know that "all things work for the good of those that love Christ." So, with that said, we know God will use this "suffering" in ways we could not even imagine. Get some rest you two. You have earned it to say the least.

Denise A
HAPPY DANCE!!! So glad you guys are home:) Relax, recover and restore!!

Janet T
That is awesome news! I am so glad ya'll are finally home and can get some much needed rest. We have all been praying for you both and will continue to pray for Rhonda's healing and recovery.
Ya'll are such a blessing to us as well!

Pam D
Awesome news!

Suraya K

Congratulations Both of you. Rhonda now the good days begin. You will be on your feet soon Slowly but surely you will regain your strength

Jan R

Praise the Lord, you are home! Thank you for sharing your journey with us! Your story gives me hope & it's amazing to see how this "valley" has increased your faith! I'm always so deeply touched by yours & Rhonda's strength and how closely your spirits are aligned!

Blessings

Trish M

PTL!!!! Hugs to you both. Enjoy being home and just "being". Love ya!

Peggy A

:)

Julius R

PTL Scott and Rhonda. I am so glad that you have been able to be together and for having such an understanding company you worked for that was able to support you in this time of trial.

Praying for quick healing at home and back to normal life!!!

Donna C

So happy that the both of you are HOME! Praise the LORD!!!

Relax, Relax, Relax... Rhonda, may your healing still continue, regain your strength and health...

Scott, so glad you are there for Rhonda. Such a wonderful husband for her.

We hope to see you both when you can get to the church doors. We are still praying…

Holler if you need help with anything.

love and hugs

Nita S

So glad you are home. That prayer is answered but still praying for strength for the day.

Bobbie O

We are so thankful that Rhonda is home. Know you both will get much needed rest now. We will continue to pray. We love you all.

Oct 20
My Rhonda—Surviving a Bump in the Road

Hi…

As several of you are aware, we've had an interesting last several days.

Last Tuesday afternoon (the 14th), we saw our Dr for the first post-transplant visit… and everything looked great. We scheduled a couple of more follow-ups, and most likely a scan for this week.

The following evening, Rhonda and I went out on our "date night" to eat at the mall.. and walked a bit to get some strength building going. But overnight Wednesday, the chills started… I gave her some meds and detected no fever yet… and we tried to get some more rest. Around 5AM, I sensed Rhonda sitting up on her side of the bed. I asked her how she was doing, and heard nothing in response except the sound of her rolling off the bed and onto the floor as she passed out.

As I worked with trying to help her, she passed in and out of consciousness several more times. When I finally got her back into bed and somewhat comfortable, I checked her temp and it was approaching 105. I tried several times to get a blood pressure reading on her with our home machine (even tested it on myself… and it worked fine)… but it wouldn't give me a reading. I called the dr's ofc… and they told me to call 911.

My emotions got the better of me as I knocked on Charlie's door to tell him an ambulance was coming to pick up Mom. I thought we were past all of this stuff.

The paramedics were very impressive… and I had to mention to them that right now our son Jordan is in paramedic school. They couldn't get a bp reading either, but measured her temp at 105.6…

So… to shorten the story a bit… Rhonda was taken to the ER at Baylor Dallas where they poured fluids, antibiotics, and stimulant into her to bring her temp and bp back to where they needed to be. She was transferred to the ICU in the afternoon, and by the next morning (Friday), everything was back to normal. Whew. Thank you Lord.

We got transferred to the cancer hospital late that night. They determined that bacteria was growing in her central line appliance, so that was pulled out… and was replaced with a picc line. In spite of the great counts on Tuesday, her 'baby' immune system didn't have what she needed to fight this bug off… and we're so thankful that the hospital doctors and staff knew just what to do to bring her through it so quickly... PTL!

And today... she was discharged... and we are back home... again... and ready for even more rest... still whirling from how fast it all came on... and went away.

Thank you Lord for watching over my girl... again. And Thank you all for the continuing prayers, cards, and messages. We draw strength from your support.

Our plan (with the dr's blessing) is to keep our reservations and retreat to a cabin in OK this coming Sunday for the week. We are very much looking forward to a time of true R & R.

You all please have a good week... God Bless,
Scott and Rhonda

Responses

Roxzanne M

Scott, you and Rhonda are an inspiration for people to believe in our Lord. Thank you for sharing your life with all of us. I pray for your whole family all of the time and thank God for bringing you guys into my life. Give Rhonda a big hug from me. I love you guys.

Sylvia A

So sorry about the bump on the road but glad to hear that's all it was.

I will pray for safe travels as YOU WILL make the trip to OK. We'll wait for a full report on your trip.

Enjoy your time and may God's Angels accompany you.

Jane B

Thanks so much for keeping us posted. We are praying for you and know that God is faithful.

Enjoy your retreat.

Peggy A

Oh my goodness. So glad all is well. I hope you are near a hospital when you go on your little trip… just in case. Take care.

Maw-in-law

We didn't hear all of that. So scary. Glad God answers prayer. Thank you for the update, and we'll continue to pray & thank God.

Sending our love,
Mom & Dad

Jan R

Amen! Have a wonderful relaxing week!

Bobbie O

So thankful she is home. We will continue praying for her. Julie let me know she went back in.

Patti S

Praying for a peaceful and restful respite for both of you. So thankful Rhonda is once again back home.

We love you both.

Oct 23
from Terry

All, Rhonda and Scott are back at the Doctor's office. Rhonda is running a fever of 104 today. Scott believes that she will likely be admitted into the hospital. Please pray for their strength.

Responses

Patti S
Lord please let them rest and heal!

Lupita O
Just to let you know, I keeping in my prayers every night, and you are in God hands, because all people, who loves you, we are praying for you!!!!

Vic and Donna C
Praying always for healing, strength and rest… for them… and for the doctors to find out what's causing this fever.

Julius R
I am so concerned to hear about this setback. Just prayed again for complete recovery and return to normal life. Will continue to pray daily for y'all.

Nita and Fulton S
Father, thank you for holding Scott and Rhonda in your strong, gentle hands.

Oct 24
My Rhonda—Bump #2

Hello…

We are here… again… in the hospital. :(

After being discharged on Monday, we made it for only a few days before the fever and chills hit again yesterday (Thur) morning. I had gone into the ofc for a couple of hours early, and when I got back… after listening to her unsettled but deep sleep for a while, I leaned over and touched her forehead. Oh boy.

I was able to rouse her… she was more responsive than the last time (PTL!)… so… with fever over 104… I quickly packed up some things and used the wheelchair to get her into the car. I was determined not to go through ER this time if possible, and was hoping we could just get into a hospital room right away.

That kinda backfired on me and I ended up having to roll her over to the clinic where she was assessed. They ordered a transfusion after seeing her platelets were very low… and while we were waiting, the fever broke… and she was much better, tho exhausted.

The drs (and we) needed answers… so they ran many tests… finally getting to our hospital room yesterday evening (they just had one room open up). To this point, all results are good (including a perfect PET scan from Wednesday… PTL!).. but we are waiting for the tests that take a few days to finish. This may be a liver thing that Rhonda's had at times since the first cancer treatments… a fever for a day or two, and then it's gone with no real explanation of what caused it. Anyways… we knew we couldn't take a chance with fever in her present condition.

So… In light of all this… and with a cry in my heart… I called and cancelled our cabin in OK where we were planning to be for the week starting Sunday afternoon. Sigh. Even if Rhonda jumps up and feels great tomorrow morning… with these fever episodes happening, we don't need her to be in a cabin in the woods a couple of hours away from our medical care. We're not out of these fever woods yet.

So… thank you for the continuing support, love, and prayers… we will get there one day… and finally put this all behind us. But not just yet. The Lord continues to be our strength for each day… each challenge.

God Bless… take care… and please have a good weekend!
With our Love,
Scott and Rhonda

Responses

Carolyn D
So sorry that Rhonda is experiencing these "bumps" on her road to recovery. I believe that Dr. David Jeremiah had the same - or at least close to the same - treatment that Rhonda has received. The good news is that it is successful! I continue to lift up both of you in prayer. Hope to see both of you after Rhonda has regained her strength.

Janet T
Thank you so much for keeping all of us up to date with Rhonda. You two never cease to amaze me, Jim and I feel truly blessed to have

two such sweet God loving friends as you and Rhonda. I know the Lord will continue to bless ya'll and use the two of you in ways we will never imagine. I actually feel God working in each email you send!. We love ya'll and continue to pray for both of you and your family.

Blessings

Peggy A

So very sorry but so grateful that the fever occurred before you were away. Still praying!!!

Sylvia A

Aaaaaaaaaw! I was so praying for your weekend get away!

But you're right it's in God's hands and this weekend was not the chosen one for now.

Now let's pray Rhonda makes it back home soon and you can enjoy being at home. Maybe you can surprise her with a "Stay vacation" with something special. And this just makes finally getting to OK even better. :)

We know it's all in God's time.

God bless.

Bobbie O

We will continue praying for both of you and your family.

Patti S

Thank you for the update, Scott. We pray for healing, home, peace and rest. Love Patti

Greg G

Man, I know that hurt to cancel your reservations in OK. You guys will get there. We are praying for you both and your family.

Lila C

Hello my precious friends. I had to stop for a day (also been working) and take a deep breath to search for the "right" words to let you know how sorry I am you had to return to the hospital, I can vividly see you pushing your angel wife in a wheel chair to try to get care without putting yourselves through more of the hospital system. You both are so dear to my heart, so dear to everyone and I wish I could change this and you would be in the cabin. Our bond stands on the love of our savior Jesus Christ and so those are my "right" words, I love you and so does He. You are so right Scott this will take more time, it's been so hard on Rhonda's precious body. I believe with all my heart you will be in that cabin and together in your bed, that wonderful bed, you have in your beautiful home soon, but time is needed.

If I can do "anything" please let me know!!!!

I love you both!

Standing! Standing on the promises.

Oct 30
My Rhonda—update

Hi,

Just wanted to give an update on what's been going on this week. We are still in the hospital… and Rhonda has been feeling pretty good the last few days. PTL! It does appear the old surgery may be the culprit for the last fever. Rhonda had an MRI on Monday… at midnight… and there appears to be scar tissue that could be causing periodic blockages. So she will have an endoscopy tomorrow to investigate and possibly use a stent or balloon to open things up. Something similar to this was done almost 4 yrs ago. We have complete confidence in our scope dr and expect good results.

Meanwhile… these fevers have apparently 'overwhelmed' her baby bone marrow cells… and they have "shut down" and need to be "re-started." Her white blood count has spiraled down and she is officially "neutropenic" again. The dr's are not surprised by this and have a plan to get things going the right way again. We don't know what that is yet.

So… we don't know how long we'll be here. They want to see that the scope helps… and we need to get these counts to come back up.

And on a more happy note… we made reservations yesterday for our 'official' 10th anniversary trip… a week in San Antonio the last week of April next year. That gives us 6 months to get past all of this as we anticipate the time of relaxation and all of the fun stuff we'll get to enjoy… the Lord willing!

So that's where we are… our 78th day in the hospital since June. We will get there… there is a plan… our Lord is in control. Thank you for standing with us through this all, your love and support strengthen us. We will keep you posted…

God Bless,
Scott and Rhonda

Responses

Terry C
Thanks for the update Scott. You are in our hearts and thoughts constantly.
Love you both.

Peggy A
Sending more love and prayers.

Maw-in-law
Thank you, Scott for the update. So very sorry she is having to endure all this and pray they find the answer soon.
We're sending our love and continue to hold her up in prayer.
Love you guys so much,
Mom & Pop

Jan R
Your faith in our Lord gives us hope & encouragement! Praying every day for you!
We love you both!

Mike M
We Love You

Jane B
Thank you for the updates and the opportunity to be a part of your prayer support family. Be assured of our concern, love, and prayers on your behalf.

Nov 3
post from Stefanie—Neutropenic

I learned a few new words this week. The first was in Scott's mass Mom update email, the rest I found online when I looked up what the first one meant. Neutropenic. Neutropenia. Neutrophil. Neutrophils are a type of white blood cells that fight infections (hi-yah!). Neutrophils are good and we need lots of them. A normal amount of neutrophils range from 1800 to 7700 (# neutrophils per microliter of blood). Neutropenia means that you have 1700 or below. Severe neutropenia is below 500. At that level, bacteria in your mouth and GI tract can cause infections. Mom only has 100.

Of course we are all very concerned about this. Any little thing could make her very sick, and she is unable to fight it off. Added to that, or maybe causing that (cause we all know that I don't get science), all of her fevers have conspired to wipe out all the good that the bone marrow transplant was supposed to do.

Right now we're back to square one, but maybe worse. She is at high risk of infection, and unable to fight off whatever comes her way. She needs to get better, but can't on her own. I went to see her on Sunday and had to wear a mask and gown.

The doctors say they have a plan for getting her back up, but they haven't shared it with us yet. Please pray that their plan would not only work but be completely amazing and restore her health and strength.

On the positive side in all this, Mom seemed to have a lot of mental energy during our visit and we had a good conversation. My job was to talk a lot so she didn't have to talk too much and worsen her sore throat. She had a list of things she wanted to make sure Charlie and I did to make sure he was ready for college, so it's good to see her with energy. I'll take that as a good sign.

As always, we appreciate your prayers. I'll post when I have more information.

Responses

Petra R

Thanks for the update Stephanie & Scott. Glad the doctors have a plan. It's amazing what can be accomplished with medicine. Pray that this is the solution and will help Rhonda build strength. Your family is so resilient and strong. Your stamina to stay positive and hopeful is inspiring. I pray for you to take good care of yourself while you are caretakers to Rhonda.

Cari R

Praying!

Nov 6
My Rhonda—Waiting

Waiting… on the Lord.

Yes… we are still in the hospital. Tonight Rhonda has gotten her 4th daily injection to stimulate bone marrow growth. When the shots started, her count was at zero… this morning it was up to 0.08. The count needs to be over 1.0 to go home… preferably over 1.5 to be able to fight infection. We are still a ways off.

The first procedure this past Saturday was not 100% successful so another procedure needs to be done. The dr does not want her to have the 2nd procedure until these counts come up… so… low grade fevers come and go each day as this bile duct area still needs to be totally cleaned out.

So we are waiting. The baby marrow cells have to get another kick-start… and we don't yet know how long that will take. We have been home a total of 11 days since we started the transplant process on August 29. The seasons have changed on us… with talk even of a 'polar vortex' hitting us within a week. I'm still sitting in the room in my summer shorts. I may need to make a run to the house for a wardrobe change. :)

So again I must say… the Lord's purposes for us here have not yet been fulfilled. They moved us to another floor about a week ago, so now we're meeting new nurses and staff… sharing our story… trying to reach out to these caregivers in some small way while we find ourselves in the fog of seemingly never-ending days in the hospital. I know I could do better… it's too easy to sit back and ask God "why?"… and allow ourselves to be consumed by our own circumstances.

But this is where our spiritual "rubber meets the road"… do we believe?… do we keep our faith intact?… do we crater in to our own "poor me" party? No. God has promised to never allow us to go through more than we can handle. We choose to believe… and hold on to… His promises. It is not an easy thing… it is not a path we would choose… but… it is the path that our Lord has us on for this time in our lives… and we know that He is always with us… and that He loves us more than we could ever comprehend.

We choose to trust Him. Not because we always feel like it… but because we believe… in His Love… His Goodness… and His Power over all.

So we will wait… wait until He determines that his purpose for us on this path is complete.

I cannot say "thank you" enough for the love and support we feel from you all. I know that some do not share our beliefs... but I pray that somehow... through these experiences of ours... the reality of our Lord will shine through for all to see His Glory and goodness... and that His Promises are True... that He is Life.

Even while in this darkness... we are always in His Light. Thank you Lord for your mercies... they are new every morning.

May God Bless,
Scott and Rhonda

Responses

Julius R

Daily I prayed for ya'll and ask the Lord for His will to be done, but I also asked Him specifically for healing and strength to fight this trial.

Peggy A

Is there anything I can do to help... with comfort items? Something I could bring to you? How is Rhonda's appetite? Can she tolerate sweets or anything fun. You name it and I can bake it or bring it. Praying for you guys.

Patti S

The disappointment you and Rhonda have faced which such bravery leaps off the page... we will never fully understand this trial.. but I am very sure that every day you have spent in the hospital you have ministered and showed absolute proof of the peace that goes beyond all understanding... that only God can give us.. Our prayers for mercy will not cease until we can change them to prayers of Thanksgiving for total healing for our Rhonda. We will trust in His timing... always.

Jan R

Scott, we are praying that our Lord will lift you & Rhonda up 'on eagle's wings' & give you renewed faith & energy to fight the good fight & win this battle! We are amazed at the strength of your spirit & the depth of your faith - we pray each day that He will make her journey easy & heal her completely. You have both made a difference in our lives & in our marriage & I am sure that you have touched & changed many others lives during this battle. The Lord said "I will never leave you or forsake you!" Thank you for sharing your faith with us - it makes us stronger!

Jim F

Thanks for the report. The Lord has carried you thus far and He will continue to do so. We love you and are praying for you.

Clifton W

I don't know how you are able to keep your spirits up, but you are an inspiration to all. I am thankful that you put your complete faith in the Lord. My prayers continue to be with you and Rhonda.

Deborah M

What can we do to help? Does she need socks? lotion? tooth paste and tooth brush? good smelling soap? What can she have that makes her feel better??

Please let us know how we can lift her spirits.. and yours :)

Sylvia A

You finished the first path last time around, let that be your constant reminder that you CAN and WILL overcome this journey as well.

As you stated, God wasn't finished with His purpose quite yet.

Stay strong, try to rest and leave the praying for us prayer warriors!

Lupita O

Remember God is always with you, you see 4 footprints when you walk with Him, and when you see only 2 footprints, is because He is carried you in His blessing hands.

I'm always remember you on my prayers, with love!

Drew C

Scott, your updates are such compelling reading. I feel your words calling me to go deeper in faith in my own challenges, following your and Rhonda's courageous footsteps as you seek the Lord with all your hearts. I hope you have saved each of these emails; they would make a great book or devotional someday. Who knows – maybe part of His larger purpose in this is to increase the faith of those who are watching and drawing inspiration from your courage and perseverance. One step at a time, dear brother.

In Christ

Denise A

Oh Scott, we are so sad to read this. Please let us know if you guys need anything at all. And please take care of yourself! I know how demanding it is being the caregiver… please take some breaks for yourself. Love you both!!!

Cindy H

I can't imagine all the pain and suffering that Rhonda has had to endure from the surgeries she has had. Bruce and I have been praying that God will heal Rhonda's body and bring her out of this VICTORIOUSLY!

Scott, I pray that the Lord will give you and Rhonda the wisdom and discernment you both need to know when it's His will for you to "keep on believing" in the face of apparent defeat. Teach them how to open the door for You to work wonders their lives. Father, I pray that you will reveal to Scott and Rhonda how putting their hope in You, Your Word, and Your goodness will open the door for them to receive all the blessings You have in store for them. Remind them how maintaining a hopeful attitude can be the best antidote for discouragement and despair.

Scott, you and Rhonda are in our prayers daily!

Love you guys

Marc A (*Kurt/Denise A's son*)

Hello sir, no words can comprehend what you are going through. You are a great inspiration when talking about the Lord. My family and I will continue to pray for you. You don't have to reply, I know you are very busy. Have a good day sir.

Nov 9
My Rhonda—Looking Up

Our Lord is Faithful and True…

Just wanted to give you all a quick update. The neupogen shots finally started kicking in and her neutrophil count is well into the normal range. PTL!

What this tells us… is that her marrow transplanted cells have not been damaged by all of these fevers… that they are capable of multiplying with the injections. The next steps will be to stop the injections… get that 2nd procedure done (hopefully in the next couple of days)… and hopefully the fevers will stay away and her counts will stay up… and we can start thinking about going home again.

Thank you so much for the encouragement, support, and prayers. Thank you for standing beside us.

I will keep you posted…

God Bless!
Scott and Rhonda

Responses

Cindy H
Praise God!

Patti S
Wonderful news! Our hearts are all with you both!

Greg G
Heck yeah! Great news. PTL indeed.

Cathy G
Yes, yes, yes!!!! Praise the Lord! Tell Rhonda I am looking forward to our girl's lunch out!! We have been diligently praying for this and will continue to do so. We love you both!

Jan R

Praise God to whom all Blessings Flow!

Will keep praying!

Peggy A

PTL!!!!

Myra P

Thanks for sharing the great news! PTL!

We will keep on praying for your family and for Rhonda's healing.

Pam D

She is in our prayers

Suraya

All my Best wishes and Prayers are with Rhonda and you through this trying time. Through God's Grace you will be home and Rhonda will be well soon.

Donna and Vic C

You both are always in our thoughts and prayers. What a roller coaster ride. Praying that there will be great improvement so the roller coaster can take you both to your house (home) and remain there!!! No getting off the track… We love good news and prayerfully you can return to church soon. Praying that by Christmas you both can attend the Sunday School party.

Thank you so much for these updates and showing us your strength, will, determination and most of all, FAITH!

We all should learn from your experience!

God Bless and love

Bobbie O

Sounds very encouraging. We have been praying for you all and will continue to do so. Hope and pray she can come home soon.

Lila C

I love you both so very much and want you to know you and your updates have given me faith I did not have before. You are right, we stand, we don't have a pity party, but it is hard. I am so very sorry for all of your suffering. I am standing for the Smiths

Nov 18
My Rhonda—Home

Hi there... after another 24 straight days in the hospital... we are home again. :)

After an extended time with no fever... Rhonda was discharged yesterday evening. It was soooo nice to be back in our own bed last night!

We are still needing to be somewhat careful. The second procedure was not a 100% success... they were not able to install a drain or stent. So she still may be susceptible to a fever coming on. Also... the initial neupogen injections put her counts in the stratosphere... but when the injections stopped, her counts came down pretty quickly, and she got another injection for a boost the day before we discharged. So... we're going to limit exposure to the public (no walks around the mall, etc. for now) and keep a mask on for a while. Her marrow has still not kicked it into high gear.

So now... we have a follow up on Thursday... and may be getting weekly injections to keep counts up until her marrow has a chance to recover more fully. She also has a boatload of pills to take for the next month to try and keep those bad bugs knocked down. And after such an extended stay in the hospital, Rhonda is pretty weak… so we will be working on building strength. It will be a process…

We praise the Lord for bringing us through such a time… and finally back home again. Some of the nurses and staff really connected with us and were touched by our story and our commitment to be together through it all.

And thank you all… again… for your prayers, support, and encouragement. Our hearts are strengthened by your love and concern. We know many of you also have sickness and/or heartache in your own lives… and our prayers will continue for you and yours too.

God is great and His goodness knows no end. We often do not understand His ways… or timing… but regardless, we choose to put our trust in Him!

God Bless!
Scott and Rhonda

Responses

Pamela D
Thanks for keeping us updated and know I'm praying for all of you.

Terry C

Thank you Scott and we love you both. You are in our hearts, our prayers, and our thoughts. Thank you for your strength and faith through this journey. God protect and bless you both.

In Christ's Love

Mel and Mella S

We are so glad you are home... again. May this "home visit" be a longer healthier one. Thank you for keeping us up to date. You and yours are in our prayers always.

Jan D

I am so glad to hear that she's home—actually, that you're both home... Good news!!

Sylvia A

Hi Scott and Rhonda so glad to hear you're home. Praying Rhonda gains strength soon to enjoy the upcoming holidays with family. Being surrounded by your family is the only gift one needs.

My mother's health is declining quickly and we have placed it in God's hands. It's hard to understand but as you state we have to put our trust in God.

Bless you both, try to get lots of sleep now.

Mike M

We continue to pray for your family on this most difficult journey.

Very much looking forward to seeing you guys.

Please give Rhonda a hug for me.

Bobbie O

So thankful she is home. Will continue praying for you all. Know you both are thrilled to be back home. Love you all.

Nita S

Yeah, Hallelujah, Praise the Lord, Amen!

Jane B

I am praying especially for you all today!
With love

Donna C

Such awesome news that you both are home! I pray that Rhonda will continue to heal, get well, regain strength and both of you get uninterrupted rest. Stay close to home so ya'll don't catch any nasty bugs for this time of the season. No setbacks allowed!

May your home be your protection with God's hand and love.

I'm not for sure if I had mentioned this, but I think I have, that I forward your emails to my dad as he is so tenderhearted and loves the way you both are so strong in this situation. I still forward your emails to my sister Debbie, for encouragement in her battle...

Nov 20
My Rhonda—Another Fever

Hi there...

Well... this time we got to stay home for 3 nights... until the fever came again. It kept her in bed all day Wednesday, but then the fever broke overnight... PTL! We went to our scheduled appt this morning with Rhonda still very weak... but alert and able to get around a bit... and her blood pressure was low... low enough to have the dr put her back into the hospital and contact the scope dr make another attempt at getting the biliary drain in… to keep the fevers away.

So… here we are… back on the 7th floor in the transplant unit… with Rhonda getting loaded with fluids and antibiotics… yet again. The good news is that her other counts were not laid low by the fever this time… that they are even better than when she was discharged on Monday… PTL for that!

So… we're hoping that the scope thing happens in the next couple of days… and maybe we can still be home for Thanksgiving. We kinda begged the dr to not put us back in… but he was concerned that the Rx antibiotic did not keep the fever from coming on, and he wants to see if the scope dr can work some magic and get this taken care of once and for all.

So… we're sorry to deflate the joy that many of you shared with us about being home… but we're not there to stay… yet. And we thank you, once again, for your prayers on Rhonda's behalf. Our Lord has a plan… and this hospital stuff will come to an end in His perfect timing. He will continue to be our Strength to see this through to the other side, and one day this WILL all be behind us.

Thank you and God Bless..
Scott and Rhonda

Responses

Sylvia A

Keeping you always in constant prayer.
((Hugs))

Quinn W

Scott, so sorry to hear this. Still in prayer…

Mike M

Continued prayers for Rhonda's full recovery.

Jan R

God will carry you on eagle's wings to that sweet place of complete healing! We hold you close in our prayers.

Denise A

So sorry to hear this Scott. You are both in our daily prayers as you know :) Wish we could help you. Thank you for the updates as the kids are always asking us how Ms. Rhonda is.

Greg G

Praying for strength and the ability to wait on the Lord. Man, I know it's tough. Hang in there.

Cathy G

Thank you so much for keeping us all updated regularly and sharing your heart and story as you walk through these difficult and trying days. We rejoice with you both for the praise reports and thank God for giving you good news to encourage you. We continue to keep you in our prayers.

Donna C

Gee whiz!

I just prayed that the doctor in charge will get what needs to be tweaked to get Rhonda and all medical issues taken care of and back where she needs to be, at home gaining strength each day. We want you to be home for Thanksgiving!

Tell Rhonda, Vic and I said hi. She is always on the Gideon prayer requests that we send out and are mentioned in the Garland Camp Gideon meetings.

God Bless - love in Christ

Jane B

Thank you for keeping us informed. We are thankful to be a part of your prayer army and are trusting for strength and healing.

With love

Nov 22
Post from Stefanie—Ups and Downs

After 24 consecutive days living in the hospital (this time), Mom and Scott returned home on the 18th! They couldn't release her until she was consistently fever free and had those numbers back up, Mom got another injection before she was discharged to help keep her neutrophil count up, and they need to limit her exposure to germs, so she won't be out much and wherever she does go, she'll have to wear a mask.

So that was good for a couple days, but after three nights, the fever came back. Mom stayed in bed all day Wednesday and the fever broke. The fever didn't wipe out her numbers; they're even higher than they were when she was discharged! Mom had a doctor's appointment Thursday morning, and her blood pressure was low, so the docs admitted her.

The doctor is going to try again with the scope to put in a biliary drain in order to keep fevers away, and Mom and Scott are hopeful that it will be really soon and Mom'll be healthy enough to return home before Thanksgiving.

Pray:

1.   That the drain would work without any problems.
2.   That the fevers would stay away—for real this time.
3.   That Mom and Scott could be home in time for Thanksgiving (and stay home).

Responses

Marie L

Prayerful thoughts that Rhonda will be fever free and with Scott can share Thanksgiving at home and remain there. Prayers extended to the family as you continue to support one another. May the love of our Heavenly Father continue to be a source of strength and guide you to the good health you deserve. Keep the faith my friend. Your Aussie friend.

Amy G

Scott and Rhonda, prayers continue for you. You are true warriors fighting on the front lines. Your faith and trust in The Lord is beautiful and inspiring. And I know it is what sustains you. Love and hugs to you both!

Lourdes H

Stephanie, thank you so much for the updates. I know this journey must be frustrating. It seems that you guys take three steps forward and two steps back. I am happy to see that the trend is that she is getting healthier. We all wish it could be faster but I am still thankful that the trend is going in a positive direction. We will be praying. All the very best for your mom, you, and the rest of your sweet family.

Nov 23
My Rhonda—Procedure Done

Hi,

After a long day of waiting, Rhonda finally had the procedure to install the biliary drain/stent yesterday evening. The doctor said that everything went great and, with wonderful pain meds, she had a comfortable night and is doing well today.

So… now we wait and see if it's done the trick.

After a recovery period, we're praying that the fevers/pain from surgery 5 years ago are… no more. We're praying that these fevers that have delayed and prolonged her transplant recovery… are gone. We're praying… and looking forward to… getting back home in a few days to get back to our lives and to the building of strength… if our Lord is willing and it is in His timing for us.

Thank you for your love and prayers on our behalf!

God Bless,
Scott and Rhonda

Responses

Terry C
Father, we are in agreement with Scott and Rhonda's prayers. We ask that out of your mercy you will answer these prayers. We look forward to the restoration that you will bring. We ask that you strengthen both Scott and Rhonda. Father, may you touch Rhonda's

body and bring healing and strength to her. We give you the Glory for what you have already done and will do.

I ask this in the powerful name of Jesus!

Julius R

Praise the Lord... for He is good and cares for His flock.

Pam D

We are praying that this does the trick finally!

Mike M

All things are possible with our GREAT GOD

Lila C

I am sending Rhonda a hug and I think about you both so so often. This will help her, I pray. I pray she is eating and drinking more and feels like doing so.

I love you both dearly,

Standing

Bobbie O

Thanks for the update. Pray this will keep those fevers away. Know you are both anxious to get home.

Nov 25
My Rhonda—We Give Thanks

Hi,

Just wanted to get you all an update for you before the holiday weekend...

Rhonda is still recovering from the Interventional Radiology procedure on Saturday and it is most likely that we won't be going home any time before late weekend or next week. The actual installation of the drain had much more impact than the 'lookaround' procedure they did the first time around and the need for strong pain meds has been pretty steady.

In our chat with the dr this morning, he wants to be satisfied that the fevers are not trying to come back... and he wants Rhonda on oral antibiotics for at least 72 hours before we leave for home. That tells us that home by Thanksgiving is not possible. We are disappointed... but we also want to do the right thing... and not find ourselves coming back again after just a few days at home... we want to be able to stay there.

But we are thankful for so much that our Lord has blessed us with... our kids and family... incredible friends... jobs and homes for all of us... and yes... our health. I'm amazed at how much Rhonda has been able to withstand these last several months... I'm so proud of her! And we don't have to look far (esp in a hospital) to see others in circumstances the same... and much worse... than ours. We feel that we've received "world-class" care here... and our insurance has been a huge blessing... and the support of my mgrs and co-workers that enables me to be with Rhonda 24x7... and I could go on and on...

God is good... His Grace is amazing... His Faithfulness is unwavering... His Love knows no end.

Yes... we are so Thankful for what God has given us... and brought us through.

And we pray for you… that your travels over the holiday will be safe… and that you'll bask in the goodness and thankfulness of sharing the time with those you love. Me and my Rhonda… we'll be together too. :)

May God Bless you and keep you… and may He cause His face to shine upon you.

Thank you for blessing our hearts,
Scott and Rhonda

Responses

Patti S

You bless our hearts and we will count your friendship as one of our blessings this thanksgiving and always… prayers always for the two whose testimony strengthens us all. We love you

Peggy A

Do you need anything? What kind of a Thanksgiving are you going to have? Will the kids bring special food? Let me know if I can help in any way.

Sylvia A

Wishing you and Rhonda many blessings this Thanksgiving.

Pam D

Sorry to hear she won't be home for Thanksgiving and am praying that this last procedure puts an end to the fevers. We all signed a card for her last week. We are thinking about both of you.

Bobbie O

Thank you so much for the update. Sorry you won't be able to come home for Thanksgiving but what a wonderful Day of Thanks when she can come home. Love you all.

Jim F

Scott, thanks for keeping us informed. Your emails are always so uplifting. I am very thankful for your friendship and look forward to the day when we can enjoy fellowship a little more freely.

Nov 29
Stefanie's post—Thankful

Give thanks in all circumstances; for this is the will of God in Christ Jesus for you. 1 Thessalonians 5:18

This holiday season, we are thankful for many things.

We are thankful that Mom is getting better. It's moving slower than we've hoped, but her fevers have stayed away for longer now, most of her numbers are up and staying up. The whole family met Mom in the hospital on Thanksgiving Day and Mom was able to sit up in her wheelchair for over an hour before she started drooping. We left when she became visibly tired, but an hour and fifteen minutes out of bed is a sign of major improvement, and we are thankful. The hour we did have was enjoyed by all as we watched Mom's favorite grandchild run around and squeeze into awkward nooks in the waiting room. It's been a long time since the whole family had gotten together, so we are thankful for the reunion and the time to catch up on each other's lives.

We are also thankful—VERY thankful—that Mom is in remission! That's right: Remission. After having slow-growing lymphoma for the last five years, this latest round of chemo did a major Ninja-kick to the cancer and it is gone! With all the neutrophils and fevers and platelets going up and down, my parents neglected to tell me that Mom was officially cancer free a month or so ago. (Thanks, guys!) We are always thankful for good news, and we are thankful that remission means that once the fevers, blood pressure, blood counts, etc, have all stabilized, everything will be moving uphill again. *Hopefully* we won't have any more hospital visits or bad news for another five years or more!

We are thankful for Scott, and for his employer and co-workers, who allow him to work from the hospital on a daily basis. When Mom is in the hospital, Scott lives in the hospital room. There is a couch/bed in the room where he sleeps, and the refrigerator and wifi allow him to eat and work. We are thankful that Scott is not only able to be with Mom every day, but chooses to spend every day with her. Whether at the house or in the hospital, Scott makes sure Mom is taken care of.

We are thankful that Charlie is moving forward in his education. He'll be transferring to a four-year program in the Spring, bringing him closer to career options and doing what he loves. We're thankful that he has a steady job that will contribute to his educational expenses and will graduate with minimal student loan debt. We are thankful that his work schedule allows him the time to be a full-time student.

We are thankful that Julie has her own apartment and has the opportunity to work on her writing projects. We're thankful my step-brothers are moving forward in their jobs and that both families will be expanding soon.

We are thankful my job situation is improving and that my proximity to being debt free gets closer every month.

We are thankful for every single family member, friend, friend of a friend, and complete stranger who has prayed over us, for Mom's healing, for our family as we've worked through all of this, for the doctor's hands and plans, and for every step of Mom's healing process. Thank you for joining us in this process. Thank you for your petitions and prayers during the low times, and thank you for celebrating the victories and praising God with us during the high times.

Finally, the last I heard, Mom should be returning home at the beginning of the next week. I'll update you again when the day gets closer and we know for sure if she will be ready and able to return home. When she does return home, we will continue to celebrate God's Greatness and our Thankfulness with all of you.

And let the peace of Christ rule in your hearts, to which indeed you were called in one body. And be thankful. Let the word of Christ dwell in you richly, teaching and admonishing one another in all wisdom, singing psalms and hymns and spiritual songs, with thankfulness in your hearts to God. And whatever you do, in word or deed, do everything in the name of the Lord Jesus, giving thanks to God the Father through Him. Colossians 3:15–17

Responses

Lourdes H

Thanks Stephanie for the update. So happy to hear of all the good things in your lives. Even happier to see how firmly your family is grounded by faith. Give your mom a big hug from us!

Mary B

Praise His holy name for this wonderful testimony and news. Thank you for letting us be involved in the praying for Rhonda and for all of you. So thankful that Rhonda is cancer free and that she will be able to go home soon. Blessings abound in the midst of difficult times—God is so good!

Marie L

What an inspirational piece of writing. It is indeed an honour to read and to share in the strong faith which radiates from your family. I am thrilled that Rhonda is improving and is in remission from the cancer. Faith in Jesus definitely works wonders. May Jesus Christ who dwells in each of us and who is never far continue working in the most beautiful and comforting way He has already. God bless each and every one of the family and Scott you are precious.

Amy G

Amazing! Rejoicing with you with what God has done! What a blessing to read this post tonight! God is Good!!!

Wanda J

So appreciate the update and many more prayers sent and lots of love.

Mom and Dad J.

Sandy L

PRAISE THE LORD!!!!!! This is the best thing I have heard and a HUGE answer to my prayers!!!

LOVE to ALL of you

Vicky S

So thankful for the news! We praise God for all the blessings he is bestowing on your family, and rejoice with all of you!

Dec 5
My Rhonda—Home

Yes… we are home.

After another 2 weeks in the hospital, Rhonda was discharged yesterday. We so thankfully collapsed into our incredibly comfortable bed last night and conked out… with Rhonda sleeping almost until noon.

We came home with another bagful of meds… incl 3 different antibiotics… those drs are determined to do their best to keep the fevers away. It has been about 10 days since she last ran fever… and we're praying that there will be no more. We have a follow up with our dr next Tuesday… and will have an appt with the IR (interventional radiology) dr in a couple of weeks so they can check on the drain.

So for now… it is a time to rest… to slowly build strength and endurance… and get ourselves acclimated back to home life. We gratefully look forward to it!

Thank you for continual prayers and support. You all are one of God's greatest blessings to us!

Please take care and God Bless,
Scott and Rhonda

Responses

Lila C

Hi, Terry told me you were at home! We are so happy for you. You are both precious, so so precious! Please let us know if you need something PLEASE!!!

With great love

Jan D

Nothing like "Home Sweet Home"… Good news to hear…

Patti S

God bless you both… praying for rest, peace, comfort, restoration.

Bobbie O

Praise the Lord!!!! So thankful she is home. Pray the fevers stay away and you both get some badly needed rest.

Peggy A

Glad to hear you are home. Prayers for continued healing.

Myra P

PTL!

We are happy to know that Rhonda is doing well and back home.

We will continue to pray for Rhonda and your family.
God bless

Terry W

Glad to hear you are home in your own bed and that in itself shows how strong you are and how love, family, friends and faith helped. may your recovery to your full strength be just around the corner. God bless you all and special hugs go to Scott and Stephanie. welcome back Rhonda

Marie L

Absolutely thrilled to hear you are home, Rhonda. It is a very gradual process and you are doing wonderfully well. Keep in touch with your inner tortoise. Remember slow and steady wins the "race." Will keep you in my thought and prayers. God bless you and your family.

Susan H

This is great news. I can only imagine how wonderful it feels for you to sleep in your own bed. It sounds like you are getting much needed rest. Take it easy, don't push it too hard. Make it a slow easy climb back to recovery.

God bless you and your family

Dec 18
My Rhonda—What a Week

Hello,

Well… the good news is that we are still at home… PTL! However… my poor Rhonda has really been put through the ringer this past week or so…

Our first follow-up after being discharged was on Tuesday, 12/9. And in another case of "déjà vu all over again"… Rhonda fevered the night before. So the biliary drain didn't keep fever away… and the huge doses of oral antibiotics didn't keep the fever away… mercy.

But… the fever was completely gone by the time our afternoon appt took place… and her counts were good (PTL!)… so the dr made us a deal. He would not put her in the hospital, but if she fevered again, he wanted to put her back on IV antibiotics. He had us make an appt for Friday the 12th with his PA to see how she was doing.

So guess what… the night before the appt, she fevered again. So… they started her on the IV meds for 7 days. In order to stay out of the hospital, we've been going to the clinic every day since the 12th.. just finishing up today. Exhausting. There were times I wondered if we'd been better off going back into the hospital for it.

Also… yesterday she had her follow-up with the IR (Interventional Radiology) dr to check the drain… and they finally figured out that, yes, that was a stricture (narrowing) that needed some help. This is what the GI dr told them 2 months… and 3 procedures… ago. So… in January sometime, Rhonda will have a procedure where the IR dr and the GI dr will collaborate and each do their part to finally get a stent or balloon to fix this in a more permanent way. In the meantime, Rhonda is in pain from the procedure to check the drain yesterday, and still has the drain to deal with for the next month or so.

All this has been a chore to work through for her… for me… but… we are home… and very much looking forward to enjoying a brief, yet wonderful, time of Christmas celebration with our kids next week. The strength just isn't there for much people interaction time just yet.

This whole thing has been a challenge from the start... and things seem to keep happening to prevent Rhonda from being able to move forward much... but our Lord has brought us through it all and we are looking forward to a special holiday time and a new year that we hope will mark the beginning of a march towards more strength and health... and fewer dr visits... and NO hospital stays.

We pray that you all will enjoy the holidays too. The season is so special to us.

Thank you again for your prayers, love, and support. May God Bless you and your families in a very special way this season!

Love always,
Scott and Rhonda

Responses

Mike M
Hey Scott
Is there anything I can help you with? Please let me know.
We love and pray for your family.
Please give Rhonda a hug for me.

Patti S
You are always in my prayers, Scott... your love for each other makes my heart rejoice. We love you forever... Merry Christmas.

Trish M

Scott, just want you to know I've been waiting on every update you send and praying for you guys daily. I can't believe all Rhonda and you have had to endure. But yet you don't question anything and handle it all with grace as you guys have always done. I know you appreciate all time together and hope you'll be able to enjoy time with the family over the holidays. I'm praying for a much much better new year for you guys. Sending hugs.

Denise A

So sorry Scott you guys are having to go through all this. Our thoughts and prayers are with you both as always! Merry Christmas!!!!

Bobbie O

So sorry she has had such a hard time. I remember when Gary went through his second cancer and all they said might happen after his forty rounds of radiation did and then some. He still doesn't have the endurance he once had. I told you all that to say HOLD ON. God loves you and many others love you too. We are praying every day and will continue to do so. Give my precious friend a hug for me and tell her I love her. Merry Christmas.

Dec 21
My Rhonda—Here We Go Again

Hello,

Yes… we are back in the hospital.

Rhonda started fevering again in the wee hours this morning. It did spike pretty high, but my real concern was a high level of pain around her biliary drain that would not go away with our pain meds.

It made me suspect an infection… and so a trip to the oncology triage assessment center at 5:30 this morning.

Her counts and vitals kinda jumped around for a while after we got here, and they ended up putting her in ICU when they couldn't get her blood pressure to come up. The good news is that her bp is up by 20 points or more… and that this is a different ICU that will allow me to stay with her 24x7… PTL times 2!

They don't have a definite answer for the fever (which is now gone… PTL #3!)… but they suspect either the biliary drain… or her picc line… so they will replace her picc line tomorrow and wait to see what the biliary drs have to say.

So here we are again. We would surely like to be home for Christmas… but it is nowhere near a given at this point.

Thank you so much for your continued prayers! Sometimes, I hesitate putting out another update because we've been going back and forth between steps 3–5 to get past this… and I hate to continue to burden others with our troubles. We know that we all have troubles at times… and we do our best to pray for those who are also beset by hard times. We are being constantly reminded that some troubles are longer lasting than others…

We will continue to wait on God to lead us through… and past… this… praying that it will happen… in His time to fulfill His purpose.

I will send out another note when we know more… but if it's not in the next couple of days… please have a wonderful Christmas celebration with your loved ones!

God Bless!
Scott and Rhonda

Responses

Pamela D

Scott, thank you so much for the updates! Even if it's six times a day!! We can always look at the updates when it's convenient or not at all. But I for one want to know how to pray specifically for all of you.

Melinda H

Hey Scott and Rhonda! It's always good to hear from you and get an update. We continue to pray for ya'll. May God pour out his blessings upon you during these difficult days! He's in control. A song comes to mind Fear not tomorrow, God is already there, He's charting the course you'll take, He sees each hidden snare, He's waiting to guide you, thru each burden and care, Fear not tomorrow God is already there.

We wish you a Merry Christmas!

Patti S

Dear ones we love you and would really covet the updates... They keep us close to all in heart and soul... praying praying praying... and no matter where you are on Christmas I know you will feel the love of Jesus always

Usha A

My best wishes and prayers for you and Rhonda.. Hope and pray that you will spend a quiet Christmas at home.

Maw-in-law

Ty Scott for all the updates. We all need to know when these things happen so we can pray in the right direction. Your problems are our problems. We're in this together. Love you both so much and hope you're home for Christmas

Jan R

We are so grateful that you faithfully continue to share your journey with us! it shows us how to pray specifically for you & how The Lord is answering our prayers. Your emails reveal your deep faith in our Lord & His sovereignty & control over everything that happens in your life. And that testimony has been a great witness to me & Julius! Thank you again for sharing! We will be praying for healing & that you can be home for Christmas!

Blessings

Lila C

I beg you "not" to ever having feelings that you could burden us with any news, IT'S WHAT WE WAIT FOR, we don't love only during the easy times, these valleys make us stronger and even though our love is already great for you, its greater because of these hard times, I mean to say we suffer when you do and we have joy when you have joy, like the Thanksgiving picture. I am so very sorry this is horrible exhausting suffering. I am watching my sister and aunt suffer and the pain just makes me love them more. I suppose pain is love as He loved us with pain and suffering on the cross. If I can come please just say the word. Scott I love you and Rhonda. PLEASE keep me posted, please.

Standing

Lupita O

Scott and Rhonda, no matter where you are going to be for Christmas, what is count you are going to be together, and we are praying for you, and GOD is always with you, no matter where you are.

We love you all.

Sylvia A

Hi Scott, so sorry to hear Rhonda's back in the hospital. But I'm glad you're wise enough to know when it's time to head back so she can get the care she needs to get better soon.

Yes you're right we are all beset with hard times and put to test our faith as well. But we all know that nothing is impossible with Christ, and we place our prayers and faith in His hands.

Please tell Rhonda I said merry Christmas, and the same to you as well.

God Bless

Donna C

So sorry that ya'll are back at the hospital! I pray that the doctors get it right. I pray that the doctors seek wisdom from God so Rhonda doesn't have to keep going thru this and You! What a wear and tear on nerves. May stress stay away from you both and pray that soon Rhonda will be in your own home, NO MORE HOSPITALS!

Tell her hi for us and we miss you both!

Mike M

Hey Scott

Do not for one second think you are burdening us with news about our precious Rhonda.

We all love and care deeply for you and your family and are saddened by these circumstances.

My continued prayer to the Lord is for a full recovery for Rhonda and strength for your family.

You are the most fantastic husband and father and the way you have handled the situation is truly remarkable. We all take encouragement from you.

I deeply respect you as a friend and brother in Christ.

We love you. Hang in there. We are all praying for you and Rhonda.

Deb M

Please keep sending updates. I think of you every day.

Jim F

Scott, I am so sorry to learn of this apparent setback but, as always, am greatly inspired by your love, joy, peace, patience, kindness, goodness, faithfulness, gentleness, and self-control -- all fruit of the Holy Spirit in your life!

Thanks for keeping us informed.

Judy R

Hey Scott, excuse me but we care how you and Rhonda are doing. Please keep sending messages!

Fingers crossed, thoughts and prayers, you'll be home for Christmas. :)

Peggy A

Sending love…

Bobbie O

Please never feel like a burden. Moses needed Hur and Aaron to hold up his arms when he got tired when in battle. All of us want to be your Hur and Aarons. Gary and I couldn't have made it without them. We all want to be a part of this hard time in your life. Most of us have been there. Give her a big hug for me.

Nita S

Please, please, please. Your news is not a burden. It is our privilege to pray and support you. This way, we know exactly how to pray and be specific. And we do pray that the source of the fever can be identified and treated effectively. If there is ANYTHING else we can do, please let us know.

Love to you both

Dec 21
post from Stefanie—Déjà Vu

Mom had a fever again, so she's been going to the clinic every day for an IV with antibiotics. They've been very happy to not have to be in the hospital.

BUT last night mom had another fever with strong abdominal pain. The doctors suspect an infection where her biliary drain is. We've been here before, haven't we? Her blood pressure is low (again) and she's in the ICU (again). Scott said that she's stable, but the doctors want to be careful. We like careful, but we also like being healthy at home.

If we haven't hit 100 days in the hospital yet, we will this week. Christmas is in four days, so I'm not sure what this means for our family's Christmas this year. After 100 days, including Thanksgiving, in the hospital, I know none of us wants Mom to have to spend Christmas in the hospital as well. Our prayer this week is that Mom can spend Christmas (and the rest of the year, and all of 2015) at home, healing, recovering, and strengthening.

Responses

Dirk B

I am at a loss for word. My heart aches for you all and I have no way to help. All I know is God sits on the throne and that He is love. For God sooooo loved the world…

Romans 8:26—In the same way the Spirit also helps our weakness; for we do not know how to pray as we should, but the Spirit Himself intercedes for us with groanings too deep for words; and He who searches the hearts knows what the mind of the Spirit is, because He intercedes for the saints according to the will of God.

Debbie B

Let's all lift this request up to the Father.

Father we come to you to lift up a friend in need of your touch. Father you are already touching Rhonda—you are with her daily and we thank you for your strength and touch that you have already bestowed to your precious one. But for her and for her family we are asking for a special Christmas Blessing—would you grant Stephanie's request that Rhonda could spend Christmas at home and the family together. We ask this in the precious name of Jesus. And we thank you.

Amen

Lourdes H

Sweet Rhonda, many sincere and thoughtful prayers are being said at our home for you and your family. Hang in there, Tiger. I know this is enough to try the patience of any normal person. Luckily, you are an extraordinary person. Big big hugs

Peggy A

So sorry to hear you are in the hospital again. I hope they can get the fever/infection remedied so you can be home for Christmas.

Sending prayers.

Merlene

Prayers are coming your way, Rhonda. I know that your faith and strength have gotten you this far and will continue. Love you

Dec 22
My Rhonda—A Better Day

Hi,

Just a quick note to let you all know that Rhonda's fever is gone and her vitals are good and stable... so they moved us out of ICU and back into the cancer hospital. PTL!

The drs are still assessing and figuring out a game plan. The picc line replacement ran into a wall when her veins went into hiding when approached by a sharp object (a part of her history)... so other options are being discussed. Until we know the dr's plan, we won't know how long this hospitalization will last...

And thanks so much for the many who responded about our updates... your words of support were truly uplifting to our hearts today. :)

I will let you know when the docs know what their plan is...

God Bless
Scott and Rhonda

Responses

Denise A

PTL!!!!!!!!!! Thank you for the updates, know we are all praying for both of you! We love you! Merry Christmas!!!!!!

Peggy A

Home for Christmas… I hope!

Sally T

Glad she's out of the ICU, hope they get you home soon and this is the last stay.

Take care of both of you. I told Rhonda I expect you here for Thanksgiving next year.

Cathy G

We are praying regularly for you both. Thank you for continuing to send updates to us all.

We will check in with you all tomorrow.

Love and prayers

Greg G

Man

I'm getting your updates and Cathy and I are praying for you and Rhonda. I know this is probably the ultimate test any of us could ever face so we are praying for peace, discernment, supernatural patience and strength, and joy in the midst of it all. Hang in there Scott.

There is a purpose in this. Stay the course brother.

D'Ann C

Praying for Christmas Blessings for you all!

Lila C

Hi, Scott thank you for the update, I hope you can feel how we are in thought and prayer for you both.

Please keep us posted as best possible. This is the hardest. I know your faith is strong and yet I weep for this pain for you both. You are our precious and our dear dear friends. Father please heal Rhonda…

I love you so

Jan R

Praise God for His grace & mercy!

Bobbie O

Hope you hear the plan soon. Pray she continues to improve quickly. Thank you again for keeping us in the loop.

Dec 24
My Rhonda—Procedure

Hi,

We were just surprised by our scope dr stopping by to tell us that the IR team is going to do a procedure this afternoon to try and stretch out the biliary stricture and see if that solves Rhonda's fevers.

So… please offer up a prayer that all goes smoothly for Rhonda and that this time we will have the results we are needing… no more fevers!

Thanks and God Bless!

Scott and Rhonda

Responses

Maw-in-law
ty, Scott for that information. We definitely will be in prayer.
Give her our love
Mom & Dad

Lila C
I now know why my mind was "just" about you and Rhonda this morning. We are "stopping" to pray "together" now. I love you both so very much.

Lupita O
Scott I just pray for you and drs that GOD, bless them with wisdom to help Rhonda, and hoping this would be the last time for you in the hospital.

Lynn B
Wishing you the best with the procedure.

Clifton W
Praying. Rejoice in the birth of Jesus!

Sally T
Prayers

Terry C
Lila and I have prayed and will continue to do so.
Love you guys.

Suraya K
I am praying that all goes well for Rhonda today

Cathy G

> We are praying, Scott. Thank you for the update.
> Love and prayers

Peggy A

> Sending prayers and healing.

Donna C

> Thank you Scott for updating all of us!
> Just prayed for a mighty outcome, that this is the answer to get Rhonda healed.
> Thank You, Jesus for always being with us no matter what. Rhonda needs healing, strength. Please be with Scott and family as they also need strength to help Rhonda. Please give everyone comfort, knowing that this procedure is what it takes to get Rhonda healed. AMEN!
> God Bless

Julius R

> Will do. Praying now.

Nita S

> You got it!

Bobbie O

> Will be praying for you all. Pray this will help. Let us know.

Sylvia A

> Just left Christmas Mass and offered a prayer for Rhonda's healing.
> Merry Christmas.

Dec 24
My Rhonda—Recovering

Hello and Merry Christmas!

The procedure went smoothly and quickly (please pray that the pain will subside quickly too). They used a balloon to stretch the narrow part and inserted a larger drain. So now we wait and see if any fevers come on after we go home... not sure when that will be. Maybe next week sometime.

Thank you for the amazing prayers, love, and support... and have a Blessed Holy-day with your loved ones. All of our kids are planning to come and see us tomorrow... what a blessing that will be!

Love you... God Bless...
Scott and Rhonda

Responses

D'Ann C
Good news! Praying. Merry Christmas!

Maw-in-law
We hope we can hear from you tomorrow if you guys are able. We won't be having our Christmas until tomorrow.
Merry Christmas.
Love you all so much,
Mom & Dad

Jan R

Merry Christmas, Sweet Friends! We really miss seeing you as well! When you are up to a visit, let us know! Still enjoying our new grand baby in San Antonio!

We pray for Many blessings to be showered on you both!

Lila C

Just got home 1223, very tired, but went right to my computer to see if you had updated us. Thank you with all my heart. We are praying this will be the relief, that ends these horrible fevers and what comes with them. I will going to bed and praying for Rhonda's pain and continued healing. How are her blood counts post bone marrow transplant? I am so happy you will see family, for Christmas. Pictures if you can and want please? We love you!!! so so much. Thank you again for the update. I am so sorry you are still in this, but it's going to clear the way for remaining at home and healing. Rhonda's suffering is not understood… tonight at their church was a huge stain glass of Jesus in the garden of Gethsemane, I do know He knew we would suffer and oh how He loved us, on his knees in prayer, in pain, bleeding, His precious blood shed for "us".

Great love to you on this Holy Day and every day and minute

Cathy G

Merry Christmas, Rhonda and Scott! We spent time in prayer this morning for you. We hope you have a peaceful day with your family and That God will bring relief from pain along with healing to Rhonda.

Love and prayers

Greg G

Merry Christmas to you both.

Bobbie O

Merry Christmas to you all as well. Pray this will solve her problems with the fevers. Hope you all will be able to come home soon.

Patti S

Merry Christmas Scott and Rhonda!

Pam D

You both are in my prayers.

Donna C

Hope things are looking up today! Still praying for healing and no more fevers!

Please let us know if we can help in any way.

Love and God Bless

Dec 31
My Rhonda—Looking Forward to the New Year

Hello and Happy New Year!

Rhonda's time of rest and recovery has been moving along… and today we got word that she will be discharged on Friday, January 2… we are ready… and PTL!

The discomfort from the drain thing is under control (thank you Lord!). The drs want her here for 2 more days so she can complete the IV antibiotics regimen… and we will be sent home with no rx antibiotics to take… another PTL!

So… 2014 is coming to an end… and we look forward to a much better 2015. We know that we will still have clinic visits, scans, and finishing up (and removing) the drain thing… but we pray that the fevers and hospital stays will be over as we move past all this… and look forward to building strength… esp for our anniversary trip at the end of April. :)

Please have a safe and fun new year's celebration… and thank you again for your support and prayers to help strengthen us for this long journey. We've needed every bit of it.

May God Bless you and yours in the coming year… 2015…
Scott and Rhonda

Responses

Myra P
     Happy New Year!
     We are very happy for all the great news that you are sharing with us. We will continue to pray for Rhonda's healing and recovery and for your whole family.
     God bless!

Cathy G
     Thank you so much for another update. Such encouraging news!! We have been thinking of and praying for you both this past week. We look forward to seeing you soon.
     Happy New Year! May 2015 be FULL of God's richest blessings and healing.
     Love and prayers

Peggy A
     Happy New Year! Yay!!!

Sylvia A

And a very blessed New Year to Rhonda, you and your family.

Bobbie O

So thankful she is coming home. Wonderful news.

Patti S

Praise the Lord indeed… We love you all and Happy New Year!!!

Denise A

YEAH for going home!! Happy New Year!! Love and Prayers from us as always!!

Donna C

HAPPY NEW YEAR TO THE BOTH OF YOU!

Glad you both will get to go to your home tomorrow! yes! PRAISE THE LORD!!!

God Bless

Lynn B

Good news! I bet you both are looking forward to be back in your home again!

2015: The Difficult Path to a Final Solution

Jan 7, 2015
My Rhonda—Same Song… New Verse

Hello,

Several have asked so I wanted to send out the latest on my Rhonda. Our original discharge date of Jan. 2 was delayed by the on-call dr being very cautious when some counts changed that morning. It looked to be self-correcting by the next day, so we came home Saturday, the 3rd. :)

The first couple of days were up and down… and then here comes more fever and tummy pain last night. It always seems to happen the night before a follow-up appt. I had to give her such heavy doses of pain meds, it kinda threw her into a disoriented state where it was difficult to focus and function. :(I called the clinic to let them know what to expect when we came in… and they asked us to get there asap. I wasn't real hopeful we'd get to come home.

When we got there, we got the IV antibiotics and I asked if we could get those set up to administer at home. The drain thing seems to be a bacteria magnet… but we'll have it for another 4 weeks when it fully heals and can be taken out. But… the good thing is that her blood pressure stayed up during the fever, so the drs are more comfortable letting us stay at home. I'm hoping the home meds will work out… or else we'll need a permanent room at the hospital.

At the end of it all today… they did let us come home. PTL! But… we will be going to the clinic every day for the next few days (she did need a neupogen shot too due to the fever knocking down her neutrophils) so they can watch her counts… and then maybe set up the home IV meds for a while.

So… we are home tonight… and so relieved to be here! Thank you for your concern and prayers… for rejoicing in the little victories… and feeling the frustration of the setbacks. We know that our Loving Father hears our pleas… and He will continue to give us strength to weather it all until we come out in victory on the other side of this time of challenges.

Well, winter is definitely here. It's supposed to be 17 degrees in Dallas tonight… I had to cover the orange tree Rhonda's mom gave us. Please keep warm and safe in the extreme weather… and…

God Bless to all…
Scott and Rhonda

Responses

Usha A

My thoughts and prayers with you and Rhonda.

Cathy G

Thank you for yet another update. We continue to pray…… you both inspire Greg and me by your love and commitment to each other and to the Lord in spite of all you've been through. Rhonda, we pray that God will continue to give you strength and healing as you fight this disease. We love you both and look forward to seeing you when you are able.

Love and prayers

Terry and Lila C

My Lord. Our Lord. He knows. We don't. We do know he will continue to give you the strength you need to get to Rhonda's healing. Scott and Rhonda I don't know what to say, except I am so so sorry you both must suffer like this. I love you both and pray daily for you. I am happy you can have treatment at home, could they draw the blood too so Rhonda can stay out of this cold?? Please continue to keep us posted. We wait. We stand. We love. If we can do something please let us know.

Bobbie O

Glad she is home. That helps both of your spirits I know. Sorry she is having such a hard time. I remember how helpless I felt when Gary was struggling those two years and we would get over one thing and be fighting another. I remember quoting Ps. 4:1 alot. Hear my cries oh my righteous God. Give relief to my distress. Have mercy on me and hear my prayers. There was a song that came out during that time that God gave me as well. Somebody's praying me through. God is there, He cares and so do we. Give her my love.

Linda S

Thanks Scott for the update on Rhonda. Hope she is able to stay home where you both can relax in your own setting and that the drain heals very soon.

Suraya K

Hi Scott and Rhonda Thank you for the update you are always in my prayers.

Patti S

How are you all doing? Praying you have been able to stay at home and rest...

Jan 7
Stefanie's Caring Bridge post (Scott's update plus her comments)

I thought Scott's title to his update was very appropriate, so I stole it, and most of his update. :) We'll start with my narrative and end with his medical notes.

Mom went back into the hospital (as you read last time), and was there for Christmas, our post-Christmas cross time zone Skype with family, and New Year's. We got the whole family together for Christmas, in her room this time, and enjoyed family time, gift exchanges, and a rousing round of "The Twelve Days of Christmas". A smaller crew of us met again a few days later to Skype with Mom's side of the family, and Mom enjoyed getting to see everyone- especially the new addition to the family! Although I wasn't with Mom and Scott for New Year's, I'm sure they celebrated like the party animals they are! Fortunately, Mom was released a few days ago and has enjoyed the comforts of home. Mom had been on some super major pain killers (only administrable while she was monitored in the hospital), but had gotten well enough that she didn't need them anymore. Yea! Less pain and more home time!

And now for a medical message from the person who always knows what's going on (aka Scott —"Same Song" update; see above):

.

.

.

One set of numbers gets better, and another goes down. Mom's on the worst see-saw ever, so please keep praying for healing. Please keep praying for Mom's increased health and that she will soon be well enough to return home, and stay home, and be "normal" again. Well, normal doesn't mean so much in our family. Our dictionary doesn't exactly have that word. I think one of my aunts tore that word out of the thing years ago. But healthy would be nice. Pray for healthy, comfortable, healed, ambulatory, and mobile.

Thanks again for your prayers. We appreciate them all and trust that God will respond to them in His awesome way.

Responses

Vicky S

Praying without ceasing for all of you, confident that the Lord's will of complete recovery be done!

Marge B

Praying for you Rhonda! May the Lord bless you and keep you and your family in 2015!

Petra R

Stephanie: Thank you for taking the time to post an update on your mom. I'm so glad that your family was able to get together and celebrate Christmas in a festive manner. That must have really cheered up your mom. How fortunate modern technology allowed your mom to visit her family and visually see Sarah's newborn daughter. I can imagine the smile your mom wore after seeing her. Your family's resilience and strength really demonstrate the power of faith and prayer. I'm adding my prayers to the community prayer circle in hopes that your mom will soon feel some relief from this vicious cycle and experience steadfast progress toward health. I'll pray for your mom to gain strength each day, so she can soon be home on an ongoing basis. I also pray for your family that you take good care of yourselves while being your mom's caretaker. My prayers are with you

Barbara C

Rhonda I am lifting you up now in the Lord! Lord Please give Rhonda relief from the pain she is having and also let her not get discouraged! I pray that you know how much you are loved and that God is in control of each and every tiny little detail. We pray for complete healing and that all of this can be behind her! Lord you know every cell in her body and we ask right now to lay your hand on her and heal her in the name of Jesus! I thank you now for Rhonda's life, her family and her doctor's and the strength that she shows during all of this! Please let her be comfortable tonight and sleep the whole night thru while her body is healing!!!!

Merlene

Rhonda and family—I want you to know that you are ever on my mind and in my prayers. Please know that we are all concerned for your recovery and very glad that you have such a wonderful family support group. If there is anything at all that I can do, please let me know. I will come and stay with you if you want and do what I can.

Terry W

glad you are still hanging in there and pray that there are more up days than the downers… and that you have a wonderful support team with you… praying that soon there will be no down days… take care. God bless, and may you finally knock this out of the ring and get to be the winner that you deserve to be.

Jan 18
Prayer request from Scott to SS class

I also want to share about our Rhonda… just to you in our beloved SS class. We have continued to go to the clinic every day for

IV meds… and she has also continued to fever nearly every day. This morning we were hopeful because she had not fevered since Friday… but then this evening it came back. We are scheduled for more IV treatments the next 3 days, with an oncologist appt on Tuesday… but I think we're going to take tomorrow off. The meds are obviously not working when we've taken them for 12 consecutive days… and the daily trips to the clinic have further drained Rhonda's limited strength. So tomorrow we will rest and enjoy the holiday together… and then Tuesday we'll see if the dr has any more ideas of what we can do differently… even if we have to go back to the hospital for a time. Please pray with us that the dr will have the wisdom and insight to know which path to move to next.

We also want to discuss pain meds with him. The current med has not been effective and has made it almost impossible for Rhonda to have a mind clear enough to even log into her computer. After the drain procedure on Wednesday, the drs there gave her a new pain med that helped her to feel better than she has in weeks… and it lasted several hours… and with a more clear mind. We are asking our dr to consider moving her to this new med. Please pray that this may work out too.

This time has been very trying on our physical strength… and our faith. It seems like the prayers for help are not being heard. With our days being so caught up by just trying to help Rhonda be comfortable, it's been hard to maintain any time for spiritual things. We know that our hope is in Him… but much of the time we cannot feel His Presence in all of this. We would love to be able to come to church for fellowship and to be recharged… but we've been prevented by Rhonda's sickness and physical weakness.

We are so thankful for your constant prayers… and know that you are with us in spirit always… and look forward so much to seeing you again one day soon.

In His Love,
Scott

Responses

Lila C

Oh my, my precious friends… I have felt like our Rhonda was having a harder time and that you both must be beyond drained. I think about you all the time… Rhonda and Scott, I worked today and then went to church to hear Patti's son in law sing and music does minister greatly just when you think "how can we do this!" I don't know how you have been standing this strong… I can say the mountains and valleys are horrible, I am truly so sorry, we must just breathe and claim ourselves as a child of Jesus. I agree, take the day off, this is all way too much on you both. I pray this medication will come just as Rhonda needs it. Pain is never fair!! I am not able to have any right words, but the name of Jesus… Is there anything I can do?? I have wanted to hear from you so badly, time runs in together… things are a blur, but my heart and love for you both are so "clear" Thank you so much for being in touch.

Rhonda and Scott I am going to pray that you have a fresh touch, of His strength, I know it's so hard to be this strong every second when suffering to this extent for so long!!

Terry C

Scott, we are praying for both Rhonda and you. We will pray that God would intervene with the Doctors providing your care. That God will grant them wisdom and that they might look at all alternatives for what is causing the fevers. We will pray that God will help them determine different medications that might eliminate her fevers. We will also pray for relief from the pain and that the pain medication she had the other day would be available for her. We love you and can't imagine the suffering and struggles you are battling. I ask right now that God would fill you with His presence and that the Holy Spirit would lift you up. I also ask that Jesus intercede and that He would ask for you the care, love, lifting up and sustaining that you need. I ask that our High Priest would pray on your behalf for what we don't know or understand. I pray for His presence and that you can feel Him in this very moment.

Love you both so very much.

Your brother in Jesus

Patti S

Dearest Scott… We think of you always and you are in our fervent prayers.. how we miss you… is there anything we can do… Anything we will be there… We love you and pray for you to come out of the desert… you are our heroes

Donna C

You both are always in our thoughts and prayers. Praying that Rhonda will gain strength and that you both hold on to faith in Jesus.

Praying that Rhonda will be able to get the meds to fight off pain and fevers. For doctor's wisdom! Please Lord, heal Rhonda…

Lord, give them the comfort, rest and energy they need daily.

We miss you both!

Love and hugs

Jan 20
My Rhonda—Some Promising Changes

Hello,

I wanted to update you all on what's been happening, and some changes that we hope will lead to some true steps forward.

Today we were at the clinic for IV meds for the 13th time in the last 14 days. Yesterday, on the MLK holiday… we took the day off for some much needed rest. Rhonda has also continued to fever almost every day… they start up with chills in the evening or wee hours… and then fever peaks and they are gone within 6–8 hrs. These daily trips to the clinic, and daily fevers, have really drained her strength further.

We also met with our oncologist today. He has agreed to set us up for home IV meds asap. The only 2 days that Rhonda has not fevered in the last 2 wks was when she was able to get extra rest… one of those days being yesterday when we played 'hooky'. We managed to convince the dr that her body also needed more rest to keep the fevers away. He concurred. PTL! :)

Also, Rhonda had a check of her biliary drain last Wednesday. She was dreading it because she had always had lots of pain after these procedures. But this time, they tried a new pain drug… that not only kept her from pain, but also helped her to feel better than she had in weeks. After some nudging at the clinic the last few days, our dr wrote her a Rx for this med today. We are fixing to try the first dose tonight. The dosage may need to be tweaked, but we are looking for wonderful results.

So… we are hopeful that with fewer trips to the clinic (we hope that the home treatments are set up by the weekend)… and more time to rest… and a better handle on pain… that we are 'turning a corner' in this lengthy saga… and moving finally into a time of rest and strengthening.

This is what we are praying for… and we do so much appreciate your prayers as they join with our own. All this that Rhonda has suffered through has been at the hands of men… the treatments, the chemo, etc… but our Lord is the Great Physician… the Great Healer… all healing comes from His Grace.

This is what our Rhonda needs… this is what we pray for.

Thank you for your notes and messages of love and concern… for standing with us as we feel our way through this desert of weakness… carried only by His Strength… until we can get to that place of healing and strength… not for ourselves only… but strength to reach out to those around us. This, we know, is His desire for us…

I'll keep you posted on how the changes go… thank you!

Love and Blessings,
Scott and Rhonda

Responses

Lila C
Thank you for this update! I prayed for this medication for her, please let us know how much this helps her Scott. You both are a great part of our hearts and life and to hear anything is precious and

Rhonda's mind body and spirit are sacred and I am humbled to know about you both. PLEASE let me know if I can do something???

I love you both,

Standing

Jan and Julius R

Praise for promising changes! Thank you for faithfully emailing despite your own lack of rest! We will continue to pray for rest, strength, no pain, and complete healing. Your faith gives us courage & strengthens our faith! God has a plan - plans to give you hope & a future. God's grace & mercy are greater than anything we can imagine! We love you two & are covering you with our prayers.

Blessings

Patti S

Thanks so much for the update. This is encouraging and we pray for this time of rest and refreshment for you both… and an end to the fevers.

Mike M

We Love You Guys.

Terry C

Thank you Scott for this wonderful news. Praise God that you can get some well needed rest. Love you guys

Bobbie O

So thankful she is doing better. You always get more rest at home. Will keep praying for all of you and thank you so much for letting us know how she is doing. Give her a hug for me and when she is better and stronger would love to come down for a short visit.

Lupita O

I'm so, sorry this take soo long, and she keeping fighting with fever, but GOD, is holding both of you on his blessing hands, hoping pretty soon all this be beyond.

Jan 25
My Rhonda—Finally

Hi,

I just wanted to send a quick update…

As of this past Thursday, we are now administering Rhonda's IV meds at home… PTL!!! This includes the 2 we've been getting for the last 2 weeks at the clinic, and a 3rd anti-fungal that they started her on last Wednesday after a culture of her biliary fluid checked positive. We're hoping that this last med will be the silver bullet in taking out her fevers. She has fevered some since Thur, but much milder, low-grade temps… PTL!

Also, the drs doubled the new pain med dosage when we couldn't see any results with the first dosage… she's still not pain free… but we're getting closer. PTL!

So… now we don't have to be at the clinic until Tuesday… and should only have 1 or 2 visits per week… no more daily trips! PTL!!! So we can finally work on resting and strength-building… emphasis on resting.

Thank you for your continued prayers and support… we are finally moving forward… slowly… but definitely in the right direction…

Thank you Lord!

God Bless,
Scott and Rhonda

Responses

Cathy G

We are so grateful to hear both of these most-recent updates on Rhonda. Greg and I have been trying to figure out what we could do to help you all during these difficult days…

We are praying for you… have been, and still are. Please give our love to Rhonda.

Patti S

Wonderful news… we all wait for your reports. We love you.

Sandy L

Thank you so much for the update!

I know y'all are concentrating hard on getting Rhonda the rest she needs!

Please let me know if there is anything I can do to help.

Peggy A

Thinking of you always!

Sylvia A

Rhonda and Scott, one step at a time towards your April get away. God and the rest of us will be at the cheering line cheering you both on.

Have a blessed week!

Lila C

Thank you for the update. Scott it looks like the direction is right and I am happy you don't have to get Rhonda out. You both need rest so badly, I could see how exhausted you were, please let me know if I can bring any food that sounds good to you both please…

I love you both so much

Jan R

Thank you Lord!

Donna C

We are so glad and encouraged by this news about Rhonda. We continue to think about the both of you and pray.

Pam D

That is good news.

Greg G

That's great news Scott. Cathy and I are praying for you guys. Please let us know if there is anything we can do—meals, errands… etc.

Suraya K

Through God's Grace and Mercy Rhonda will get stronger and better soon. Praying for you

Denise A

PTL!! So happy to hear this news! Love and prayers for both of you!!

Bobbie O

So thankful she is doing better and now getting more rest. Pray she will get stronger each day and will not have the pain she has been fighting. Thank you for the update.

Pamela D

Yes, thank you, Lord, for your great grace to all of you, Scott and Rhonda. Still believing and praying for all of this!

Feb 1
My Rhonda—Corner Turned

Yes!

We had an appt on Friday to check Rhonda's labs… and her counts have started rebounding like crazy! Hematocrit up over 30%… platelets up 40%… etc… The nurse practitioner told us that this is what happens when there are no infections. Rhonda hasn't fevered for a week. It seems that we have finally "turned that corner"…

Let the healing begin! PTL!

We have both been exhausted… sleeping in when we can (without those daily appts)… napping… resting… recovering from those weeks and months in the hospital. Rhonda's strength still has a ways to go… but she has made great strides in the last week with her ability to focus mentally… and has even kicked off a few 'Words with Friends' games! That's my girl! PTL!

The initial orders for the home IV meds are due to expire this coming week… but I think they will most likely be extended. Our next appt is not until Thursday. :) We do still have this biliary drain thing that we hope can be removed soon. We hope to hear what those drs think this next week.

Yes... God has been Faithful and is bringing us back from the dark desert that we have been wandering in... slowly back to a life where our strength and energy are not consumed by battling through the sickness and pain and the constant attention of hospital staff... and into a time of recovery.

So now we will rest... and work to gain strength... and enjoy the quietness of our new home life (the last kid, Charlie, moved to his college dorm this past week... the nest is empty!)... and look forward to our 10th Valentine's Day... Anniversary... and our San Antonio trip in about 80 days!

Thank you again for your prayers and support. Your love has helped to carry us through to this point. It is so wonderful to be able to relax... and breathe deeply of the goodness of our God... our Lord and Savior... without feeling the urgent need and desperate pleas for strength to get through each day. Thank you Lord!

Please have a good evening and a great week! God Bless!
Scott and Rhonda

Responses

Jan R
Oh what sweet music to my ears! Praise to the King of Kings!

Maw-in-law
wow!! Overwhelming news.

Love you more than words can say. Can't wait to see you eye to eye.

Jim F

This is awesome news, Scott! We rejoice with you. Praise the Lord!

Lila C

Such a true expression of real suffering, the deepest of valleys and yet "light" He is light, and yet as we see in Job and so many places in the Word of God, this suffering is such a part of our walk. I will never understand why you, the most precious, with the greatest of faith must walk through this. But we won't use such needed energy except to rest as you said. Deep inside I felt my girlfriend gained strength by not getting out in the Jan. weather every day and as you knew Scott, oh how you both needed this. This is the most encouraging letter! Thank you so very much. Please know I stand that Rhonda is recovering for the life you will have together, and yet I will always acknowledge suffering as it is a part of me as a nurse and my families and my own. It's so real, it's so often second to second.

I can't express how much I love you, I pray you just know. Thankful…

Standing

Usha A

Great news! Keep the good news coming. God bless!

Greg G

PTL. That's what I'm talking about.

Patti S

always in our prayers

Peggy A

So happy things are going better. YAY.

Clifton W

Sounds like a good report. PTL

Sandy L

This is the best news I've heard in a long time!!!! THANK YOU JESUS!!!!!!!!!

Lupita O

I'm sooo happyy!!!! to hear this wonderful news, very careful when you go to the next appointment, specially this days, when everybody is sick, and days with flu everywhere, Yeah, way to go!!!!

I'll keep praying for you!

Lynn B

This news is fantastic!

Donna C

Hey!

That's awesome news! So good to hear positive info… a BIG sigh… of relief… We are still praying…

Denise A

PTL!! I can't express how happy we were to read this email :) Still praying for you both and doing a happy dance for you guys!!

Myra P

Thanks for sharing the good news Scott! Our Lord is Almighty and great! PTL!

Bobbie O

So thankful things are going better. We pray for you every day and will continue to do so. Tell her I am looking forward to when she gets stronger and she is up for a visit. I have really missed seeing her smiling sweet face.

Pam D

That is AWESOME news!

Feb 3

post from Stefanie—Home Sweet Home

So, Mom went home. And STAYED home! It's been a long time since I've been able to say that! Aren't you excited?

When they first went home, it was pretty much just for the nights because Mom still needed the IV meds and they would only administer them at the hospital. Between transportation, waiting for the appointment, receiving medicines, and getting back home, each (daily) visit took between 6–8 hours, not exactly the restful day Mom needed. After about two weeks of that, however, they allowed Scott to administer the meds at home. So Mom's been able to get MUCH more rest now, which has also kept the fevers away! Yea!

Being home really agrees with Mom. As of Friday, Mom's hematocrits were up 30% and her platelets were up 40%. Mom has even returned to the interwebs, wording with her friends. And we all know that even in recovery, even on meds and with minimal energy, she can still word it up so good that we'll groan when we see that 100-point word on our boards. So Friends, beware: the words are coming! And they may quite possibly destroy you.

Mom and Scott are hoping the biliary drain will be removed soon, and then we will be even further down the road to recovery! Mom's energy is still low, and Scott is still staying home with her every day.

I'll leave you tonight with one more happy thought: When I visited Mom last week, I noticed she was growing hair again. Yea! Mom said that she knew she was doing well when she was having a bad hair day! So there you have it, Mom can have bad hair days again. :)

In conclusion, we are very excited about this new development, are praying the numbers continue to improve, that Mom continues to feel better and regain energy, that all goes well with the drain removal, and Mom returns to "normal" soon. Many thanks for all your past and future prayers.

Responses

Teresa M
    Thank you for sharing! Praying for her

Petra R
    Hi Stephanie: Thanks for sharing such wonderful, hopeful news. I'm really happy for Rhonda, you and your family. I bet your mom now has some point loaded medical terms to play in her Word games. Praying your mom continues to get stronger and this move home is a sign of better things to come.

Lourdes H
    So glad you're home, growing hair, and killing me on Words with Friends. You are amazing.

Vicky S
Such wonderful news!

Feb 8
My Rhonda—Recovery Continuing

Hi,

Just a quick note on our appt this last week…

On an extremely exhausting Thursday this past week, Rhonda had her 2nd PET scan since the transplant… and an appt with our doctor. The scan was set for 7:30 AM, so we had to get up at 5:30… and the dr appt was at 3:30 in the afternoon. What a long day…

Anyways… the scan results were beautifully clean… no trace of the "bad stuff"… PTL! And in our afternoon appt we learned that her counts are continuing to climb, climb, climb by leaps and bounds. PTL x 2!!

The exhaustion of the day did bring about (we think) a short bout with fever overnight Friday… due to Rhonda just still being a bit frail. We will get past this in time. We will have some nice weather for the next few days… so we will be taking some walks to work on gaining strength. :)

So… we continue to be on track. The IV meds were renewed for another 2 weeks… and probably past that… until we get that drain thing out. Our Lord is bringing us back into the sunshine after the darkness of the valley. We give Him all of our praise and thanks!

Thank you for your prayers and encouragement! God is loving us through you... :) Have a good week!

God Bless!
Scott and Rhonda

Responses

Cathy G

Praise the Lord!!!!!! We are so happy to hear this, Scott. Be assured of our continued prayers, and please tell Rhonda I am looking forward to our next lunch and girl time.

Patti S

Praise God!!!

Sylvia A

Rhonda and Scott, yes PTL is exactly right. We're reminded that God has a purpose and plan for everyone and I've always believed God has chosen the 2 of you to be examples for all of us of the wonders of Gods miracles and that thru prayer all is possible.

Peggy A

I love good news!

Greg G

Great news Scott. It sounds like you might be turning the corner? We will continue to pray God gives you endurance. I'm proud of you brother. Rhonda has a good godly man.

Lila C

We thank God for the positive news!! Thank you so much for letting us know. Please know how often everyone wants an update. I am so sorry for that long day and am so thankful you might be able to be outside, the sun shines over my precious friends. I miss my girlfriend! I love you!!! Standing

Sandy L

We are doing a Happy Dance for this AWESOME news!!!! THANK YOU THANK YOU THANK YOU JESUS!!!!!!!

Jan R

Oh, Happy Day! God is Light & He's bringing the Light back for your healing! Wonderful news!

Jan D

My only response to this is... YEAH!!!!!

Bobbie O

PTL. Such encouraging news. Thank you sooo much for sharing. Tell her will continue praying and hope to see you and her in the neighborhood walking as she works toward getting her strength back. Tell her I love her and am looking forward to a visit when she gets stronger.

Lupita O

I'm glad to hear this good news, please take it easy, don't overdue, rest, Scott you need to rest too, and I'm praying for you!!!

March 11
My Rhonda—Three Steps Forward… and a Step Backward

Hi there…

I know that I haven't sent anything out for a while so I want to briefly share what's been going on and what's coming up for us…

The first couple weeks of February, things were really moving along great! Rhonda felt well enough to work on building strength… walking for short shopping trips… and even to attend a Wednesday evening service at our church. We were on the way… and it felt great!

But lately we've been reminded that we are not there yet. Rhonda had a procedure to check her biliary drain on Feb 26… we told the dr that she was doing well, and we wanted that thing taken out. It didn't happen that way. The dr told us that she was afraid that taking the drain out would make Rhonda more sick again. That took the wind out of our proverbial sails.

And then… the fevers started coming back anyways. Go figure. Low grade at first… but then a couple where she hit 102 or more… ugh… what's going on here?

So… our oncologist is wanting to get us into an Infectious Disease dr to get an opinion on continuing the current Rx regimen (we're still doing the IV antibiotics at home… for like 6 weeks now) or changing things up. They've been working on it for 2 weeks now and still no appt.

But… the potential game-changer is now officially on the schedule. On March 30, the IR doc and the GI doc will combine talents in a procedure intended to remove the biliary drain and put in a stent. This was first mentioned to us in mid-December.

So… our prayer requests are… that the fevers go away… and that this appt on the 30th will be successful and put the final nail in for getting past all of this and moving on… oh please let it be Lord!

Thank you for continuing to check up on us and keep us in your thoughts and prayers. We are asking for you to lift us up to our Lord… and the doctors… for success in this procedure. And we know that you will be with us… thank you!

Spring is finally just around the corner… and Rhonda and I will celebrate our 10th anniversary tomorrow (after the doctor appts). I am so thankful for the privilege of sharing life with my best friend!

Please have a good week… God Bless!
Scott and Rhonda

Responses

Lila C

Thank you for the much wanted update. I am broken hearted about these fevers. Rhonda and Scott, I feel the procedure on the 30th will help Rhonda and we will speak and believe and stand that Rhonda will be healed. It's time, and spring will be a new and wonderful time for you both. It's time. I love you with all my heart. So we go forward with great faith in our Lord Jesus Christ, and with a precious love He gave us for one another. Scott thank you for letting us (me) know about my girlfriend. I miss Rhonda greatly. I had hoped her visit with Georgya was perfect, I hope the fevers weren't at that time. Must close, exhausted. I am going to bed and will not rest without prayer time for you and Rhonda and the healing Christ will give you.

Pam D

The two of you have been so amazingly strong through all of these ups and downs. Both of you are in my prayers.

Sandy L

PRAYING PRAYING PRAYING!!!!
We Love you both sooooo much!!!
Happy Anniversary

Sylvia A

Uplifting you and keeping you both in my daily prayers.
Happy anniversary and many more.

Usha A

Happy Anniversary and many happy returns! God bless!

Suraya K

You are in my prayers. May all go well with both of you

Myra P

We will continue to pray for Rhonda and your family.
Have a happy wedding anniversary to you and Rhonda! God bless you both.

Mike M

Dear GOD

I pray that you remove this burden from Scott And Rhonda's life!

I ask this in the name of your son Jesus, AMEN.

Donna C

So glad to hear from you! I'm happy that there are still continued plans of action to get to the point where all of this will be behind
you both and get on with more enjoyable things. God is still good, I
choose to believe that this is His plan... Just wish it didn't take soooo
long, perhaps there is a reason?

God Bless you Rhonda & Scott!

love and hugs

Jan R

Happy Anniversary dear friends! Lifting you both up to our
Lord & asking for complete healing!

Bobbie O

Thank you so much for the update. We will definitely keep
praying. I know this has been a long journey for you both. We pray
the doctors will be successful for the procedure and Rhonda can start
getting her strength back. Congratulations on your 10th Anniversary.
Give her a hug for me. Love you all.

Patti S

Thanks for the update... you are always in my prayers

Cindy H

Father, I pray that you will heal Rhonda of any more fevers, that
the doctors will be able to remove the biliary drain and put in a stent
on March 30, and that this procedure will be a success and restore
Rhonda to good health!

Happy 10th Anniversary! Maybe we could go on a double date
after Rhonda and I feel like eating again and are healthier. Heavenly
Father, please let it be!!!

Jane B

    Dear, dear Rhonda and Scott,

    You both continue to be in our thoughts and prayers.

    We love you and care very much for you and all your family!

D'Ann C

    Happy late Anniversary! Hope all are feeling well today. I pray for you and Rhonda every day and appreciate specific prayer requests.

    I'd like to bring over dinner for y'all sometime next week. Let me know what day would be the best and what Rhonda will/can eat and how many are at your house these days. Have a blessed day.

Barbara C

    Hello Rhonda I can't tell you how terribly sorry I am that you and your family are going thru this. I think of you often Rhonda and when I do I stop and pray. You are an amazing woman. I know God is carrying you thru this day by day. We may never know why this had to happen but God does. You are a hero to so many. Paul had his thorn to carry. He asked several times for it to be removed and it wasn't. God knows what He is doing. You are so fortunate to have such a loving and understanding family around you. I love when we know specific things to pray for- such as your upcoming procedure. I can do that! Please know that you are not forgotten. You are on many many prayer lists! I am praying for a complete recovery. In His name, Barbara

March 29
My Rhonda—Monday is the Day

Hi,

Just wanted to send a note to ask again for your prayers to cover Rhonda's procedure tomorrow. We want our Lord to guide the minds and hands of the drs and staff… and for the stent to be placed successfully… and that it will fix what it is intended to fix… as in "no more fevers."

Rhonda has really been pushing this last week… tromping around the mall a bit.. walking into the clinic for her appt (instead of the wheelchair) for the first time since… last fall… August even? We even made it to our 2nd Wednesday night church service since January. Yet… every time she pushes… she pays for it with fever and exhaustion that lasts a day or two. It makes it difficult to keep any momentum going.

So… tomorrow's the day. We are scheduled for around noon. I will send out another update as soon as we can tell how it all went.

Thank you so much for your prayers… support… thoughts… well-wishes… acts of kindness and encouragement that you have showered us with. And we know that we stand on a solid Foundation of faith in our Loving Lord… and are especially thankful for His great Gift to us… and during this season too where He willingly laid down His life for us… and then demonstrated His Power over death by rising again. That He could care so much for a worm such as I is the crux of a Love beyond my comprehension.

Thank you all… for being vessels of such a Great Love…

Numbers 6:24–26 New King James Version (NKJV)
24 "The LORD bless you and keep you;
25 The LORD make His face shine upon you,
And be gracious to you;
26 The LORD lift up His countenance upon you,
And give you peace."

Love you all…

Scott and Rhonda

Responses

Cathy G

Thank you so much for the update on Rhonda's procedure tomorrow.

Please continue to be assured of our prayers for you both. The Lord is using your perseverance through all of this to encourage us all.

We love you both!

Clifton W

Just prayed and will pray for this procedure.

Greg G

On it Scott.

Jim F

Have prayed and will pray again tomorrow.
Joshua 1:9

Lila C

Thank you Scott, yes its Easter, the stone was rolled away. His blood was shed for us, your words "care for such a worm as I" are so clear and true. I am humbled beyond words watching you and Rhonda. I thank God for you all, He gave us love in the midst of it all.

Love and standing

Jane B

You are such terrific people, and we are always so blessed by your messages and reports! Bill and I count it a privilege to be included in your communications and requests for prayer, and we are praying for strength for both of you and for Rhonda's complete healing. We love you!

Sandy L

Praying for both of you continuously!!

Lots of Love

Denise A

We are praying!!!!

Lupita O

Dears brother and sister in GOD name, I will keeping in my prayers specially tomorrow at noon, that GOD, bless all the staff of drs and nurses around Ronda for wisdom and knowledge to know to do it the right way to handle the situation…

With love

Pamela D

Praying that God uses this to show how big and gracious He is as He brings healing for you both.

Suraya K

My best wishes and prayers are with you

Myra P

We will pray for Rhonda's successful procedure today. Our Lord is Almighty. He will heal and strengthen Rhonda.

Mella S

Our thoughts and prayers are with you today and always. Chronic fevers (and wheelchairs) are not easy to deal with for anyone. The fatigue can be overwhelming at times for even the bravest of souls. God bless.

Bobbie O

We are praying. Let us know how she does. Hope and pray this will stop those fevers and she can start getting her strength back.

Barbara C

I read this posting and had to chuckle a bit, seeing myself in Rhonda's actions. I suffer from several health issues. When I "feel good" I always overdo it. Always. Of course, I don't end up in the hospital, but I do end up in bed missing out on life and trying to sleep and regain my strength. Rhonda- I love you. I love your spirit. I love your outlook on life. I love your determination. I love your personality. You are an inspiration to so many. You are like the ever ready energy bunny. You just keep going. Well you just keep being you!!! In the meantime I am praying for that complete healing. I am praying for your procedure tomorrow. I am praying that God's holy spirit will just shower over you with his love and holds you in his arms as you go thru this.

Merlene

I will keep you in my prayers always. I commend you both on the way you have kept your faith and perseverance. Love you and thanks for the update.

Wanda J

Give our girl our love and prayers that this will fix the problem for good. Wow she is such a trooper! Most people would just say forget it I am tired and not going through another procedure of any kind. Not Rhonda, she is as much determined as the day it started. We love her so much and praying for her and you Scott as you are there for her! We appreciate you! Love momma and daddy J

March 30
My Rhonda—No Stent

Hi,

Just wanted to let you all know… that we did not get the results that we had hoped for today. The dr told us that they just couldn't get the stent to do what it needed to do… to open things up in the stricture area. But… they did find that the existing drain had "clogged up" somewhat and so they replaced it with one that was bigger. We are hopeful that clearing this up will at least make the fevers go away for a while.

They are exploring other options… and may bring Rhonda's case up before an "interdisciplinary" panel to discuss what may be workable for us. As for now, we are back on the 6 week schedule of getting the drain thing checked.

So... we were pretty bummed when we first learned that the drain was still there... but we know that our God has a plan and we continue to trust in Him to work all of this out one day. In the meantime... we are hoping that fevers are gone... at least long enough for us to enjoy our San Antonio trip coming up soon! :)

Thank you again... and again... and again... as our final resolution seems to always be a few steps away from us. Our Lord will deliver... in His time.

We will keep you posted... please have a good week...

God Bless,
Scott and Rhonda

Responses

Lila C

My dear friends, I don't have words, I love you and I pray Rhonda's pain is under control, gone. He will make a way. Is there anything I can do?

I love you with all my heart, standing

Patti S

We love you both and we will pray. please know that.

Sandy L

We are praying for you both!!!

Peggy A

So sorry Scott... continuing to pray for all of you.

Donna C

I'm sorry that the procedure wasn't the answer but I'm so glad to hear that there are still plans for something else and that is perhaps what God wants to take place because God knew there is something else to look for?

I just love how you both have such Faith to keep on keeping on!

We will continue to pray and we keep Rhonda on the Gideon's prayer requests list..

If there is something other than praying we can do for you both, please let us know.

Love in Christ

Terry C

Prayers and love for you both.

Bless you all. I am asking God to heal Rhonda and to do what the doctors have not been able to do for her. I am asking He opens the blockage and remove the fevers so she can gain strength. I will continue to pray for this. Hopefully we can see you Saturday. That would be a special blessing.

Bobbie O

Thank you for letting us know. So sorry it didn't work out as planned but pray this will take care of those fevers. Hang in there.

Lourdes H

Dearest Rhonda, so very sorry you did not get the results we all wanted to hear. But it seems that resolving that clog may give you some relief in the short term. We are so thankful for all of God's small tender mercies. Please keep us posted on how you are feeling in the days to come. Big hugs

Vicki D

Thank you for the update Stefanie! Rhonda and Scott, I'm so sorry the surgery didn't work out as you were hoping. We will continue praying for you and your family.

Amy G

Prayers continue for healing. Thank you for the update.

April 12
My Rhonda—Daily Fevers

Hi…

I just wanted to give you all a quick update on how Rhonda's been doing. Well… she has had a fever almost every day since the last procedure. They have been more mild as time goes on… but still spiking at times. Fighting these every day has sapped energy and strength and made it difficult to maintain any gains we had previously made.

So… this past week we both realized that our planned San Antonio trip in a couple of weeks would be too much to handle at this time. That will have to wait for another day when we have strength for an adventure. As a wonderful replacement, God kept a cabin in Oklahoma open for us until we were ready to change our plans. It is a gift and miracle that we found a cabin at our beloved state park for the same date range that the San Antonio trip was to take place… and we are both REALLY looking forward to a week in the woods and the small town nearby to relax and rest! Thank you Lord! :)

The drs have still not told us of any other plans/attempts to fix Rhonda's stricture… we continue to ask God every day to fix it… in any way that He sees fit. And we are also thankful every day for the amazing support we receive from so many… Thank you!

The Lord continues to bless our hearts in so many ways… kids… grandkids!… protection… friends… at church… at work… so many blessings to count that our hearts fill to overflowing. Yes… we would love to get past these fevers… but when we look at how our God has gifted us… we can hardly complain or say "poor me." He is so good to us…

Please have a good week… we will keep you updated. Thank you again for your love and support!

Scott and Rhonda

PS—Our second grandchild, Everly Jordan, was born on March 14. :)

Responses

Sandy L

Praying for both of you!

Patti S

Thanks so much for the update… we are praying always and are delighted to know you will be enjoying your time at Lake Murray this weekend.

Jane B

Dear, dear Rhonda and Scott,

You all are remarkable and such a blessing to all of us who get to hear from you! It is obvious that the Lord certainly is "your strength". Be assured of our continued love and care for you and, certainly, prayers for both of you. As well as healing, I will focus on prayers for strength and energy in time of need.

With love,

Jane and Bill B

"… we also…, do not cease to pray for you, and to desire that ye might be filled with the knowledge of his will in all wisdom and spiritual understanding; That ye might walk worthy of the Lord unto all pleasing, being fruitful in every good work, and increasing in the knowledge of God; Strengthened with all might, according to his glorious power, unto all patience and longsuffering with joyfulness; Giving thanks unto the Father, which hath made us meet to be partakers of the inheritance of the saints in light:" (Colossians 1:9–12)

Jan R

What a testimony of Faith! So grateful that you & Rhonda will be able to get away! Will keep praying, praying & praying some more!

Love you both

Cindy H

Father, I pray that you would heal Rhonda's stricture, heal whatever infection that is in her body and causing her to have fever, and restore her body to good health! Help Rhonda and Scott to trust you in every situation and depend on you for strength and comfort. May they feel your love, peace and joy always!

Myra P

Hang in there. Everything will be good soon. We will continue to pray for Rhonda's healing and to regain her energy & strength.

Bobbie O

I woke up early this morning and prayed for Rhonda. Gary and I do every day before he goes to work but during the early hours He put on my heart to lift my special and precious friend in prayer. I know how much He loves both of you and I know He is in control of all that is happening. I am so thankful you are able to go to Okla. It will be so good for both of you. Thank you for the updates.

Mike M

love you guys

May 3
My Rhonda—Amazing Grace

Hello,

Well... we just got back yesterday after a week in our cabin in the woods... and we had an amazing time!

In the days prior to the trip, Rhonda's daily fevers were waning... but still hitting hard at times... like 102 two days before we were to leave. At that time, I almost considered cancelling even the cabin trip... but I knew we had to give it a try... we both needed it too badly. So what does our Lord do for us? In the last 10 days, Rhonda has had fever a grand total of one day (this past Thursday... after a looooong day of hitting several stores in OK)... one day! We were both ready for a day of rest at that point. And, believe it or not, the pharmacy even overnight delivered the IV meds to the state park office, so we could have what we needed and not miss a beat... amazing! Thank you Lord for holding these fevers off and allowing Rhonda to have the strength to enjoy our week's getaway... Amazing Grace... Amen!

So... we're on a sort of 'roll' here. PTL! The IV meds end tomorrow... don't know yet if the dr will renew the Rx... our appt is this coming Thursday. We'll see. Also... we're about due for another "procedure" to check Rhonda's drain thing... and those always seem to set off a string of fevers. We'll see... nothing scheduled yet.

And... we have seen that the GI/IR docs have not been able to fix Rhonda's biliary stricture... so we have felt led to investigate another option... and have made an appt with a surgeon on 5/26. We certainly don't relish the thought of a surgery... but we need to get rid of this drain thing so we need to explore other means to reach the desired end. Please pray with us for God's direction in this.

In the meantime... while the fevers are at bay... we are going to work to build strength and stamina. Our neighbor told me last week on the phone that she had read that it takes the body a full 6 weeks to fully recover from a single 24-hr fever... 6 weeks! I would bet that in these first 120 days or so of 2015... that Rhonda has fevered for 70–80 of those days. Guess that's why it takes years to recover from this stuff... once the fevers have really stopped. Mercy.

So... we will see what the spate of May appts bring to us. Rhonda's counts have remained strong and we are very thankful for that. Thank you for your continued love, support, and prayers... we always know that God is with us... it is also comforting to know that you all are too.

Please have a good week... God Bless!

Scott and Rhonda

Responses

Sandy L
 Praise The Lord for a great week and for the pharmacy that got the medicine to you!!!
 We saw Rhonda's video this morning at the end of the church service. It was so good to see my sweet friend even if on a video!!!
 We miss both of you sooooooo much!!!
 Prayers still going up!
 LOTS of Love

Denise A
 I am so happy to hear you guys went on your vacay! God is Great!! Of course we are still praying daily for you both. You both are an inspiration to our family.

Sylvia A
 PTL! Glad to hear you were able to make your trip to the cabin. Congrats.
 My mom turned 80 today and we celebrated her bday. And this after we were told last Christmas her journey might be at its end. Only God knows our fate and it's all on His hands and timing.
 I continue to keep you in my daily prayers.

Jan R
 Amens and Prayers! Love you two!

Trish M
 Oh wow! This is such great news Scott!! Praying it continues!!!

Donna C
 Hey!

So good to hear that the both of you were able to get away to your destination! We saw Rhonda's video at the end of the worship service yesterday. What a surprise and a blessing for her to give a message about her situation and how prayer works and why prayer is necessary. We are still praying for her to get the answers to get her well.

Thanks for the update!

love and hugs

Quinn W

Hello Scott, so so so glad to hear that you all were able to enjoy your cabin trip! To God be the glory......

Bobbie O

Thank you for the update. So thankful you got the much needed time away and that it all went well. Yes, God is truly good all the time.

Will be praying for wisdom as you seek this second doctor. Pray all goes well and that she has a wonderful Mother's Day.

June 8
My Rhonda—Moving Toward a Solution

Hello,

We hope that you are doing well as summer weather (after record rains for a month) is finally settling in around here.

Rhonda has been fighting to hold her own, but a rash of fevers has kept her from gaining the strength we had hoped to have by now. These latest fevers started with a horrible lack of communication between myself, the dr's ofc, and the IV med pharmacy where Rhonda ended up being without her IV meds for 72 hours. During that timeframe, she fared pretty well, but the day after we started the meds back she was violently ill… almost like she had had a chemo treatment. The worst stuff didn't last long, but it started a trend of fevers over the following 2 weeks that have drained much strength from her. She is doing better these last couple of days, but has lost ground with her physical strength. We hope to have a break so she can work back up to where she was a month ago… able to walk into the clinic.

The "solution" mentioned above involves our visit with the surgeon. We were impressed with his knowledge and attitude in wanting to gather info and history before deciding on a course of action. He told us that we need "someone to pull all of the information together for a decision… and I don't mind being that guy." Pretty good stuff to hear on a first visit. His office then called us this week to schedule Rhonda for a follow-up appt and specialized CT scan… and also to let us know that the surgeon had spoken to all 3 or 4 of our doctors and that all had concurred… surgery is the only way to fix this.

That surgery will involve removing the part of the liver that has the bad bile duct. He told us that this is a rare condition and that he wanted to try and figure out what brought it about. He also told us that he would prefer for Rhonda to be stronger before undergoing the surgery… so this is another huge reason she needs to be without fevers so she can work to build strength. The dr spoke of waiting a couple of months, which would be around the end of July. Our next appt/scan isn't until the 22nd, we hope we can get a good start on strength by then.

The dr told us that the surgery would make Rhonda "feel like you've been hit by a truck"… we don't relish that at all… but are looking beyond that to a life with no daily IV drugs, no fevers, no biliary drain line, no picc line… and the strength to be involved in our family and church life… things we've missed out on for the last year (June 7, 2014 was Rhonda's first chemo treatment).

So… again we call on you prayer warriors to offer prayers up on Rhonda's behalf… for no fevers… to gain strength… and to come through this surgery with 100% healing so we can finally put this chapter behind us.

Thank you for your amazing support and encouragement! We see that soon a 'stick' will be put in the ground to mark the turning point for my Rhonda… this surgery… and the watchcare of our Lord through it all. Of this, we remain confident. He is the Healer… the Great Physician. He loves Rhonda even more than I do… amazing Love will carry us through it all.

May God Bless you all! We are so thankful for you!

Love you,
Scott and Rhonda

Responses

Clifton W
Thanks for the update. I do pray for yaw'l daily, but will intensify my prayers on your behalf.

Bobbie O
So many times I walk Peanut right in front of your house and think of you all and pray for her. So sorry she is going through all this.

We love you all and pray all this will help Rhonda get back on her feet again. We really miss you both.

Drew C

Praying for you two!

Pam D

I will be praying for her and her doctors.

Donna C

Good to hear from you. Although it seems to be a rough time again, I'm so glad to hear about the new doctor you have and the plans and how upfront he is with you both as what to expect. Praying for strength and fevers to go away enough to have that much needed surgery. We all can't wait until Rhonda can feel like she's on top of the world and you both can get back to a much needed normal life. Always thinking about ya'lls situation and praying for answers, solutions, and good health.

love to you both

Lila C

Yes dear Scott and Rhonda, love will see you through. Thank you for letting us know, I know every ounce of energy you both have is to take care. I do wish I could do more for you. This has to be the way to healing, I am so very sorry Rhonda must endure more, this just has to be it! I love you both with all my heart.

Peggy A

Still praying for you guys. Thanks for the update.

Lourdes H

Dearest Rhonda, I am so sorry you have one more major hurdle to go through. However, I am so happy that you have Scott as a soul mate to support you through all this. I already started praying before writing this post and pray often for your health but I will have focused prayers this summer for your strength and endurance during these months' trials. I hope you and your family feel the Lord's comfort and presence at all times. I hope laughter and happy times regularly find their way into your life as well. Big warm hugs, dear friend.

Petra R

My prayers are with you as you prepare for this surgery and pray this becomes the real turning point for Rhonda's health. You have been so amazing in keeping up the fight. I can imagine there are days where the exhaustion and frustration seem to have the upper hand. It's at those times, I especially pray your guardian angels hover over you with buckets of love, comfort, patience, support and energy. I'm glad you found a doctor whose communication style, knowledge and thoroughness gives you new hope for a better future down the road. Wishing you the best in banishing the fevers and building strength for the surgery.

Vicky S

Praying and sending our love!

June 22
My Rhonda—No Reason to Wait

Hi,

Hope that you all are doing well. Just wanted to bring you up to date on things...

The surgeon has completed his "due diligence" and all parties agree that a surgery is needed to fix the stricture issue. He also asked for a biliary tube check/exchange procedure to gather tissue samples, which was performed this past Friday. Unfortunately, these procedures always unleash the 'pagan hordes of bacteria straight from the gates of hell' and give Rhonda some very rough times of fever. So... the last 4 days have been tough... with fevers/chills coming and going at all times day and night. I don't know if we've gotten more than 3 consecutive hours of sleep since. It will get better.

After the effort of our CT scan and follow-up appt with the dr today, Rhonda is fevering yet again. These fevers have really robbed her of any strength that she had been able to build up, and when the dr saw her, he asked if we wanted to put her in the hospital right away. We told him that we've been working through it all and would prefer to stay home until surgery. He also told us that he believes her radiation treatments back in 2009 are the culprit that messed up her bile duct. That part of the liver is right on top of the pancreas area where the radiation was targeted. Interesting... and thankful that nothing else biologically-speaking is going on to cause this.

He then told us that he would like to put her in the hospital 10–14 days before surgery to give her super-nutrition, therapy, and more antibiotics in an effort to keep fevers away before the surgery and give her a chance to gain some strength. We are in hearty agreement with this and thankful for it.

So... he will be putting the wheels in motion to get her admitted around whatever surgery date he can schedule. Our oncologist offered to have her placed in the oncology hospital which is much more spacious and comfortable than the older buildings when I'm staying with her. The surgeon agreed, explaining that she would be in ICU for a time after surgery, and then could go back to a regular room.

I am amazed… and humbled… by how much my Rhonda has physically been having to go through with all of this… and still keep her attitude of thankfulness. I don't know that I could have personally handled what she has endured. This was reinforced at about 6 AM this morning. I had prayed that she would have no fever so she could get rest for the appt, but that was not His plan.

She had been fighting the chills for about 2 hours and had herself bundled up too much, causing the fever to go way up. Within 30 minutes of pulling off covers and downing a whole bottle of water, the fever suddenly broke and was gone. I was surprised that it had left so quickly, and Rhonda said "He knows just what we need and when we need it." My eyes instantly welled with tears to witness the amazing grace she has been showing through this whole trial. Yes Lord, you know just what we need.

Thank you again for your amazing support. We still need you to stand with us and send your prayers on Rhonda's behalf. This surgery will not be an easy thing to endure. It's a major procedure.

After the fever broke this morning and we were trying to settle into a time of rest, I heard a song that again brought tears to my eyes. We always play soothing music as we go to bed to relax our minds and souls, and this artist we've played nearly every night during this past year. Joanne Hogg is the lead singer for the Irish Christian group, Iona. She put out her own recording last spring and we find it beautiful and relaxing. It's kinda become our 'theme' music during this time. The last song (In That Moment) speaks beautifully of what it means to have a 'heart set free' from the burdens of this life… burdens that our Lord longs to help us with… every day… every moment. Here are the lyrics…

> Brave boy walking to the front of the stage
> Hands wrapped around a snow white dove
> Both of you tremble in front of the crowd
> And your mother is watching, so calm and so proud
>
> Your hands move forward
> And you let the bird fly
> My eyes look upward
> And gaze into the sky
>
> And in that moment,
> I suddenly see
> A picture of love
> And what it means to be free
>
> And now I stand watching the dove flying home
> And I'm praying for another to come
>
> My hands move forward
> Waiting to receive
> All that's been promised
> Everything that I believe
>
> And in that moment,
> I suddenly feel
> The embrace of love
> And my heart set free
> (johoggmusic.bandcamp.com)

I personally want to "fix" everything (seen that commercial with the guy saying "I got this" about everything?)… and it's many times hard for me to let go. But so much is out of my control… it's such a needless expense of my energy. My God is always waiting, wanting me to give the burden over to Him. Too many times I refuse… it's my responsibility, I think… "I got this." But those times that I can let go… when I'm at the end of myself… it's a beautiful and freeing thing (as stated in the last 2 stanzas above).

I will share details and dates as we learn them. The Light is at the end of this tunnel, and our amazing Lord is saying… "I got this."

With much love and thankfulness for you all,
Scott and Rhonda

Responses

Roxzanne M
Scott and Rhonda, I just love your commitment to God, and putting your lives into his hands. Thank you for sharing your life challenges.
It makes me thankful and helps me to look to God more than I have lately. God is definitely using the two of you to bring other people to him. I will be praying for you both.
Take Care and God Bless both of you.

Sylvia A
Scott and Rhonda, you are a testament to all of us. We will continue to be your prayer warriors.
God bless you both.

Sandy L

We are praying daily for you and Rhonda!!!
God's got this!

Jan R

Thank you for sharing that beautiful song! Continuing to pray for you and that God will provide what you need! Humbled & awed by your steadfast faith in our Lord!

Donna C

We appreciate you updating all of us. I tell you that I don't know if I could go through all of this but if I ever have to, I will go back and reflect on this journey you both are going through and pray to God to help me through it like Rhonda and Scott did and with their faith that God is in control.

It is very encouraging how this doctor has what you said, due diligence... I wish that this doctor was found sooner but perhaps there was a reason he wasn't? After it was mentioned that the doctor thought that the radiation treatments were a culprit that messed up her bile duct brought me to my past when my former husband was told that it appeared that the radiation treatment in 1973 had damaged the arteries to his kidneys which led to complications. While radiation treatments help in one respect, not so good in others but I'm so glad that the doctor has come to the conclusion why the bile duct is the culprit.

We still continue to put you both on the prayer requests in the Sunday School class and on the Gideon Garland Camp prayer requests.

I also thank you for sharing the song by Joanne Hogg. I haven't heard of her and don't know if Vic has either, but I'll make sure to bring this singer to his attention. He likes to hear this type of music especially if it has the Irish accent. I tried to find the song you both like on the internet and couldn't find it but I did like her message in other songs.

Keeping you both in our thoughts and prayers.
Also, with love and much thankfulness for you both!

Bobbie O

Thank you so much for the update and I am so thankful the doctors have a plan to help her. She's been through so much and is an inspiration to so many. Tell her we are praying for all of you and we love her. Gary and I are wearing bracelets in honor of her and my brother-in-law who just found out he has ALS or Lou Gherig's disease. It says "No One Fights Alone." Thank you for keeping us in the loop.

Julius R

Just to let y'all know that we are still praying for healing, comfort, and strength daily. His will be done.

Patti S

Thank you so much for this update, Scott. Yours and Rhonda's journey has been a light to so many… this e-mail just pierced my heart… so achingly beautiful. You are always in my prayers.

Our love to you both

Jane B

With love and prayers for strength and healing

Mike M
Love you guys

Vicky S
We are keeping all of you in our prayers!

Merlene
Thanks for the update Scott. I commend you both on your diligence and faith. I pray each day for you both knowing that you have turned this whole situation in God's hands. Just want you to know that I have not forgotten your daily struggles. Love you

Terry W
Hope that you can kick this thing in the butt finally instead of it you. I will add my prayers to you and your family as I miss our conversations. Stay strong for each other and may the crying times lessen. God bless you all

July 20
My Rhonda—Going In

Hi,

Hope that you all are doing well!

So... Rhonda will be going into the hospital one week from today... Monday the 27th... to start her nutrition/strengthening regimen. This is all we have a date for at this time... no surgery date is set to our knowledge.

Rhonda has had some really good days... and some really rough ones.. and many days that have been somewhere in between. She went for almost 10 days without a fever, and then has fevered every day for the last week. She just can't get any momentum to build strength. We hope the hospital time will be a help.

All of her counts continue to be well-anchored in the 'normal' range… which is a very good thing… PTL! We just have to get past these next several weeks… and some days it's difficult to see the other side of the procedure that is drawing closer every day. Our Hope is continually on the One on whose shoulders we are being carried.

So… we continually pray for no fevers… for a chance to build some strength… for the Lord's Hand to be on the drs, nurses, and staff to guide and give them insight to "fix" this… and for our faith to be strengthened to ride this through to the end… striving toward that Light standing at the 'exit' of this valley… to stand strong on the Foundation and hope of better days ahead.

We did, through Rhonda's sheer will and determination, get to go to Sunday's preaching service yesterday… and it was wonderful just to experience the joy of sharing time with God's people! We so much look forward to going every week again soon!

That's all we know now… I will let you all know when the surgery date is set. Thank you again for standing so faithfully with us through this journey. Your support and encouragement truly bless our hearts!

Please take care… and God Bless!
Scott and Rhonda

Responses

Sylvia A

Hi Scott and Rhonda. I continue to keep you both on my daily prayers.

Jane B

Thank you so very much for the update. You are loved and prayed for!

Kathleen S

We wanted yall to know we think of you often. We wish we could come by but with the girls being germ pools we don't want to risk adding those germs to Rhonda's recovery. But because the girls are growing like weeds I thought y'all might like to see some recent pictures. We love you both very much!

Clifton W

Thanks for the report; I have been wondering how it's been going.

Bobbie O

We will continue to pray for you all. I pray for her every day and think of her when I walk Peanut close to your home. Gary and I pray for her each morning before he goes to work. This has been such a hard journey for both of you and we pray things will start getting better and she can get stronger. Your continued faith has been an inspiration for all of us. Give her our love.

Sandy L

I can't wait (as I know you cannot either!) for all of this to be in the past!

We are still praying for both of you!!!!
I am so thankful for the 10 days without fever!!!

Peggy A

Thanks for the update. I do think about and pray for you guys often. I hope this regimen will really help Rhonda. You guys have been through so much. I will be praying for you and Rhonda.

Mike M

Thanks Scott for the update.
We love you.

Cindy H

Scott, Bruce and I have been praying for Rhonda daily, that God will strengthen her body, protect her from the fevers, and enable her to go into this next surgery in good health. Of course, we pray that He gives the doctors wisdom and guides their hands during the surgery. We also pray for God to strengthen you, physically, mentally, and spiritually!

Pam D

You both are in my prayers.

Donna C

So good to hear from ya'll. So happy to hear that the both of you got to go to preaching last Sunday. We pray that the nutrition and strengthening regimen is just what she needs that the next steps after this will be the final answer to health restoration! Amen!
We love ya'll and miss you!

Mella S

Our prayers will be going with Rhonda Monday. May this regimen do even better than expected.

Petra R

Thank you for taking the time to post the update. It's always good to learn how Rhonda and family are managing this marathon. You continue to show great courage, resilience and determination in the face of uncertainty. Will pray that the hospital stay will help Rhonda develop the strength required for this next surgery and post-surgery days. Wishing you many blessings, Petra

Lourdes H

Praying so very deeply for you, sweet girl. Wishing I could give you a hug.

July 26
post from Stefanie—Tomorrow

Mom goes into the hospital tomorrow. The first goal is to get her strength back up via quality nutrition, and then her body will hopefully be able to handle the surgery better.

To recap, this surgery is to remove the infected part of her liver that has initiated her monstrous fevers, caused her pain for the last five years, and prevented her from healing from this last round of chemo. We are hopeful that this is the correct diagnosis for this recurring issue, and that it will solve all her problems. I mean, we don't expect some miraculous overnight healing, but if this surgery removes the source of all this pain and all these fevers, I think it'll feel like a miracle to all of us! And God is in the miracle-doing business anyway, so why not?

I know Mom is looking forward to having the energy to spend time with all her kids and grandbabies, and I think we're very close! As far as I have heard, we don't have a date for surgery yet, but it was supposed to be 10–14 days after entry into the hospital. Given Mom's history of hospital stays that always get extended, even if it's 20 days, it will be for Mom's health and strength. After the surgery she'll stay in the hospital to recover and HOPEFULLY this time, without infection, she'll enjoy recovery without daily three digit temperatures and low neutrophils and blood counts. HOPEFULLY, she will recover well, quickly, and fully.

praises

- that God is always in control
- that Mom will be able to stay in the same section of the hospital before, which has a decent sleeping set-up for Scott, who goes wherever she goes
- that Scott's work has been so generously flexible with his schedule these last few years (really, for the last six years)

request

- that Mom would gain the needed strength and healing pre-surgery
- that the surgery would be effective and without error, incident, or problem
- that Mom's healing/recovery would be both complete and quick, so she can return to enjoying life and not merely surviving it

Thanks again for every single one of your prayers and support. I'll update again when we have more information or updates about the surgery and recovery.

Responses

Marge B

Rhonda, Peggy and I were talking about you this past Saturday. We were remembering our great visit with you in Dallas a year ago last February. Marcus and his family are here visiting in Georgia from Dallas. We will be praying for you to get the strength you need for the upcoming days. The Lord is faithful. I just pray you will have comfort and peace to enjoy your beautiful family as you wait on the Lord. Love, Marge

Dirk B

Glad something is going to be done. Rhonda and you all are always in our prayers.

August 2
My Rhonda—Date Set

Hello,

Friday is the day. After telling us "week after next" for several days, the surgeon changed it up and has been telling us for the last couple of days that he has scheduled her for this coming Friday, the 7th for the surgery. We are in the cancer hospital now, but will be in a surgical recovery area after the procedure.

The week has not been an easy one... but the Lord has been our Helper (including helping Rhonda's picc line to work in the middle of the night to save her from a "stick") and Rhonda has made the best of things. We are both more than ready to get past this and move on down the road to having the energy and strength to enjoy life and family… including little Mable Mae who eldest son David and wife Jillian have been gifted with through adoption just this last week. God is so good to us!

Our first night here in the hospital, the lab tech (who would've had to do the "stick") gave us an amazing testimony of how God had healed her from multiple sclerosis… a condition for which there is no known cure. She looked at Rhonda and said, shaking her finger at her… "Don't you listen to how you feel or what the drs say, you just start thanking God for your healing right now!" It was a wonderfully encouraging and uplifting experience.

So… thank you again for your prayers and encouragement… and thank you Lord, in advance, for healing my Rhonda. :)

I'll send out another update sometime after surgery…

God Bless,
Scott and Rhonda

Responses

Jim F
    Scott, we're standing with you in faith!

Cathy G
    We're praying… thank you for being so faithful in your updates. We are so grateful that when life is so difficult, and circumstances are

beyond our control, God is still faithful. Please be assured of our constant prayers for you and for Rhonda.

Love and prayers

Peggy A

Wow! Praying hard that this will do it. You have all endured so so much.

Donna C

Your update is encouraging! Praise the Lord! We are still praying for Rhonda's strength and healing up to, during the surgery as well as afterwards. Also Scott, for your strength for taking care of your precious bride. We are anxious for the both of you to return to church on a weekly basis!

God Bless you both

Trish M

You guys have GOT THIS!!! Praying for success, quick healing and that Rhonda can feel like Rhonda again very soon. Please update us when you can. In the meantime, please know that you have many, many people praying for your family.

Merlene

Rhonda, I love you and know that God will be with you and your family through this next procedure as He has been throughout this whole illness. You have put up a terrific fight and I cannot believe that it is all for naught. Just know that you are in my every thought and prayer. Love you dearly

August 7
My Rhonda—Surgery Done

Hi All,

Just to let you know that the surgery for Rhonda went well today, although the surgeon's findings were somewhat a "mixed bag."

The good news is that everything went without a hitch… and more quickly than anticipated. Also, after running some tests, the dr removed less than he thought he may have to remove. He also said that the section that was removed looked "really sick" and that its removal would most likely help her to feel better after the recovery.

The surprise downside was that the dr unexpectedly found cirrhosis which caused him to pause and reevaluate with consult before continuing with the planned procedure. After he told me about this, I did some quick research to see that it involves scarring of the liver and no real cure is available, although it can be slowed down and minimized a great deal.

In the short term, the dr said that the cirrhosis would probably slow down the recovery from the surgery. We don't yet know what long-term implications this may have.

So… Rhonda is pretty sore after surgery and is spending the night in recovery where I cannot stay with her… so I am at the house for the night. She is scheduled to be moved to a regular room in the surgical hospital in the wee hours tomorrow morning where I will be able to stay with her again.

I'll send more later as we find out more... and see how the recovery goes. Please pray for comfort and speedy healing from the surgery. Thank you as always for your wonderful support!

And thank you Lord in advance for sending healing down for my sweet Rhonda!

God Bless!
Scott and Rhonda

Responses

Cathy G

Thank you so much for sending this update tonight. As I told Georgya, I've been working at my computer tonight watching for updates to come in about Rhonda. I'm so glad to hear the positive things that have happened today. We will continue in prayer tonight for you both – you've both been through so much, and I pray that God will grant you peaceful rest tonight and for Rhonda, freedom from her pain tonight and rest so that she can begin the healing process.

Our love and prayers to you both

Sylvia A

Scott thanks for the update I had Rhonda in my prayers yesterday. Continue to be her warrior, let us storm the heavens and leave the rest in God's hands for He is almighty.

Denise A

We are so glad the surgery went well. We are praying for complete healing! We love you guys!!!!!

Greg G

    We are praying Scott. Thank you for the update.

Clifton W

    Thanks for report. Prayers continue going up.

Lila C

    Hello to my precious friends. Scott how is Rhonda's pain? No worries if you don't answer. I wanted to say I love you both and think about you all the time. Is there anything I can bring you?? Please let me know…

Bobbie O

    Thank you so much for the update. We will continue praying as she recovers from this surgery. Pray she heals quickly.

Pam D

    She is definitely in my prayers. Sounds like they found the issue and I pray this resolves her issues!

Maw-in-law e-mail to Stefanie for posting

    This is the update as I know it for a gut wrenching day. It started at 3:30 for me. Couldn't sleep; had to get up and pray for my daughter. She went into surgery at 9:00 midwest time. The doctor was surprised (??) to find cirrhosis to her liver (so many pills over 6+years). One option was to abandon going further with the surgery. But after conversing with some of the top notch doctors, they continued. The good news is that there was no need to take half the liver. There was fungal infection to a portion of the liver due to the biliary duct being clogged. Pretty sure that that was the cause of the continued fevers. They removed that portion of the liver, and she tolerated the procedure much better than I dreamed she could. She'll be in recovery overnight due to pain meds. But it appears she will mend. Let me take a moment to thank our Heavenly Father; and another moment to thank all of you for your prayers. God Bless all of you.

Thank you.

August 12
My Rhonda—Working Through It

Hello…

Hope that you all are doing well.

I just wanted to give an update on Rhonda's recovery these last few days. She is my trooper and has worked hard to do what is asked/ expected of her (limited exercise… eat this… drink this… blow into this… take this med… etc.) while the staff are still trying to figure out how to keep her pain down to a tolerable level. This evening I think we're closer as Rhonda is now resting with her heart rate under 100 for the first time today after a nurse revealed to us that she could take two of one of the pain meds instead of just one. I wonder why the other nurses failed to mention that…

She also is still running low-grade fevers with all that goes with that… some chills… feeling cruddy. The drs are wanting to keep the antibiotics going for at least 2 weeks after surgery so we have more than a week at least of that to go yet. Today her red blood counts were a bit low, so she is receiving a transfusion. Not a surprise after a major surgery.

On the good news front… there are no complications from the surgery and from the outside anyways, all is healing well. The sur-geon told us that if pain and fever can be managed, she could go home as early as next Monday. That would be wonderful, but she has much to overcome to get to that point. We also checked online and made a phone call last night to reserve a cabin in OK for mid-October. We had a similar reservation last year and were not able to keep it… this year it will be different. :)

The best part of our day today was a word of encouragement… from the room-cleaning crew. A sweet lady… probably pushing 70 yrs old… came to clean the room today and as she was leaving, she poked her head back into the room to tell Rhonda that the suffering would only last for a short time and that God is helping her to be strong. She also said that our surgeon was a wonderful guy and very skilled at what he does. Then she mentioned that she used to work on the bone marrow transplant floor before she was transferred to this liver transplant area… so we asked and she knew our oncologist too… and told us what a great and skillful guy he was. Only God could engineer things like this… and speak words of encouragement from a godly, hard-working lady like this who knew both of our drs. Rhonda and I just looked at each other after she left and basically said at the same time… 'That was a God-thing'. How amazing and wonderful to receive a word of blessing from a lady most of us wouldn't even notice. It's clear to us that cleaning these hospital rooms day-in and day-out was not just her job… it is her ministry. Thank you Lord for speaking through the lowly and humble to remind us how you never forsake us… that You've got this!

So… we don't know how much longer we will be here… and we may end up moving back to the cancer hospital… but we will still thank the Lord for Rhonda's complete healing. We are blessed to have great doctors, but He alone is the Great Healer. The drs administer harsh drugs, and cut and remove stuff… but through the power to persevere and healing, the Lord will bring us back to a place of good health.

Thank you again for standing with us through this. Please have a good evening… God Bless!
Scott and Rhonda

Responses

Maw-in-law
Thank you, Scott for the wonderful update. We also know better how to pray.
God bless you both and pray that tomorrow is a better day.
Love you

Jan R
Our God is an awesome God! He knew you needed some encouragement & he sent it in a person just like himself—a humble servant!
Continuing to pray! Love & miss you two!

Jane B
Thank you for keeping us posted! You all are certainly in our thoughts and prayers

Peggy A
You guys have been through so much. I pray so hard that Rhonda can get well forever and you can be done with all of this. Please know I do keep you in my prayers.

Melinda H

It's always good to hear from you and get an update!! We are still praying for Rhonda and hope she has a speedy recovery and things will start looking up soon!! I was up at the office last week and missed seeing you!!

Please continue to update us!! Praising God for those special moments and encouraging words!! God is in control even when we are in our darkest moments. He is there!!

Bobbie O

I am so thankful she is getting better and pray she can come home soon. Yes, it was a God thing for the lady to give you just the right words you needed. We saw that as well through Gary's two times with cancer. We will be praying for her healing and her strength to return. Tell her I love her.

Donna C

This is wonderful news! AMEN!

I'm so thankful for your updates as I always wonder what is going on with ya'll.

It's good news that things are improving…

Take care and God Bless!

Lupita O

Scott and Rhonda, I'm praying for you, I really respect you and I have a very highly admiration for what's you'll passing through, I'm passing through hard time in this time of my life, and now I realize is nothing compare with you, GOD, is blessing us with this hard times to making us strong, I agree with the lady you are talking about, and with our friends praying for us, and making our friend-ship stronger…

I love you and praying for you, through these hard times

Mike M

We Love You Both So Much.

Thanks for the update.

Nancy P

Thanks for the update, Scott. It's nice to know how to "specifically" pray for Rhonda. Give her a hug from me when she's feeling better!! Continuing to pray!

Merlene

So happy to hear that progress is being made. No matter how small, any positive progress is a miracle. Thank you for keeping us posted and I will keep you praying for a speedy and full recovery. Love you guys.

August 17
My Rhonda—Not Yet

Hi,

Just to let you all know that did not make to 'early train' to the house today. Starting last Thursday, Rhonda started fevering a bit more (slightly over 100) which resulted in a flurry of tests on Friday. A CT scan showed some lingering fluid as a result of the surgery and the drs were pretty sure it was infected because the whole area had been.

The Infectious Disease docs were wanting to pull a culture of the fluid, but her white counts have been moving significantly back towards "normal" (not there yet) so the "wait and see" approach is being taken. So... Rhonda is continuing to work through fevers and chills... eating some... and thankfully her pain is largely lessening, but still wearing on her.

We did have a time yesterday when she was out of bed for extended periods... sitting in the room... taking her out for a spin in the wheelchair around the hospital floor. Under more pleasant circumstances, we would really enjoy more the view of downtown Dallas from the 14th floor here. We always tell our nurses and staff that the next time we come back, we'll bring cookies. It hasn't happened yet, but it will. :)

So... our next tentative going home date would be by the end of the week... and we are hoping and praying for that. A nurse who has taken care of us for several of our days here came by to visit today after her 2 days off... just to chat. She's a single mom with a 13 yr old daughter who's looking for more in her life. She gladly accepted Rhonda's contact info... on the back of a business card from our church. :) We pray that Lorena finds what/Who she is looking for.

Please have a good evening... thank you so much for your love and support!

God Bless
Scott and Rhonda

Responses

Sandy L
We are praying, praying, praying!!!

Lila C

Thank you my dear friends! I think about you both every day, throughout the day. I just know this is Rhonda's turning point for healing. It will take time, but it's coming! I wish I could come see her. I am sorry I haven't asked to come more often. I love you both with all my heart. Thank you Scott for the update, it means more than you could know!

Bobbie O

We pray she gets to come home soon. Know both of you are anxious to leave the hospital. We were out walking Peanut last night and Gary began to pray for her. Rhonda is on the top of our list and we pray she gets to come home soon.

Barbara C

Continuing daily prayer for complete healing for you Rhonda. May you be covered today by the holy spirit. God knows exactly what you need at any given moment in time and as you read this (or as it is read to you) I pray for the Holy Spirit to give you comfort and understanding as to what is needed at this exact moment. You are an inspiration to so many and you are not forgotten. Love you my friend!

Mary B

Praying for God's healing and peace for all of you.

Merlene

Still praying for you and still love you

Teresa M

God bless you! Always in my prayers

August 22
My Rhonda—Home

Hi there,

Yes… we are home! PTL!

In the hospital we were both so exhausted… never getting more than 2–3 hours of sleep at a time. I told one of the drs that I felt like I was experiencing some interrogation tactic where they try to break you down by giving you just enough sleep to somehow function each day, while waiting for you to finally break down and confess to all sorts of things you've never heard of just to get some more rest. Looking back, it's a bit comical… but we were miserable.

So… Wednesday evening I asked Rhonda if she wanted me to push hard to get the drs to discharge by the weekend. I knew they'd have to set up home meds again, and the coordinator from the clinic who's been handling it was out of town for the rest of the week… so I figured they'd need some time to get all of that set up. Rhonda told me not to push for anything… so we just resigned ourselves that they would discharge when they were ready… and maybe looking at another 5–7 days in hospital. Ugh. So… we prayed that God would give us strength and we'd leave it up to Him and the drs.

Well… at 6:00 the next morning, the first dr visited and said… 'Looks like you may be going home today'. I was in shock. Then more drs came in saying the same thing. And the Infectious Disease dr said that his office would set up home meds. And by 4:00 we were rolling out the door. Isn't God amazing? He just wanted us (Me!) to let go and let Him take over. Wow!

Just before we left, the nurse I'd mentioned before, Lorena, came by to see us and give Rhonda a hug. She is very much looking forward to keeping in touch as soon as Rhonda is up to facing Facebook and her laptop again. She told us again how much it meant to her to meet us. God always has a purpose in all things.

So... the IV meds didn't get to the house until 9:30 PM and that kept us up for a couple more hours. But... we got to sleep in our own bed... for the first time in 25 days. Thank you Lord!

And now... we rest... and gain strength. Rhonda is very weak from her ordeal. The pain is being managed by us keeping the meds going around the clock. She has not fevered hard since we've been home... another PTL! A therapist will be contacting us next week to help us get her started back to getting around the house on her own. It will be a process... but the worst is behind us. PTL!

So please continue to pray for the pain to be managed and for strength for Rhonda to be able to work to get her mobility, and a healthy appetite, back. We are so thankful for all of the prayers and support! And we are so thankful to our Lord who is always with us and gives us strength to endure all.

We love you... God Bless,
Scott and Rhonda

Responses

Jim F
Great news! So glad that you got to go home. The Lord is faithful.

Terry C

Thanks for the update about both of you. PTL that prayers are answered and things are progressing. Scott, I know there is still a long way to go. We love you both and pray that the Lord will renew your strength. We also pray about Rhonda's pain, fevers, and infections daily.

Your brother in Christ.

Patti S

Praise God.. cannot wait till you are back in class with us! We love and miss you!

Sylvia A

Glad to hear you're home, rest now and remember there is power in prayer. We storm the Heavens for Rhonda's recovery.

Pam D

That is awesome news!

Bobbie O

I am so thankful she is home. I have been out of town and what a wonderful email for me this morning. We will be praying and let her know again I love her and pray for her each day. Thank you so much for the update.

Jane B

Thank you so very much for keeping us posted. We praise the Lord that you are able to be home and continue to pray for strength and health for all of you.

With love

Barbara C

God is so good! Thank you Lord for answering this prayer with a YES!

Terry W

So glad that the Lord answered your prayers Stephanie, and Rhonda I'm doubly glad you get to rest in your own home and soon, with God's help... and your medical team and family... you won't ever have to go thru it again. Cured of all of it... no more pain or fevers, or chills, or weakness. I wish and pray for that for you. God bless you and yours

Susan H

This is great news Rhonda and Scott. God is so gracious to us. We know that all things work to his good and according to his purpose, he needed you to touch this nurse's heart and show her his love through your life.

May God Bless you as you rest and heal. You are so precious to so many.

August 31
Stefanie Caring Bridge post

After only a few days of being home, mom said she was up for company and missed us, so Julie, Charlie, and I went over on Tuesday (8/25/15). In the past, our visits were less than thirty minutes and we left when mom was trying too hard to stay awake. Last week, however, her eyes were closed for most our THREE HOUR visit, but she was awake and aware because she regularly asked us follow up questions. It was good to see her up for a little bit of conversation, even though it was clearly difficult for her. She has had no major fevers since being home, and has gotten quality sleep now that she hasn't been interrupted by doctors and nurses throughout the night.

Responses

Nichole B
     Thank you both for taking time out of your busy schedules to keep family and friends informed. It's greatly appreciated! I pray aunt Rhonda feels better soon.

Wanda J
     Thanks so very much for the updates. Rhonda and you Scott and the family remain in our prayers! Give her our love and we are praying for a miracle

August 30
My Rhonda—Back In

     Hi,

     Well… we enjoyed being home for the last 10 days… but tonight we are back in the hospital. For the last few days, Rhonda has had constant nausea… not able to keep meds or anything else down. So finally today she said 'enough' and we went to get checked out at the cancer hospital's assessment center. And… they are admitting her so they can run tests.

     The good thing is… no real fevers since we last left the hospital on the 20th… and her counts remain strong. PTL for that!

     So… the first scan will be coming shortly… and hopefully they'll find something and resolve it quickly so we can be home in a few days.

So again... we thank you for your support and encouragement... and more prayers. We will get there... one day. And thank you Lord for Rhonda's full healing that we will experience... soon.

God Bless
Scott and Rhonda

Response

Patti S
We are all standing with you. God bless and keep you both.

Petra R
Thank you for sharing. Glad to read that you had at least a week at home and time for extended, enjoyable visits with family members - what a boost for the spirit! Really happy to learn the fevers have subsided and the blood counts are strong - great signs for hope. My prayers are with you as you wait the test results to understand the source for the nausea. I pray that your hospital visit is short and you're home soon.

September 13
My Rhonda—Waiting

Hello,

Well... it's been 2 weeks since we came in with Rhonda's nausea... and we had hoped to be back at home by this time... but, as we've seen before on this road, healing is not a speedy process.

The reason behind the nausea (which is much better now), is because Rhonda's digestive system is in "shock" after the surgery...

or it has "gone to sleep." When she eats, the process goes to a certain point… and stops. The medical term is an "ileus." It's like a section of her system is temporarily paralyzed and has to rest and recover. The great unknown is… how much time will this take?

We just don't know.

So… we are in the hospital… again… for an undetermined amount of time… again. We have reservations for a cabin in OK the week of Oct 18, and still hope to be there. But we also had reservations at the same place in 2014… for the last week of October… and had to cancel. We will see.

We know that God has a plan… and that "all things work together for the good of those who love Him." So we will wait on His timing… again. We are fortunate to be in the more spacious cancer hospital… with a great staff and doctors working diligently to care for my Rhonda. Thank you Lord for the little things. And thank you Lord that you love Rhonda even more than we can imagine. And thank you Lord that we are on the path to her complete healing… one day… in your perfect timing.

And thank you all for continuing to undergird us with your prayers and encouragement. It is humbling to know that we remain in the thoughts of so many. We are blessed to have you 'in our corner'. The day of healing will come.

Love you all… God Bless!
Scott and Rhonda

Responses

Trish M

I'm so sorry to hear this Scott. You guys have endured so much. And Rhonda's body has gone through so much. I hope her digestive system starts responding. I pray faithfully for you and your family. Life shouldn't have to be this way. I sure hope you get to sneak away in October. Hugs to both of you.

Greg G

Wow! Prayers for Rhonda and you Scott. I know the uncertainty has to be weighing on you. Man, please let me know if there is anything we can do personally for you guys—need any groceries, check the house, water lawn/plants/flowers, clothes… etc. Let us know.

Nita S

We often say "Wonder how Scott and Rhonda are doing?" Thanks for sharing with us.

We love you, too.

Donna C

I just can't imagine all of this that Rhonda has to go through and how you are handling this… But, I know you both are trusting God…

Thank you both for your positive attitudes no matter what. It helps me with mine!

Say hi to that precious wife of yours for me!

God Bless and Love

Bobbie O

Please let her know that we continue to pray for her as well as so many others. This has been a long and difficult road for all of you and know that we lift you up in prayer and love all of you. Give her a big hug for me.

Virginia T

Please give Rhonda a big hug and kiss from her Miami family. We are all praying for her!!! Let her know that Dalia sends her Love too!!!!

Lynn W

Gary and I are praying for you both - Rhonda healing and Scott love and patience. Love you, Lynn and Gary.

Barbara C

Oh Rhonda I am so sorry that you have ileus! Having worked in the medical field for so many years I have seen my share of patients with ileus. It is painful. I am praying that your digestive system wakes up and you are no longer in pain or are nauseous. I am praying you will be well enough to go to the Cabin! I know many people are praying for that and the Lord certainly hears our prayers! Praying diligently! Love Barbara

Ellen C

Scott thank you for the update. My heart goes out to you and Rhonda for all that you guys have gone through. I pray every day for all of you. I know I haven't seen Rhonda in several years but she is still dear to my heart. Tell her that I still love her.

September 29
My Rhonda—Moving Towards Home

Hi,

I just wanted to send a quick update… all things are moving towards going home on Friday! PTL!

After a rough weekend (including some hurtful comments from a new dr who had been brought in)… we made some med (and dr!) adjustments… and decided that we needed to be back home. Today is day 31 in the hospital… after 25 days earlier around the surgery.

It is enough.

So… all things that have needed to happen have fallen into place… 1) removal of almost 2 liters of abdominal fluid greatly reduced the pain level (and the fluid had zero infections!)… 2) we're starting to cut back on pain meds… 3) All of the drs have 'bought in' and supported us in discharging Friday… 4) all antibiotics were stopped as of today (no fevers in weeks!)… 5) the ileus is going away (never thought we'd be so excited to hear a growling tummy)

It's like God said… "It's time!" :)

So… we're excited at the prospect of getting our lives back… family, church… and even making it to the cabin in OK in a few weeks. It has been a long haul… and we're not all of the way back by any means… but it's a huge step. God has been so gracious to carry us through all of this. We are so thankful to Him… and to you all who have carried us in your hearts and thoughts and prayers.

God Bless and please have a great week!
Scott and Rhonda

Responses

Jim T

Thanks for this report—this is great news. Praise God!!!
Continued prayers…

Patti S

We love you dearly… praying always.

Sylvia A

PTL!

Penny F

You two have been through more than anyone could imagine, and through it all you kept your faith. Patience is a virtue. If only more people could practice what they preach. Give Rhonda a hug for me. I am so glad things are looking brighter. Keep looking towards the hills from where cometh your strength.

Response to Penny from Scott

Whenever I share with the drs and nurses (or anyone) about how my company is allowing me to work from wherever to be with Rhonda during this time, they are amazed. Thank you for being such a huge part of allowing this to happen and giving me such flexibility for my work hours. We thank God every day for this gift from my co-workers and managers, and Rhonda looks forward to seeing you all at a lunch or something sometime soon. Thank you so much for your prayers, support, and friendship!

… God Bless!

Julius R

Hooray. Praise Our Lord.

Cindy H

Praise God from whom all blessings flow and for hearing our prayers!

Jan R

It's time! You've been there long enough! Praying God will make it happen! Love you both!

Nita S

To God be the Glory! Can we have a fireworks show?
We love you

Pam D

That is awesome news!

Myra P

We are very happy to hear all the good news about Rhonda. God is Almighty! PTL!
We will continue to pray for Rhonda and your family.
God bless.

Kat S

So excited to hear this!!! Please let us know if there is anything we can do to help y'all's coming home!

Denise A

That's good news!! We are still praying for you both!

Jane B

Thank you again for the report. Again, you are in our thoughts and prayers.

We love you all.

Terry and Lila C

Thanks for the update and Praise to the Father for both of you. Good news and we look forward to complete healing, strength and restoration for you both. Love you guys!!

God Bless you both.

Barbara C

Yay—"It's time!" I am praying all goes on schedule for you Rhonda to be coming home on Friday. That in itself will be the best medicine of all! God is so good! So sorry you had a problem with the new doctor-some of them are so smart but absolutely no "bedside manner". Their approach to patients is not something that can be taught in Medical School! Praying for you daily sweet lady!

Terry W

Hallelujah, finally great news... being home and cutting back on meds. Enjoy your time at the cabin Rhonda you and your family have earned it. may God still bless you and keep you. My prayers are still with you all. may your days be sunny and pain free

Nancy H

yeah! Many blessings on the upcoming days outside. That sounds so restorative and marvelous. Hugs!

Lourdes H

So very thankful to hear the good news. I'm especially happy to hear that there are no signs of infection and that pain medication can be reduced. Such a very good sign that she is healing. Thank you so much for the regular updates. It's wonderful for all of us who live out of town to get regular reports. Hugs for you, sweet Rhonda.

Teresa M

Thank you so much for the update, I'm so happy that she is going home. God is awesome! I will continue praying for you and your beautiful family. God bless!

Wanda J

What an answer to prayer! No fever!!! Prayers continue and are so happy you are finally headed home! Thanks so much for the great update, just what we have been waiting to hear! Love, Mom and Dad J.

Vicky S

Wonderful news, we've been praying for this day!

October 4
My Rhonda—Home Again!

Hello,

Yes! We were discharged on Friday and left the hospital at 4 PM… and we don't plan on going back! Friday night was busy with Rx runs, etc., and the TPN IV nutrition wasn't delivered to us until almost 10, so we didn't get that started until last night.

And we continue with NO fevers… not much appetite… and limited strength… but Rhonda blew me away yesterday with strength to walk all around the house (holding my hands). I am so proud of her effort! I didn't think we'd get to that point for a week!

So our main prayer focus is for appetite and strength building. There is no pain and very little nausea, and we are so thankful for that too! She does have a feeling of restlessness at times which is probably med-related… and we're looking for the magic combination there.

We also had a treat on Thursday at the hospital when our oldest son David came by and brought little Mable Mae. Rhonda got to hold and feed her for a few minutes. And then last night another unexpected visit from Jordan and his little ones. So great to see and hold our grandbabies! And Stef and Julie are coming over today. It's so great to be able to be a part of our family again!

So we are planning on our OK trip in a couple of weeks and looking forward to a time of true relaxation. Our Lord has been so good to bring us through this… it's great to know that better days are ahead!

Thank you again for your prayers and support!

God Bless!
Scott and Rhonda

Responses

Lupita O
Dear Rhonda and Scott, I'm so happy to celebrate all this blessings with you, I'll keep praying for both of you that GOD, bless Rhonda with health, and don't back to the hospital, anymore other just for check-up.
Hugs

Sylvia A

Good to hear you are home! I will keep you in prayer.

Praying she has strength to fully enjoy your upcoming trip to Ok.

Julius R

Praise goes to Him whom we trust. Rhonda, praying you'll be able to have the strength to enjoy Oklahoma.

Bobbie O

I am so thankful you all are home. Tell her I love her and give her a big hug. When she is up to it would love to come see her for a short visit. Thank you so much for letting us know. Yes, God is good.

Lynn B

Great News! I am amazed how strong you both have been throughout journey.

Sandy L

This is FABULOUS news!!!!

Thank you so much for sharing Gods Blessings!!!

Lots of Love and prayers

Terry C

Thank you for the update. Great news. God bless you both as you continue to recover.

Myra P

I'm so happy for Rhonda's continuous recovery and regaining her strength back.

God bless you all.

Trish M

AWESOME!!!! Made my week! Will be praying for continued strength and that Rhonda's appetite increases. I feel it in my bones… this is the beginning of putting all of this behind you guys!! Love you!!!

Peggy A

So happy to hear this GREAT news!

Barbara C

This makes my day! I will continue praying that each day you have more and more strength! God is so good to hear and answer our prayers!

Teresa M

I am so happy for Rhonda! I will continue praying for a full recovery. God is good!! Blessings.

Terry W

Hallelujah!!! Great news can't beat it. May each day be better than others and may the weather for the trip be perfect. You guys deserve the break and refreshing of the spirit with the beauty of God's creation—nature. God bless and keep you well… aw heck, better than that pre sick health.

Susan H

Great news continues to flow from you. Praise God that he answers our prayers. It will be a great blessing to hear how Rhonda continues to gain her appetite and strength.

Bless your family and the special time you have at the cabin in OK.

Marge B

Praise the Lord! Rhonda, Peggy and I will be in Dallas again to see her grandbaby this weekend, 10th and 11th. Don't know if you will be up to anything by then. Just know I am praying for you! Message me on facebook if you can. Love!

November 4
post from Stefanie—Still Home and Beginning to Heal

I am happy to announce that Mom is still home. She's been out of the hospital for about two or three weeks, including a weeklong trip to Oklahoma. She's been able to go to church and run a few errands with Scott. So far they've only gone to church on Wednesday night, as it's shorter and easier on Mom, and they've enjoyed being back in church.

Although Mom is still not strong enough to move around on her own, she has been able to walk for a few minutes on the treadmill (with supports to hold onto), so we know that she is getting stronger! She has had a few small fevers, but not as bad as they have been in the past. Mom was also able to be a little more invested in conversation, so all in all, I can see how she is beginning to heal. I can also tell that she is discouraged by how weak she still is. Studies show that recovery from chemo takes 2–5 years. Last time around, Mom had three years of healing before the cancer came back, and it took the whole three years to return to a mostly normal quality of life. Mom has been through a lot more this time, been a lot sicker and much weaker. This is where you guys come in. We (all of us humans on this planet) need prayer every single day. Mom needs prayers right now for continued healing and strength, for encouragement to keep going, and for hope and joy to keep her going strong in this process. We don't know how long it will take before Mom and Scott can return to a "normal" life, but we pray that however long it takes, that God is sovereign over it and will provide comfort and joy through the process. And that it would be a quick, smooth, and pain free process.

Mom has PET scans coming up that will show whether her lymph nodes are growing or not (we need them to be not growing.)

As always, thanks for your continued prayers, love, encouragement, and support.

Responses

Cynthia DL

I was thinking about you the other day wondering how you were doing. Prayers will be sent from me to you for the healing of your body, your mind and your soul. I pray that you smile every day for I truly believe that smiling heals your body. Please get well soon.

Take care.

Vicky S

Praying always!

Susan H

Praise God he is watching over such a special woman. May God continue to give you strength through the journey ahead toward your "normal". May he bless you and keep you close in his love. While at times it is hard not to get discouraged we know who holds us in his hands. Through our joy God gives us the strength to get through those rough patches. We see life so differently and the beauty of God's creation in everything around us. It is beautiful to behold. I am rejoicing with you that you are out of the hospital and on you way to normal.

Ps 91:1–2 He that dwelleth in the secret place of the most High shall abide under the shadow of the Almighty. I will say of the Lord, He is my refuge and my fortress: my God; in him will I trust.

Merlene

Love you Rhonda and prayers go up for you today for a complete recovery.

Lourdes H

Praying for you. Repeatedly. I am so happy you are taking those baby steps towards healing. I am so very thankful that finally we are trending in the right direction. You're small but you're scrappy. You are fighting a good fight, little girl. This doesn't surprise me. You have a long history of surviving tough times and doing hard things. Wishing you and your family all the very best. Big big hugs.

Marge B

Praying for you Rhonda! Love, Marge

December 14

post from Stefanie—Stronger

FYI: You should find a song about strength on youtube to play and listen to while you read this.

It's exciting to see how much stronger Mom is getting. I can tell that Grandma and Grandpa's visit last week did her much good. Mom and Scott have gone to Wednesday night church a few times recently, because there are fewer people and less time to be "on", but they went to church on Sunday morning. Mom was even up for a family dinner out at a restaurant last week. Awesome! I've noticed Mom eating a little more, too, and she's walking on the treadmill for a few more minutes at a time and at a higher level (eight minutes at level 4) than before (before was two minutes at level 2)! Yea!

Mom is doing considerably better than when she was in the hospital: she is noticeably more alert and can handle much more conversation and keeping up with people. She's getting back on Words With Friends, which means y'all are going down! Don't say I didn't warn you…

Mom's next doctor visit is this Wednesday, so please pray that all is well inside her and that God continues to heal and restore her, body and soul. As always, we appreciate your prayers and trust that God hears them and responds and is in control of everything, whether or not we understand.

Much love and many thanks.

Responses

Petra R

Stephanie: Thanks for posting such great news! This has to be the best Christmas gift for your family. I'm so happy for you and your family that Rhonda is consistently showing signs of healing. Your mother has been a true warrior and shown great courage during this battle. It's so nice to know she's on the road to recovery. Your family has been amazing through this entire process. You've all shown great unity, perseverance, and love for your mother. Your faith is an inspiration to all who want to learn about the power of prayer and faith. Your support for your mother has made a big difference in her recovery.

Susan H

This is such awesome news to hear and a wonderful miracle. Our God is truly in the miracle business His healing power cannot be restrained. It is my prayer that he continues to heal and strengthen you. I wish you and your family a Merry Christmas as we celebrate the birth of our Lord and Savior Jesus Christ.

Barbara C

What a wonderful update! Rhonda it was so good to run into you a while back at Albertson's-that was such a nice surprise! I thought about it all week. I've been praying for a miracle, and then to see you in the store was like walking right into a miracle! While I'm sure it was good for you to get out, I can't even explain what it did for me to see you. It was like witnessing first hand God's work! Enjoy this Christmas Season-I'm sure it will be a special one for your whole family! Merry Christmas!

Vicky S

So thankful she is getting stronger—never doubted it would happen!

Lourdes H

You're right Stephanie. She is back on Words with friends and she slays me every time. Even when she's sick. So glad to hear you're doing better Rhonda. I'm looking forward to losing more scrabble games. I continue to live for the day all you get is vowels and worthless letter tiles.

Lucy G

Rhonda, I think of and pray for you often. It's good to read this.

Sandy L

I am so happy and praising my Lord for this wonderful news!!!!
Thanks Stephanie for sharing!

Dec 25
My Rhonda—Moving Forward: An Overdue Update

Hello and Merry Christmas/Blessed Holiday Season to you all!

Well… it's hard to know where to begin. I've intended many
times to get an update out to you all. Our thanks to Stef to get out a
couple of Caring Bridge notes to give some progress reports.

There has been a lot of "3 steps forward, 2 steps back" since we
were last released from the hospital on Oct 2nd…

The home TPN treatments went okay, but were very involved
and time-consuming… and known side effects included affecting
your sense of taste and loss of appetite. Seemed kind of contradictory
to us, so we stopped TPN after 2 weeks… and just before our trip to
the cabin in OK. We had a great time, but Rhonda fevered on and
off all week. Rhonda just weathered through the fevers like she had
for the last year… but it was pretty discouraging after all she had just
gone through to stop the fevers.

We mentioned the fevers on a follow-up appt with the surgeon in November, and he gave us a Rx for some oral antibiotics to
take whenever they came on. After taking the pills for a few days, it
seemed to be doing the trick… the fevers were going away. It was
still a bummer to have fever at all… but it was very encouraging
that a pill could make it go away rather than the 3 high-powered IV

antibiotics she had been on all year. But the setbacks weren't finished with her yet...

As the fevers went away, one day we suddenly noticed a 'hole' in her surgical scar... big enough for my pinky to fit in. In another semi-emergency visit to the surgeon, he determined that the surgical area had been infected underneath... most likely from all of the bad stuff that had been messing up her liver. So... when the pocket of infection was cleared out by the antibiotics, it left a hole. And the only way to ensure proper healing of the surgical wound was to partially open it back up... and pack it with gauze every day so it healed from the inside out.

So... after getting off almost all of the pain meds, Rhonda had to go through all of that again... and I got to re-pack and re-dress it every day (sorry if this is TMI). And this is what we've been going through for the last month. The fevers first... and then the discomfort from re-opening the old wound... made it very difficult for Rhonda to move much and build strength. We were in a 'holding pattern' again.

So... the healing moved forward very slowly. We decided to keep her on the antibiotics until it fully heals to hopefully head off any more relapses. Rhonda's mom and dad came for a visit after Thanksgiving and really helped Rhonda to push more than she had felt up to previously... even getting up to 11 minutes on our treadmill! Maw-in-law also cooked up a storm and filled our freezer to overflowing. No going hungry around here!

After a generous Christmas gift from Rhonda's brother and wife, we decided to go all out and spent this last weekend at a hotel on nearby lake... in the fanciest suite that they had. It was a true indulgence… and mostly relaxing after we got through the hiccups of being able to even open the door to our room. We rested and enjoyed eating out once a day… wheeling around the eateries nearby.

And the weekend must have awakened something deep down for Rhonda… cause this week she's been on a rehab frenzy. Monday-Wednesday… each day… she pushed for 18 minutes on the tread-mill. And… using the walker instead of my hands… she's been getting around the house, working to take care of herself, folding laundry… NORMAL STUFF that she hasn't been able to do for the last 18 months.

But yesterday she really blew me away. She used the walker (instead of the wheelchair) to go to a restaurant… and then to the Christmas Eve service at our church. Wow… and PTL!!! The surgical wound is still not yet fully healed… but it's getting there.

To be continued… we pray and hope!

So… I know that this has been a long note. Our hearts are full of Thanks for your prayers and encouragement… and for this special Christmas season and what it means to us… to the whole world. We really need some peace right now. God has been so faithful to bring us through everything. And we feel that 2016 is going to be a banner year for us… we've got all of these granddaughters to keep up with! :)

Thank you and God Bless… and best wishes for you all for the upcoming New Year!
Scott and Rhonda

Responses

Sandy L

> Thanks so much for the update!
> It really helps to know how to pray for my sweet Rhonda!
> I believe that 2016 will be the best year ever for your family!
> Lots of Love

Sylvia A

> I saw Peggy and Trish last week for lunch and was just asking about you both as I hadn't seen any updates and behold I was glad to see your note. Please know I continue to keep you both in prayer and glad to hear Rhonda had a good Christmas.

> Many blessings to you both and all your family in this Christmas season and always

Patti S

> God Bless you both. We will not stop praying for a wonderful 2016!

Jan R

> You continue to be a beacon of True Faith to me! God's ways are not our ways & God's timing not our timing. A challenge you are all too familiar with. Thank you for sharing your journey—the praises & the challenges!

> God bless you and your family!

Jan D

> Merry Christmas Scott & Rhonda —you guys are always in my thoughts… here's hoping for a positive new year!

Mike M

> We Love You Guys.
> Merry Christmas and a happy and healthy new year.

Barbara C

> Thank you for the update. Those infections can be nasty things! I am so excited to hear that Rhonda has a bit more energy! Greg and I are praying for complete recovery in 2016. We all need some good news with what is going on in the news! Enjoy those granddaughters!

Petra R

> Thanks for the update! I'm so relieved to learn that you're continuing to make progress and you were able to spend the holidays with family. The road may be bumpy, but you're building momentum with each step. Rhonda, you're truly amazing. May God continue to bless you with positive news and make 2016 a very special healing year for you.

Lourdes H

> I am so happy for Rhonda. There are no words. Her faith and the fight in her makes me try to be a better person every day. But I need to take a moment and thank Scott, whom I have never met. Thank you, thank you, thank you for being the husband you are. I am so thankful that Rhonda has you at her side. Caring for her, loving her, pushing her back to health and normalcy. You are a dear dear man. So thankful for all the good things coming your way.

Nancy H

> AWESOME!!!! All that recent energy is excellent - and blessedly normal! Praise God for whom all blessings flow. You go girl!

Terry W

I know how hard it is to beat Rhonda at any game we play so I know that she will beat this horrible illness and the setbacks. She's the champ, it doesn't stand a chance. But my prayers and well wishes just the same.

2016: The Slow Path to Recovery

Jan 12, 2016
My Rhonda—Check-Up Day

Hi,

I just wanted to give a report on Rhonda's appt today... the first oncology appt since November. Also... the first appt without her picc line for lab test blood draws. She had that removed in December at an appt with the surgeon in an important step in moving on from all that lay behind.

So... my poor Rhonda had a pretty rough last week... thanks to (we think) a bad fish sandwich last Tuesday. She ended up being violently ill all night.. and a relapse the next day when she thought she felt better, but her tummy didn't agree. Of course... all of this really drained her strength. But she still pushed to get back to her 18 minutes per day on the treadmill. When she pushed on Saturday, it was too much for her... and she ended up with fever/chills for most of the day... which took any strength she had left and was hoping to have to go to church last Sunday... but we couldn't make it happen.

So... after a week like that... yesterday she started to bounce back a bit... and we had this appt today. There was a natural dread over getting blood for labs... without a picc line for the first time in 18 months. So... the tech could not find any usable veins in her arms... and the stick came on the back of her hand... and went relatively great! Wow... whew... and PTL for those little things!

Then we waited for the lab results and to see the doctor. There have been many times when he's been hours behind schedule... but today he was pretty much on time (another small miracle for us).

As the doctor was looking at her chart and lab results. He said, "You're freaking me out a bit here with these counts." Oh… meaning, what? His response was, "I'm not used to seeing counts so 'normal' here." I said "Wow… Great!… even the liver enzymes?"… and he read us her liver counts… all in the 'normal' range when the last time they had been off literally by a couple thousand percent!

Really?? Wow and PTL again!!!

This is just amazing to us… especially after being ill all week which previously had made her counts all messed up. But now… all counts are "normal."

THIS is what we've been praying/suffering/working toward… the opportunity to get back to "normal" again. The strength and stamina are still a ways off… but with "normal" blood counts, we can look forward to continuing to move forward… and getting more areas of our lives back to "normal." Wow… and PTL!

Our Lord has been so gracious to us… my eyes are misting up even now. This has been such a long time coming. This is amazing to us. Wow.

And… all you who've been lifting us up in thought and prayer… we are humbled by the effort you have spent on our behalf. Prayers are being answered. Thank you all so much!

So.. we are cutting back on some of the meds… and the next appt is in another 6 weeks… and Rhonda plans to leave the wheelchair behind for that appt… and stroll in with her new strength that she will doggedly continue to pursue. That's my girl!

And that's our Lord!!! Wow!

Thank you again… and God's Blessings to you all!
Scott and Rhonda

Responses

Lila C

Oh my Scott, so thankful! I was thinking about you both so heavily and just wrote to her. I love you both with all my heart. Our visit was such a blessing. Thank you for calling us. Your friendship is such a gift from our Lord who loves us all. Please take care Scott and hug your Rhonda for me.

Ryan G

That's amazing news!!

Jim F

Scott, thanks so much for the update. The Lord is faithful.
Love you

Patti S

God Bless You! We will continue to pray for the normal so many of us take for granted… there is never a Sunday when we all don't ask, pray, inquire about your well being

Suraya K

Congratulations and God Bless you both. I pray that 2016 will be a great year for you and your family.

Sylvia A

Amen!!

Sandy L

Praise The Lord!!!!

Such wonderful news!!!!

Blessings

Mella S

Normal is such a beautiful word. Please may there be more normal for the Smiths. Thanks for the info.

Bruce W

Thanks for sharing Scott, This is Rhonda's turnaround year in Jesus name......

Nita S

Well, did you just hear our SHOUT for joy??? So good to hear this wonderful report. Prayers will not stop and we know God will continue to answer.

We love you

Trish M

Wow! Just awesome you guys!!! no doubt you're so, so happy with the results!!! Rhonda, keep doing what you're doing!!! You guys are amazing!!!

Always praying for you. You've got this!

Jan D

Oh, Scott... I am SO, SO, SO happy for you guys!! Such great news for you – keep it up!

Judy R

Thank you for this wonderful update!

I'm so happy for both of you! :)

Myra P

PTL! Our Lord is Almighty. I'm very happy for the great news that you shared to us.

I'll continue to pray for Rhonda's continuous healing and prayers for your family too.

God bless you all!

Greg G

Great news Scott & Rhonda! Amazing is all I can say. PTL!

Clifton W

Sounds like a great report. PTL.

Jan R

Thank the Lord for "normal" test results! Amen for your normal results!

Bobbie O

That is wonderful news. We are so thankful to God and thrilled for all He is doing and has done. Give her a big hug for me and tell her we are still praying, in fact we did this morning and we love her.

Jane B

Thank you so very much for the communications! We continue to pray for Rhonda and all the family.

With love

Dina T

Wow and Thank you God is right! I am so happy to hear her blood work came back with such positive results. Looking forward to Rhonda gaining her strength back and for both of you to move forward.

Thank you for sharing Scott. Give Rhonda an extra hug from me.

Donna C

Scott!

What wonderful news! I know you are so very happy about Rhonda's most recent progress and I hope since your last email, she is getting even better.

She is a much better patient than I would ever be! Say hi to her for us. We still keep Rhonda on the Gideon email and at the Garland Gideon camp meetings for prayer.

Thanks again for taking the time to give us the details in your update.

And God's Blessings to the both of you!

Sylvia A

My daughter Cristina sent me this testament from a couple at their church that was shared on Easter Sunday. The couple immediately reminded me of both you and Rhonda's unwavering trust and devotion in our Lord. I once said to the both of you that I believe God works thru each of us to help others and that I believed God chose you two to be an inspiration to all of us - and you still continue to be. May God continue to bless you with his mercy and love and reward you for being teachers to us and demonstrating what unconditional love is.

Nancy H

Absolutley Fabulous!!!! Rhonda you are an inspiration - and indefatigable. Scott - you are an amazing caregiver, supporter, and faithful warrior for your princess. Prayer Warriors are Fighting Hard... and I am grateful for everyone who's fed them, helped them in any way possible, covered this family in prayer, and been a blessing to them! I can't wait to see what Rhonda & Scott do next January without rehab!!! PTL! Thanks also to Stephanie..for all the regular updates, gathering of family and friends, being gatekeeper and amazing trench digger! You all bless us… and I am grateful you are in Rhonda's life. Thank you.

Susan H

Praise the Lord Rhonda. This is fantastic news for you, Scott and your family. I know you will be working hard to reach your new normal and then some.

Ps 92:1 It is a good thing to give thanks unto the Lord, and to sing praises unto thy name, O Most High.

Terry W

What great news. Sorry about the fish episode tho. Hope it at least tasted good going down lol… With God's help your strength and endurance will return and your "normal routine" will be uneventful. Take care

Petra R

Thanks for sharing your latest progress. What wonderful news! So happy for you to receive this type of news from your doctor. Rhonda, it's great to see that you're setting goals for yourself such as being able to leave your wheelchair at the next appointment. Progressing from a wheelchair to a walker is an awesome target. Scott, your dedication and devotion to Rhonda is very special. I'm so glad Rhonda has someone like you who cares so deeply for her. Wishing you the very best

Ellen C

Rhonda, I am so thankful that you are doing so well. I too, praise the Lord for his healing upon you. All of our prayers for you are being heard and I thank God that He is such an awesome God and so gracious, merciful and loving and wants us all to be healed. I will continue to pray for you. I so wish that I could visit with you in person. Maybe someday!!! Love you girl and keep up the good work.

Also I would like to thank your husband and children for taking such good care of you. Scott I hope I get to meet you someday. Men like you are very rare and I just happen to have a husband like you that takes very good care of me. I am very blessed and I know Rhonda feels the same way.

Wanda J

Wow and Wow!

The news we have been praying for and waiting to read! PTL! Love to all and Rhonda honey we love you and prayers continue!

Lourdes H

So thankful for this good news. Thank you so much for sharing! Love you Rhonda!

March 6
My Rhonda—Scan Results

Hi All,

I just wanted to share that Rhonda had a PET scan recently… and the results were 'clean'. PTL!

We also had another check-up and the lab counts are still good... PTL!

Rhonda continues to work hard at regaining her strength... on the treadmill and exercise bike 5 days a week. And this past week we actually did about 1/2 mile a couple of times on our favorite greenbelt trail. This is all wonderful but very exhausting to her. She needs a lot of rest still. And in the mornings are the greatest challenge with neuropathy in her legs/feet... which impacts her balance, so we still have to be careful... but have had no mishaps/falls. She is making great use of the walker... and we bring in the wheelchair when needed (which is becoming much less frequent). PTL!

There is still a nagging pain in the surgery area that tightens up on Rhonda when she gets up to walk. It may be an adhesion or scar tissue or...? We wish it would go away, but Rhonda soldiers on... and we are thankful for pain meds when needed. We will have an appt with the surgeon soon and hope to get more info to help it heal.

Some days it still seems like there's such a long ways to go to "get our life" back... but we know that the Lord has brought us so far... and are so thankful for what we have every day. We have been "regular" to our church services the last few weeks too... what a blessing that has been... to fellowship and enjoy our friends there again.

We also have our annual anniversary trip coming up soon... a week at a cabin in OK.
We are REALLY looking forward to that! PTL again!

Thank you again for the prayers, encouragement, help, and for checking up on us... we always know that we are not alone. Our God is loving us through you all.

Please have a good week… and thank you for being here with us… every day! We love and appreciate you all!

Scott and Rhonda

Responses

Clifton W

Thanks for the report. Rhonda is still in my prayers.

Jane B

Thank you so very much for the report. You have been on my mind especially lately.

Be assured of our thoughts and prayers!

Sandy L

This is WONDERFUL news!!!

I have so LOVED spending Sunday lunches with my Rhonda!!!

Sylvia A

Yes PTL for the clean scans and praying that Rhonda's strength continues to improve so you both enjoy your anniversary. Will continue to keep you both in prayer.

Julius R

Great news and have continued to pray for y'all daily. God is good.

Mella S

Thanks for the update. We were afraid to ask but wanted to know. So glad there is still progress and that makes me feel better.

Patti S

Praise God and may He continue to cover your every step.

Pam D

That is AWESOME news!

Jan R

Praise, praise, praise! Love you two!

Lupita O

Scott and Rhonda, I'm sooo happy that finally, everything is going better and better for both of you, and you'll see GOD is going to permit celebrate your anniversary in Ok.

I will keep you in prayers.

With love

Dina T

Such great news Scott! Please know that I think about you both often and will continue to pray for complete healing. Our God is a mighty doctor!

Lila C

We praise God for a good report. You both are such inspirations. I love you both dearly

Judy R

Thank you for the great news! I'm happy to hear that Rhonda is getting stronger, and the tests are positive.

I want to be sure to stay in touch and hear how you're doing.

Donna C

Wow this is such good news, it's the B E S T ! Praise The Lord how he's worked in your lives.

Great and encouraging update!

love and hugs

Bobbie O

So thankful her tests came back good. I am so glad she is getting stronger and you all are going to Okla. We are praying for you and know this has been a long and hard journey. Pray you have a wonderful time.

Jim F

Thanks, Scott. It blessed me to read about the progress Rhonda has made.

I hope you have a great time in Oklahoma!

Myra P

PTL! We are very happy for you and Rhonda. We will continue to pray for Rhonda's continuous healing and recovery.

God bless you all.

Nancy H

How fabulous! you go girl! I'm so very proud of you - and your family!

Teresa M

So happy your scan came all clean, God bless you always you have a beautiful family, I will continue praying for you!!

Susan H

I am praising the Lord along with you, Scott and family. It is so wonderful to hear your scan was clean. I am right there with you and the nagging neuropathy. I do hope your doctors are able to come up a way to relieve some of the annoying pain without effecting your equilibrium and balance any further. Perhaps a therapist will be able to give you some way to stretch out the area near the surgical area to relieve the pain you have when standing. I do hope you have a wonderful time celebrating your anniversary.

Praying God continues to strengthen you along your way each day,

Ps105:1 O give thanks unto the Lord; call upon his name: make known his deeds among the people.

Peggy A

Yay about the scan and numbers.

Ellen C

Rhonda, I am so happy that your scans were clean and that your blood work is still good. I am sorry about your neuropathy bothering you tho. I also have neuropathy and I can understand your pain with it. So I will now continue to pray for you but will include the neuropathy in my prayers. I know there is medication that you can take that helps to alleviate the pain but unfortunately I cannot take it. And I am afraid to try anything else. So I take the pain in stride. But God takes care of me. So keep me in your prayers also.

I love you girl!!! Take care and get well soon. And thank that wonderful family for taking care of you and for keeping us all posted on your health progress.

March 29
My Rhonda—11th Anniversary Trip

Hi,

We hope and pray that you all are doing well. I just wanted to give you all a quick update after our week in the cabin in OK.

Of course… it was SO good to get away from the house, work, etc. We just relaxed and watched movies and went out to eat when we felt like it. :) The weather started out very warm, but then went back and forth with storms and hail towards the end of the week. We're very thankful that our car was not damaged. The cabin was a bit drafty… and spring allergies were in the air… and my Rhonda had to endure a very sore throat and some low-grade fevers again… ugh. We contemplated going home early, but she is my trooper, and did her best to enjoy each day, so we stuck it out but just couldn't push forward with much of an agenda of doing stuff (except as listed above… LOTS of movies!).

Once back at home she took a few days to recover and again is working hard at building her strength… hitting the treadmill and exercise bike with regularity… 18 minutes each… 5 days a week. We've even started this week walking a very short block around the house. It's wonderful to take a walk with my girl!

We also enjoyed a wonderful Easter service Sunday at our church… even chatting with some friends that we don't see that often. We are so blessed to have our Hope in a Savior who willingly put Himself through so much… and then gained such a powerful victory over death… for us!

I also want to note that we know that there are several on this distribution who are in a time of transition. If you would like to continue to receive our "updates," please forward another email address to me. And regardless, please know that our fervent prayers are with you all.

So… thanks to all for your unending love and support! All of the "bad stuff" is behind us and Rhonda is working very hard to get her life back. As always, the Lord is our strength!

Thank you and God Bless!
Scott and Rhonda

Responses

Roxzanne M
Hi Scott, you and Rhonda are an inspiration to a lot of people. Always giving thanks and praise to God during your many challenges. I like receiving your updates. You two are always in my prayers. Thanks for sharing your lives with me.

Clifton W
Glad you had an enjoyable trip and a blessed Easter. I appreciate your updates and wish to continue to receive your updates

Dina T
So glad you 2 were able to get away and enjoy time together Scott!
Continually praying for Rhonda's strength and yours too. Thanks for the updates.

Patti S

Thank you Scott… God bless you both!

Greg G

Great to hear from you Scott. I'm glad you two were able to get away. I know that is a blessing no matter what you do. Movies are always a great way to relax and just be. Take care brother/warrior. Keep up the good fight. Give my love to Rhonda.

Linda S

Hi Scott and Rhonda—So glad to hear you were able to get away to your favorite spot in OK. I just want to thank you. You are the perfect example of faith and through all the trials and tribulation in life you have remained a constant inspiration to all of us.

Best of luck in your journey to good health and continued happiness and many more getaways to your favorite spot.

I'd love to be included in future updates.

Drew C

Scott, so grateful that you guys have finally made it through to wellness – our God is so good.

Love ya bro!

Sandy L

I LOVE the encouraging update!!! Thanks so much for the day brightener!

Jan D

Yeah Scott!! Thanks for the update… so glad she's on her way back to "normal"… one step at a time…

Jan R

God is Good all the time! Amen!

Bobbie O

So thankful you got to make the trip. Tell Rhonda I hope we can visit soon. Glad Rhonda is building her strength back. Looking forward to seeing her soon.

Donna C

So good to get an update! Happy Anniversary! Wow, 11 years!

So glad that you both made it to church for Easter and so glad that you made your Oklahoma trip.

Praise God for Rhonda's progress. So happy she has determination.

Anyway, I love your great news and keep on, keeping on and before you know it the both of you will be attending church on a regular basis!

Whoo Hoo!

love and hugs

Jane B

Please keep us on your e-mail list. We love to hear from you and are blessed to be a part of your prayer army.

With love

Barbara C

Please keep the Emails coming to me. Rhonda is on my daily prayer list and will stay there until Jesus comes for us!

Lourdes H

I definitely want to keep getting emails concerning Rhonda. We are enjoying all the good news in the latest reports. I also know she's doing well because she is slaying me regularly and thoroughly in online scrabble. Keep it up, Rhonda. Big big bear hugs. Love ya

April 24
My Rhonda—An Amazing Week

Hi,

I hope that you all are well! I just have to share what wonderful things Rhonda is accomplishing!

This week we had a follow-up with the oncologist… and for the first time in 18 months or so… she walked into the clinic. No wheelchair… no walker… just my arm to lean on. It was an amazing testament to her diligent hard work on the treadmill and exercise bike (now up to 20 mins each… 5 days a week). I'm so proud of her effort and how far she's come! She is still unsteady at times (which makes me a bit nervous), but she has come so, so far! PTL!!!

And btw… the counts and everything continue to be good… so the checkup went great! Next appt in 8 weeks. PTL!

So… today we go to church for a typically wonderful message and service… and we got to share lunch with some dear friends. Great stuff! So… I asked Rhonda when we were leaving church… "Do you want to try driving home today?" She had been thinking about and wanting to try driving again… it's been a long time for that too. So she surprised me and said 'Yes!'. Oh boy. Here go the nerves again. The last time she tried driving… about 14 mos ago… she was still very weak and fatigued… and it didn't go very well. But today… she drove us home like she'd been driving all the time… wow. Amazing!

485

With these "steps" she's been able to take... she is getting close to being "independent" again. This will be an adjustment for both of us... but an amazing step towards "getting her life back." This has been our prayer... "Dear Lord... please restore the years that the locusts have eaten." (Joel 2:25) We're getting there! PTL!

So again... thank you for your prayers. God is answering and providing the willpower and strength to make some great strides in a positive direction... and we are SO thankful!

Please have a great evening and week... God Bless!
Scott and Rhonda

Responses

D'Ann C

What wonderful news! PTL. Will continue praying.

Clifton W

Great news! Congratulations, Rhonda.

Sylvia A

So glad to hear that God continues to shower you both with His many blessings- all of God's miracles come at His time.

Jan R

What a great story! Thank you for sharing! Love you both!

Sandy L

It is easy to see Rhonda's progress! She is amazing!!!
Many MANY answered prayers!!!!
Thanks soooo much for the update!!!

Trish M

Oh wow!!! This is such GREAT news!!!! Made me want to jump out of my chair!!LOL!!!

You guys are always in my prayers. What a warrior Rhonda is and what a partner you are Scott. God Bless you guys!!!

Jane B

Praise the Lord for answered prayer! We love you and continue to pray for you.

Donna C

This is such wonderful news! As I was reading this, I could feel a smile on my face and the more I read my smile was getting bigger, No Joke! This is The B E S T email we have gotten from you in a while…

Praise The Lord! Indeed!

Tell your lovely wife hi for me!

love and hugs

Lupita O

This is amazing, this is a miracle!!!! I'm sooo happy to hear all this blessing, HE can do everything and anything.. Amen. With love

Amy G

This is SO wonderful to read!! God is faithful! May He continue to bless, heal and strengthen.

Ellen C

Rhonda I am so proud of you for the steps you have taken to get back to yourself. You have taken great strides to be well again. I praise the Lord for sparing your life and letting you get well. Just keep up the good work and let God take control. Love you girl

Petra R

Thanks for posting such a positive update on Rhonda's health. Her progress is so encouraging. It warms my heart to learn Rhonda is quickly moving toward independence and feeling empowered to try new challenges. Your faith in God and prayer is inspirational. I pray that Rhonda's hard work continues to pay off in delightful ways and you both successfully adapt to the changes this brings. Best wishes

Lynn W

So thankful to our great and mighty God for His continued healing in your life.

Susan H

This is wonderful news. It is great to hear how well you are progressing. I know how hard you are working to get your life back and move on past cancer. How awesome is our God and worthy of praise.

Psalm 40:5 Many, O Lord my God, are thy wonderful works which thou hast done, and thy thoughts which are to us-ward: they cannot be reckoned up in order unto thee: if I would declare and speak of them, they are more than can be numbered.

Terry W

this is excellent news. God definitely answered all your prayers

Lourdes H

Love this so very very much. So happy to read updates like this

Nancy H

Fabulous! Love you, and so excited you're back & healthy!

*****

Shortly after this update, we got urgent messages from Stefanie saying that Julie was in the ER due to a spinal injury. Her left leg was totally disabled, but she had some movement in her right leg. With all of the joy Rhonda and I were getting to experience with her own recovery, this heartbreaking news served to really slam the brakes on our momentum and put a damper on our spirits.

In those first days, I took Rhonda to the hospital to be with Julie several times and even logged into work a time or two as I had done when Rhonda was in the hospital. But I realized, for my own sanity, I couldn't plan on doing that every day again. So I had to come to a decision. Would I place limits and only take Rhonda to see Julie once or twice a week, or should I let Rhonda drive and go to the hospital on her own? She had only driven home from church that one time. When I took her to see Julie, we used the wheelchair so Rhonda could conserve strength and be assured of a comfortable place to sit while we visited.

I really struggled with this. Just when things were finally going good for us, this happens. I was really concerned for Rhonda's strength and safety, but how could I keep her from ministering to her daughter in such need? Stefanie was a wonderful help, going to see Julie many times and helping with errands and logistics. Charlie had been rooming with Julie for several months, and he and Stef looked after Julie's dogs and kept up with the bills, etc. But Rhonda was her "momma." Julie has a very tender heart, especially for her momma.

I decided that I needed to "turn Rhonda loose" with much prayer giving her to God for strength and safety while pleading to our Lord for no return of fevers from overextending herself. It turned out that the "momma bear" in Rhonda was awakened, and the Lord used Julie's need to fuel Rhonda's desire to work even harder to build strength to be there for her daughter. It was time, once again, for Rhonda's "mind over matter" to kick in, and it did!

Amazingly, by the Lord's wonderful Grace, Rhonda was able to drive and visit Julie multiple times a week with no huge setbacks to her own recovery. She was drained but determined to keep pressing on. Julie was very apologetic and felt bad for everyone having to scramble around to take care of her and her stuff. She really thrived on Rhonda's visits, and Rhonda knew that she needed to be there to help and support her.

After three and a half weeks, Julie was released from the hospital. She had nowhere to go where she could be taken care of, so Rhonda and I took her into our home. Dealing with meds and twenty-four-hour care for a person who couldn't get around proved to be a frantic exercise for us, and we realized that we couldn't do this indefinitely. After a week or so, a visiting physical therapist was getting Julie's vitals and found her blood pressure to be pretty high, too high for therapy. After checking with her nurse, we were told to take Julie to ER. So we loaded up everything and took her to the Dallas VA hospital where it was determined that Julie had developed an infection, so they admitted her. We were so thankful that Julie was already on disability from her military service, and the VA would take care of all her medical needs.

It was a relief for us to get a break from the twenty-four-hour care, but this also meant that Rhonda would have to drive about twice as far to visit Julie. She was moved to the VA rehab center after the infection was cleared up and was in-patient for several weeks. We also had a family meeting, and Charlie agreed to continue to be Julie's roommate once she was out of the hospital. Her current apartment was not wheelchair accessible, so Stef, Rhonda, and I launched a search for a new apartment that would accommodate Julie's wheel-chair. The Lord's favor was with us, and we found a complex much closer to our house than the previous place so it would be easier for Rhonda to make her initial multiple visits per week. Thank you, Lord, for that! But Rhonda's body could only handle so much care giving, and the day finally came where she was forced to rest and recover.

*****

June 29
From Scott to the SS Class

Dear Friends,

I just wanted to ask you to pray for Rhonda... and Julie. Rhonda has been visiting Julie in the hospital about 3 times a week for the last 2 months... and last night her exhausted body said... "enough." She came down with severe chills followed by fever... similar to last year before her surgery. The fever appeared to "break" overnight, but I have told her that she needs an extended period of rest to recover from weeks of pushing to care for Julie. She just does not have the strength to be a "caregiver." Please also pray for Julie because tomor-row was to be the day that Rhonda and Charlie were going to take her out on a "1-day pass" and go out to eat... see friends and her dogs... and see her new apartment complex. Now... that won't be happening... and Julie will be very disappointed (we don't know if Charlie is able or willing to take Julie out by himself yet and the VA may not allow for tomorrow... but it will be part of their new life together as roommates soon). It is also very hard on Rhonda to not have the strength to be there for Julie during this time. She has the true heart of a selfless mother. I'm so proud of her efforts! We also pray that this is a "wake-up call" for Julie to work as hard as she can to not depend on her mom.

The reference verse for our couple's devotion this morning was Exodus 18:17... where Moses' father-in-law, Jethro, saw Moses trying to act as a lone judge for all of Israel... "The job is too heavy a burden for you to handle all by yourself". We are taking this as a message from our Loving Heavenly Father. Isn't He amazing?

Thank you so much for your love and prayers... you all are such a blessing to our lives!
Scott

Response

Sandy L
Praying Praying Praying!!!

Response from Scott to Sandy
Thank you Sandy! After an emotional morning... things appear to be working out. Julie is handling the disappointment well. Rhonda is doing okay now too... just drained from it all. Charlie told us he's not ready to take Julie out by himself. As her roommate, he will learn. Julie is helping him with a car and a place to stay... and he will learn to help her. God will work this out too...

He is in control!
We love you guys!

Sandy L
YEA!!! So glad our prayers are already being answered!!!
Praise the Lord!!!

We love you too!

*****

So Julie was finally released from the VA hospital on July 15. We, along with Stefanie and Charlie, had been madly dashing to get everything set up and moved. It took awhile and much effort to wade and sort through everything to get it cleaned up, packed, and moved. I was on my final trip with furniture with my SUV and decided to stop for a soda and snack before getting on the highway with my load. As I was getting out of the car, a man walked up and pointed out that the sofa I thought I had secured to the roof had already shifted and was on its way to sliding right on off. Hmmm, don't need that happening on the highway (in my mind I could see it flying off and going into somebody's windshield... mercy!) So I thanked the guy and went to work trying to retighten the tie-downs. Then he spoke again, and I noticed he was standing next to a flatbed truck that was about twenty feet long. He told me that he was just returning from a morning run and that for twenty dollars, he'd put the sofa on his truck and haul it wherever I needed it to go. Wow. I told him this apartment was probably about fifteen miles away and asked him if that would even buy his gas. He said it probably wouldn't, "But God told me I need to do a good deed today." Wow. So I found a cash machine inside the store and gave him the twenty dollars after we had loaded the sofa on his truck. He said, "You don't have to pay me until we get there." I told him that I trusted him (and the sofa was in such shape that I didn't think it would be a huge loss if it disappeared). He followed me as we got on the highway that was now being spared from an "unidentified flying sofa," and we drove to the new apartment without incident. After we unloaded, I gave the man another twenty dollars, which he tried to refuse. I told him that God told me to cover his gas. One more angel our Lord sent to help and deliver us from what could have been a tragic situation. Thank you, Lord!

So now Julie and Charlie have been roommates and are doing well. We are so thankful for Charlie taking care of his sister, getting her to appointments, shopping, etc., so Rhonda doesn't feel like she has to do it all. PTL and thanks, Charlie! Stefanie continues to be helpful in many ways too. The family really pulled together to get us through this time.

The following update is when I first shared about Julie with our full e-mail support group, along with more amazing recovery news about my Rhonda!

*****

Nov 27
My Rhonda—So Many Reasons to be Thankful!

Hi,

We pray that you all are doing well! It has been several months since the last 'update', so I wanted to catch you up on things.

Rhonda is amazing. She continues to work hard and is getting her life back in many ways. When I sent the last note (Apr 24), she had just driven for the first time in 14 months. She is now running errands, shopping, etc. like crazy. Definitely got the 'driving' part back. Check!

She had several of her siblings in CA saying that they wanted to come see her. We figured it would be better for Rhonda to make a trip out there so she could see all of them at once. So… in August she flew out to CA solo and got to receive hugs from many family-members. Traveling cross-country on her own… Check!

And after being nursed along by others for so long, Rhonda had a strong desire to work to do something for others. So, after numerous inquiries and much prayer, in Sept she started teaching a GED Math class at our church. Every Wednesday night for 2 hours! There are 3 classes left in this first semester, and she's been busy creating a very comprehensive semester review for the 5 ladies in her class. Oh… and she LOVES working through all of the math! :) Reaching out to others… and TEACHING… wow… and Check!

And… for the first time since 2013, we were blessed to celebrate the October 1st anniversary (our 12th this year) of our first date… and NOT be in the hospital! Check and Double Check!!!

Also… in mid-October, we went on a road trip to IA to help our niece Martha get married and visit with some precious family. Five days and 2,200 miles in the car. Road Trip!… Check!

I simply cannot put into words how proud I am of my Rhonda… how thankful we are that she has come so far. Life is just about 'normal' around here, but we're not totally back to full strength and have weathered some heartache and challenges along the way too.

By far the most heart-wrenching event has been when our daughter Julie injured her spine around the first of May and is currently without the use of her legs. This really pushed Rhonda into 'hyper-Momma' mode, where I just had to 'give her back to God' and allow her to visit Julie multiple times a week in the hospital (just a couple of weeks after Rhonda had first driven). Our Gracious Lord gave her strength… and kept her safe… during those days… PTL! Daughter/sister Stef has been a huge help during this time, and son/brother Charlie has been an amazing roommate for Julie, helping her with those multiple day-to-day things… getting her to appts… taking her shopping… all the things that Rhonda just does not have the strength to do. We are VERY thankful for Charlie's selfless help to his sister! What a guy!

So with all that Rhonda has accomplished, we still need to be careful not to overdo it. She needs a lot of down-time and rest, and has had several bouts of the 24-hr chills/fever routine when her body is just too worn out to fight it off. Those times are NOT fun.

So we've had a couple of good follow-up appts with the oncologist with counts and everything mostly looking really good, but the liver enzymes can still get a bit crazy. So… with that and the unexplained fevers, we are on our way back to the liver specialist (hadn't seen him since 2011) to see if he can tell what might be going on. Our appt is on 12/12, and there may be a scan worked in sometime soon too. We are praying for good results in all things, and know that our Lord will continue to hold us in His Mighty Hands each step along the way… just as He has been.

We love and appreciate you all… so much… and pray that you have a wonderful holiday season as we look forward to celebrating the best Christmas Gift ever given… a little baby born and placed in a manger… who grew into the most selfless 'Son of Man' ever known… as He gave His all to make a way for sinners like me to have all the bad and ugly stuff deep inside washed clean… and the privilege of being called a child of God. To Him we always give all of the Praise and Glory… forever and ever.. amen.

God Bless!
Scott and Rhonda

Responses

Jan R

I pray that Rhonda learns to pace herself & get rest in between projects - something that I have a hard time with too! You are both such lights in this dark world - true examples of Faith!

Clifton W

Good to hear your amazing report on Rhonda. God is so good. Many prayers have been answered. Sorry to hear about Julie and pray that she may regain the use of her legs. Merry Christmas!

Trish M

You made my day with Rhonda's update! She is something else!!

Dina T

I am so happy to hear about all of these huge milestones/blessings/checked off items! Boy are we lucky to have the grace and mercy of an awesome God! :)

I am sorry to hear about your daughter. I don't think I knew that she was injured. Really cool that her brother is helping her with the day to day stuff. I will be praying for her and continuing to pray for you, Rhonda and the rest of your family.

Thank you for the update. :)

Judy R

Hey Scott I'm so happy to hear that Rhonda is out and about! :)
Terribly sad about Julie's injury, I hope she heals!

Debbie B

    She looks great!

Barbara C

    Wonderful encouraging and uplifting report! Thank you Stephanie! I will be praying for the liver scan on the 12th. It is an honor and pleasure to know your family and to be praying for all prayer requests. Rhonda you truly are an inspiration to so many people and I love seeing God's people come together to pray for you and your family. This is what God intended for His body of Christ! Love to all!

Lourdes H

    So many reasons to be thankful today. Praying for continued good news. Love ya Rhonda

Nancy P

    Hi Scott and Stefanie! Thanks for the update today. I'm so thankful for all God's doing in and through Rhonda. It's been a long, tough road, but her tenacious faith has carried her through. Rhonda is an inspiration to many of us, and I'm happy to call her a dear friend!

    Will be praying for a good report from the appointment on the 12th!

Amy G

    Awesome post!! Rejoicing with you for the amazing gift of life the Lord has blessed Rhonda with! Love the picture and the smiles!

    Thank you for the update!!

Ellen C

Scott, that was a beautiful letter honoring Rhonda. She is an amazing woman. And I am so thankful that she has come so far in fighting this illness. God is so good to all of us that believe he is faithful for all of our concerns. May you both and your family have a very blessed Christmas. And know that we love you all. Take care.

2017: Getting Our Lives Back—God Is Faithful

Jan 8, 2017
My Rhonda—2017: A New Year of Health and Strength

Happy New Year Ya'll!

That phrase has a new and special meaning to me and my Rhonda this year. We truly believe that all of the 'bad stuff' of the last few years is behind us… that we are well on the way upward and onward! PTL!

In the rush before the end of the year, Rhonda had multiple appts and scans. The most important, a PET scan, showed absolutely no sign of cancer. Then there was the MRI and blood tests for the liver drs… and another 'all clear'. Wow. Oh yeah… and NO FEVERS for the last several weeks! Yes!!! These results just confirm for us that treatments and looooong hospital stays are a thing of the past. Our Lord has been so gracious to bring us through so much… and you all… our 'support group' has been nothing short of amazing in your prayers, words of encouragement, and acts of kindness. We are more than ready now to 'pay it forward'!

And an opportunity to do just that presented itself at church a few weeks ago. A man I had never noticed before came up to us after the service and said… "We've been watching you and your wife for a while. My wife has cancer… how do you do this?" Wow. This is where we get a glimpse of what our Lord had in mind when we were going through all of that horrible stuff. Now maybe we can be an encouragement… a word of Hope… by His Grace… to others going through a similar trial. Wow. We chatted with him for a bit… and Rhonda ended up meeting with his wife… and gave her all of her hats to use until her hair grows back… and then asked her to pass them on to anyone who had need when she no longer had a need for them. Please remember this family (they have 4 kids) in your prayers. And there are several others we know who are battling this monster... too many. Please Lord, give strength and healing to them all.

So... there's this word that keeps coming up when Rhonda is sharing how her life is going now. That word is "JOY!" She's been steady in hitting our exercise machines (more steady than I've been)... playing piano... playing her oboe... crocheting... and sending out about 100 Christmas cards (each with a personal note). And we did it up BIG for our Christmas celebration at the house with our kids and grandbabies... decorations and lights up all over the place. What a time of JOY!

So... I guess I'm going to have to get a new job this year. For the last almost 3 years, I've been Rhonda's caregiver. Things are rapidly moving to a point where she doesn't need one! A couple of weeks ago, Rhonda wanted to try the stairs at church. I didn't think it was a good idea and just pulled a "reason" out of my head and told her when she could do 5 minutes on the elliptical she could do the stairs at church (she hadn't been able to do more than 2 mins at that time). So... challenge accepted! Since then she's done 5 mins on the elliptical several times... and this morning she reminded me of my 'reason' (which I'd forgotten)... and we did the stairs. Ha! Slowly, carefully, but no hitches at all (except that I'll have to get used to doing stairs again!).

This is my Rhonda's new mindset. Challenge yourself to do something that you want to do... and make it happen! Amazing! She starts her 2nd semester teaching GED Math this week, and is so excited that she can hardly sleep at night thinking about it! Wow! :)

You know you hear stories about people who came out of "near death" experiences, and it changed their life... caused them to appreciate everyday things more... and "seize the day" (as Francis shared in SS this morning). Well... that's my Rhonda... she's living it... and I need more strength just to try and keep up with her! In fact, I may need to do a Sunday afternoon nap when I finish this email. Rhonda refuses to nap... she might miss out on something! :)

Thank you Lord!!!

And... thank you family and friends... so much! Our hearts overflow with thanks and blessings for you all!

God Bless... and have a great week!
Scott and Rhonda

Responses

Greg G
Great news Scott. We are praying for the both of you. Give our love to Rhonda.

Sylvia A
God is so good, and we all knew from the beginning the He picked you for a purpose- to remind others that with God all is possible, even when we feel like giving up. And we all know that it's in His timing too.
You both have been a reminder of this to all of us. I know God will continue to bless you both and your families for answering His call.
Happy new year to you both and look forward to seeing you one day soon.

God bless

Pamela D

What a witness you both have! Thanks for sharing!

Sandy L

Praise the Lord!!! She is a walking Miracle!!!
Such a testimony to His Amazing Love!!!
We Love you both so much!

Gary W

Great news. You two have been through a tough time. God has been carrying both of you. Now you can encourage others who are dealing with tough issues. May God continue to give both of you wisdom and strength as you continue to serve Him right where you are at.

Patti S

Beautiful… we rejoice in your JOY!

Donna C

I JUST LOVE THIS LETTER! IT IS A LETTER OF JOY!
HAPPY NEW YEAR TO YOU AND RHONDA!
GOD BLESS

Maw-in-law

Thank you, thank you, thank you for sharing this. I am overwhelmed with thanksgiving and love.

Jan R

I knew God was preparing & training you both to do His work! And I can't think of anyone more qualified to be the Lord's hands & feet!

Brings me great Joy to hear how well Rhonda is doing! Love you both!

Lupita O

Aw, Scott and Rhonda!!!

Like I told you Sunday, you are an inspiration for everybody, YOU are my inspiration, last year was so hard for my family, we lost 5 members from our family, including our mom, but Rhonda is a great warrior always fighting, one time, and another one, and another one and… fighting, fighting… and you Scott always there, to support her, to encourage her, day and night, and you are a victorious couple, you are a testimony of what FAITH, and HOPE CAN make!!!

Because GOD, is always there no matter what!!!!!

This is a new YEAR, for everyone, especially for you!!!

With love

Bobbie O

Thank you so much for the update and we are so thankful she is doing so well. It has been a long journey since we first met you and Rhonda out walking several years ago. We are so thankful for all God is doing and has done in Rhonda's life. Yes, you are right when you say after going through a journey like this you appreciate and see things a lot differently. Gary and I feel every day God has given us after his last cancer is a gift.

Suraya K

I am so happy for you and your family. Rhonda enjoy your good health and enjoy this time to its fullest.

Barbara C

I cannot tell you how happy I am to read this update! Rhonda is an amazing woman and God definitely has more in store for her! The power of prayer should never be underestimated as so many people were involved in the praying for Rhonda to be completely healed! Amen and Amen! God is good all the time, all the time God is Good!

Cathy G

All I can say after reading this update is PRAISE THE LORD!!!!!!! You all have shown so much faith and trust in the Lord through this very difficult journey and you inspire us all to face our current trials and testings head-on knowing that God has the best in mind for us. We love you both!

Vicky S

A powerful testimony! Now we offer up prayers of blessings and thanksgiving for all that God has done and will continue to do through Rhonda and Scott!

Cortney S

Praise God!

Merlene

So happy to hear the wonderful update. Our thoughts and prayers have always been with you throughout this whole ordeal. I haven't ever seen anyone fight for recovery as much as you two have. Here's to continued health and happiness. Love you

Peggy A

Love this post! So happy to hear such a good report.

*****

So this is where we are as I compile these e-mails and notes. Our Lord has shown Himself to be full of mercy and grace as He has brought us through so much. With five kids and now four grand-children, we know that life can change in an instant, and it has. It's been so great to see Rhonda come back and pursue such a zest for life, but for a time, it was a somewhat difficult transition for me. To move from twenty-four-hour caregiver, it's not been an easy thing to know when to step in to help and when to step back to let Rhonda try and fly with her new fledgling wings and still limited strength, and I didn't always make the right choice. The emotional drain of the last few years had left me in a state of weary numbness. And with Rhonda's amazing progress, I was searching to see where I fit in. She was bouncing back more quickly than I was. Such times as we had been through wore us down in body and spirit, and I knew that I really needed a shot in the arm.

I know one thing that did help to hold us together (and cling-ing to our faith) was our habit to pray together every night before turning out the light. This was born out of the very beginning of our relationship, since that first date even and that very first prayer in her car. It's great to have good communication with our spouses, but it's incredibly bonding to hear your spouse's heart pouring out to God giving thanks for blessings as well as pleading for help in the difficult times. This time has always been very important to us. So every night, many of them in the hospital, we joined our hands and poured our troubled hearts out to our Savior. We prayed for strength, for healing, for freedom from pain, for mercy, and, some days, we pleaded to just get a break from the suffering when we didn't feel we could hold up any longer. We also prayed every day with tears of thankfulness for the blessings of our Hope and the encouragement and prayers of so many. Rhonda was not always able to verbalize a prayer, but we always held hands, and I would pray for both of us. I know that this was a huge factor for us both to get through all of this.

In August 2016, our pastor announced and then led our church body through a forty-day devotional book that helped Rhonda and I to get back into a daily spiritual habit. We'd had so many days of just trying to survive our routines had disappeared in the seemingly endless battle for Rhonda's health that had so completely taken over our lives. This daily devotional was a great opportunity to finally move forward and get plugged back into some sort of spiritual discipline. In addition to the forty-day book and Bible readings, I decided that I needed the extra octane boost of an Oswald Chambers devotional too. Those who are familiar with his writings are well aware that he has all of the subtleness of a baseball bat, and I needed that to wake me up and keep me moving along each morning. This regular daily time with our Lord has helped us so much to bring that "Joy of the Lord" back into our lives.

Our joy and growth has also been reinforced by discovering (and rediscovering) more music, books, and inspirational videos, which have helped to sustain the building up of our faith. In spite of the amazing progress Rhonda has made, our joy has been tempered by the prospect that she most likely will never recover her full strength and health that enabled her to jog three miles multiple times each week back in 2009 before the cancer struck. Yet we are so thankful for what we do have back and how far our Loving Lord has brought us since those darkest days.

We thought that we were a pretty close-knit couple before the cancer battle, but after going through all of this, we are truly joined as one in heart and soul. It's a true saying that adversity will either pull you together or rip you apart, and the strength of the bond I have with my Rhonda is simply amazing. She's the best friend I've ever had. I never would have believed that a marriage could be so consistently wonderful. I have been able to continue to work from home, so we are together in the house almost all of the time, and we love it! Yes, she does her stuff, and I do mine, but we love being together and finding an excuse to get up from whatever we're doing to go into the next room and get a hug and share an "I love you" with each other. What a gift from God my Rhonda is to me! Whenever I have those occasional doubts about my Lord's Love for me, I only have to think of the gift of "my Rhonda" and the tears of thankfulness will come every time.

The kids are all out of the house and pretty much on their own, and we love having an empty nest! Coming together with all of those kids at the get-go of our marriage, the alone times were hard to come by, so we are relishing this time of just being "us" (one of our favorite "sweet nothings" we share with each other is I love being "us" with "you"!). We also love the grandbabies! We love our church… and the staff (We had staff members visit us every week while we were in the hospital and are so thankful for these godly men!) and our precious Sunday School class "family" and my incredible coworkers and managers at work through the years who have all been so supportive and encouraging through everything we've gone through. God is always good. Always. But it is truly wonderful and such a blessing when life and health are good too! Thank you, Jesus, for bringing us through so much. Our hearts overflow with your goodness and mercy!

We don't know when another crisis or heartache may come, but we know that He will stay true to His promises to give us strength and never leave or forsake us. We will cling to that, and it will be enough. To Him be the glory forever and ever. Amen.

Scott and Rhonda and family and
many, many Forever Friends!
And God's Amazing Love and Grace!
May 2017

Epilogue: The Struggles and Triumphs of Recovery

It's been so great seeing Rhonda's amazing progress, but we still had struggles recovering and overcoming the ravages of those last two years. We both were spiritually, physically, and emotionally drained. After finally getting out of the hospital for good, it was still months before we were physically strong enough to attend Sunday school and church again, and I probably used Rhonda's limited strength factor as an excuse to hold us out a bit longer than we really needed to be. I just wanted to rest and decompress and find distractions to take away the numbness for a while. Missing out on regular fellowship with our home church only prolonged this time of my emptiness of spirit.

I have always loved music and playing piano/guitar, but it required such heart and effort that I just didn't feel I had the strength for it. The spiritual desert I was wandering in kept me from going to the only One who could truly help me. Instead, I spent hours watching movies and TV shows online. I got particularly entangled with one show that had very high reviews, but watching it did nothing to help my spiritual state. We'll spare the details and just say that it would not pass the WWJD test. Even so, I got hooked on watching it, and when I saw a Black Friday deal at a ridiculously low price for the complete set on DVD, I decided that I needed to order it. I did run it by Rhonda. She had heard of the show but knew little about it, and she trusted me. The order was delayed, and a couple of weeks went by and then months. I would check on the order online, and it always had "shipping date unknown," so I continued to wait for it. In the meantime, God had not given up on me.

I was starting to listen to Christian music again—mostly old favorites that were a comfort to me—and these began to warm my soul back to life again. I would even get teary-eyed at times. My heart was finally beginning to soften again. One day, I found myself sampling some newer music by the group Casting Crowns. I love their sound and the messages of many of their songs. The catchy opening piano riff of one song really caught my ear, but it was the lyrics of "All You've Ever Wanted" that really pierced my heart and set free the tears of months of hurting and fear. I listened to the song over and over again as the emotions rolled over me in waves that released everything that had been locked up inside me by always striving to "be strong" through all the days of suffering. I felt that the Lord was telling me that He wasn't finished with me yet and that it was time for me to bind up my wounds and finally move forward into another season of His plan for me. Like the prodigal's Father, He'd been waiting for me to look up, come to my senses, and come home. I shared the song with Rhonda, and she loved the beauty of it, but even more, how it had touched me. She knew I had been struggling but did not know the depths of the darkness I had felt. As we joined hands a bit later that night for our prayer time, my heart was still flowing with the grief but finally some hope too.

The next day, May 7, I woke up and found an e-mail from the Internet retailer waiting for me: "Good news, we have a shipping date for your order!" I had ordered this "manly" DVD series on November 30, over five months earlier. So here was my test: the Lord's timing is always perfect, isn't it? After my experience of the night before, I knew that it was time to leave such things behind, so I sent an e-mail to cancel the order. I bet that made them scratch their heads.

But it was still a process just begun, this spiritual and emotional time of healing for me. I did manage to maintain or maybe move forward some during this time, but I was still mostly stuck in neutral spiritually over concern for Rhonda's strength and safety and the new demands of caring for Julie's needs. Getting Julie and Charlie moved into their new apartment was a huge relief, but it was the start of the forty-day devotional book through our church a few weeks later that really helped us to get back on the path to emotional and spiritual healing.

Then an announcement in early December broadsided us when I was informed that I would be laid off from my job of almost nineteen years (along with several hundred others) at some point in the following year. It was a distressing thing to hear, but it appeared that we had some time to figure out our options. My main point of concern was being able to continue health insurance, especially with Rhonda's history. We'd heard horror stories from friends with similar situations having to pay multiple thousands per month, along with huge deductibles. We can always find something to worry about, can't we? Yet a couple of weeks later, I awoke with an inexplicably amazing feeling of peace and joy like I hadn't felt in a long, long time. I felt like God was telling me that it was going to be all right, that He would continue to take care of us in our uncertain future just as He had through those years of Rhonda's illness. When I read my devotion that morning, I was brought to tears. The day's verse was John 14:27, "Peace I leave with you, my peace I give unto you." Wow. It was another reassurance that He is near and in control. The prayers and concerns about insurance were answered just a few weeks later when we discovered that I had just become eligible for "retirement" from the company (based on an October 31 work anniversary), and by so doing, we would be able to maintain our health insurance at the same cost I've had as an employee. So the still-to-be-determined layoff date would now become my "retirement" date. And our Lord had already taken care of this insurance need even before we knew about the layoff when He allowed me to keep my job until we could receive this benefit, and we were humbled, once again, by His Provision over us.

The Lord brought us through so much that I felt led to share some of how He'd been dealing with me at our family Christmas celebration. As a testimony, I wanted our children to know how God had been working in my own heart and life. One devotional reading I shared that had really hit home with me was the realization that I don't need to be caught up with convincing others that I'm a "good guy." What I need to be striving for is to somehow create in them a spiritual hunger for the Lord. When people look at me, I want them to see God's Grace at work in me so strongly that they desire and want that same Grace in their own life. If you see anything good in me, it is only because of His Grace over me. My natural dispositions leave much to be desired. This revelation really had an impact in how I saw my relationship with others and in my thinking about putting together this book, not that I was so strong to have carried my wife through the suffering of cancer treatments and its brutal side effects, *but that the Lord is faithful… and it was He who carried both of us through these times.* We give all glory to Him. The Lord tells us through Paul that "my strength is made perfect in weakness" (2 Cor. 12:9), and we pray that it is His strength that is evident in these pages. I honestly don't know how people survive such times without Him.

We are all fallen creatures; it's in our genes, and we all need God's Grace to save us. I thank God that my "goodness," or maybe lack of it at times, has no bearing on my salvation. The Bible tells us in Ephesians 2:8–9, "For by grace you have been saved, *through faith, it is the gift of God*; not as the result of works, lest any man should boast." I am saved not by what I have done or not done but because Jesus died for me, for all of us, and rose again to prove His power over all, even death, and *by the Grace and Gift of faith, I believe in Him with all my heart.* It is only through this faith that I can have His Spirit to help me through each day, and then finally one day, when I breathe my last, that same Spirit will carry me into His Presence where there will be no more suffering or tears or pain, only the joy of being where I was created to be—with Him. This is our Hope that keeps us from despair during these difficult times, and it is this Hope that we have desired to share with you in these writings with our whole hearts.

Consider it all joy, my brethren, when you encounter various
trials, knowing that the testing of your faith produces endurance.
—James 1:2–3

And we know that God causes all things to work
together for good to those who love God, to those
who are called according to His purpose.
—Romans 8:28

Amen and Amen.

CPSIA information can be obtained
at www.ICGtesting.com
Printed in the USA
FFOW04n0157281217
44283110-43829FF